T0220959

Distributed Storage Networks

Architecture, Protocols and Management

Distributed Storage Networks

Architecture, Protocols and Management

Thomas C. Jepsen
IT Consultant; Programming Languages Editor,
IEEE ITPro Magazine,
Computer Science Instructor,
North Carolina State University, USA

John Wiley & Sons, Ltd

Other Wiley Editorial Offices

John Wiley & Sons Inc., 111 River Street, Hoboken, NJ 07030, USA

Jossey-Bass, 989 Market Street, San Francisco, CA 94103-1741, USA

Wiley-VCH Verlag GmbH, Boschstr. 12, D-69469 Weinheim, Germany

John Wiley & Sons Australia Ltd, 33 Park Road, Milton, Queensland 4064, Australia

John Wiley & Sons (Asia) Pte Ltd, 2 Clementi Loop #02-01, Jin Xing Distripark, Singapore
129809

John Wiley & Sons Canada Ltd, 22 Worcester Road, Etobicoke, Ontario, Canada M9W 1L1

Wiley also publishes its books in a variety of electronic formats. Some content that appears
in print may not be available in electronic books.

British Library Cataloguing in Publication Data

A catalogue record for this book is available from the British Library

ISBN 0-470-85020-5

Typeset in 11/13pt Palatino by Laserwords Private Limited, Chennai, India

Contents

Foreword

Having been a technical reviewer for Marc Farley's "Building Storage Networks" and Tom Clark's "Designing Fibre Channel Storage Area Networks", as well as making my own small contribution ("Storage Area Network Essentials," co-authored with Richard Barker, and published by John Wiley & Sons), I feel very much a part of the growing body of storage networking literature. I was therefore particularly gratified to be asked to contribute a foreword to Tom Jepsen's "Distributed Storage Networks."

Tom has made a unique contribution to the literature. Today, most large enterprises operate mixtures of mainframe, UNIX, and Windows servers in their data centers. All of these platforms are moving inexorably toward a networked storage concept, but they are taking their own technology directions and moving at their own speeds. It's possible to find sources of information about open system storage networks and other sources that deal with ESCON and FICON, but IT designers, implementers, and managers who have to cope with the reality of mixed environments are hard put to acquire the unified body of knowledge that allows them to deal with the different capabilities and requirements of the storage networks for which they are responsible. Tom's book does a masterful job of presenting this much-needed unified body of knowledge in four areas:

- it covers both mainframe and open storage network technologies side by side so that readers can develop a broad architectural view as they learn the details
- it covers both technology and implementation, explaining both the whats and whys of the networks themselves, and the hows of deploying them
- it deals both with storage networking within the data center and with long-distance networks, and their unique challenges and benefits

- it deals with all these topics both at the overview level (Chapters 1 and 2) and in depth (Chapters 3–11), providing real value to both executives and hands-on workers.

"Distributed Storage Networks" is also unique in that it's designed both to be read and to be referred to. The conceptual information, particularly in the chapters that cover applications and implementation, is presented at just the right level of detail for architects and implementers–enough to stimulate the thinking processes, but not the mind-numbing detail that only a standards engineer could love. Particularly trenchant in today's uncertain world is Tom's advice on security–"build it in; don't count on adding it on later." The many charts and tables are a handy reference for the inevitable "speeds and feeds" part of storage network design.

Whether you're an architect, designing your organization's first or tenth storage network, an application implementer who's concerned with reliability, performance, and security, an administrator needing an overview of the bundle of technologies for which you're responsible, or a CIO trying to make some sense of the brave new world of distributed storage, *Distributed Storage Networks* has something to offer you. It's my candidate for 2003's "If you can only have one book on storage networking, make it this one" award.

Paul Massiglia
Technical Director, VERITAS
Software Corporation
Director, VERITAS Publishing

Preface

Stored data is the most valuable asset that any organization has, and the accuracy and reliability of that data are key factors in staying competitive in today's world. The globalization of business creates a need to link together geographically separate databases in a manner that is transparent to the end user. New government regulations in the healthcare and financial industries create requirements to provide secure and reliable data backups at remote locations without impacting system performance, and to provide strategies for business continuity in the event of data loss.

Implementing these functions requires a new mindset on the part of enterprise planners and managers. The familiar computer-centric model of data processing is rapidly being replaced by a storage-centric model in which storage is geographically distributed over a large area, perhaps even the entire world. This book is intended to provide an overview of the architectures, protocols, and management functions needed to understand this new environment.

The concept behind this book emerged as a result of two presentations I gave on storage networks in 2001, at EntNet@Supercom in Atlanta, Georgia, USA, and at the Asia-Pacific Network Operations and Management Symposium in Sydney, Australia. I would like to thank the individuals who made those presentations possible, and provided me with the germ of an idea for a book: Lundy Lewis, Aprisma; Shri Goyal, Verizon; and Masayoshi Ejiri, Fujitsu Ltd. Their encouragement and support are greatly appreciated. I would also like to thank the individuals and publications who granted me permission to reprint copyright material: Monica Vago and Rose Maginniss, ANSI/INCITS; Jacqueline Hansson, IEEE; Andrea Westerinen, Distributed Management Task Force; Arnold Jones, Storage Networking Industry Association; Casper Yu, InfiniBand Trade Association; and the IBM Journal of Research and Development. And lastly, I would like to thank Paul Massiglia for his enthusiastic and supportive comments.

Acknowledgements

The author would like to acknowledge the use of the following source material.

Tables 5.6 to 5.13, 5.27, 5.28, 5.25 and 5.26 are reprinted with permission from, *ANSI INCITS 296-1997 SBCON, ANSI INCITS 230-1994 (R1999) Fibre Channel, ANSI INCITS 342-2001, Fibre Channel Back Bone (FC-BB).*

Figures 7.8 and 7.16 are reprinted with permission from, *ANSI INCITS 342-2001, Fibre Channel Back Bone (FC-BB).*

From IEEE Std 802.3-2002*, Copyright © 2002, by IEEE. All rights reserved.

Tables 5.30 to 5.33 reprinted with permission from IEEE Std 802.3-2002*, "Carrier sense multiple access with collision detection (CSMA/CD) access method and physical layer specifications", Section 3, Table 38-3, Table 38-4, Table 38-7, Table 38-8 and Table 38-10. Copyright © 2002, by IEEE. The IEEE disclaims any responsibility or liability resulting from the placement and use in the described manner.

From IEEE Std 802.3ae-2002*, Copyright © 2002, by IEEE. All rights reserved.

Tables 5.34 to 5.40 reprinted with permission from IEEE Std 802.3ae-2002*, "Part 3, Amendment: Media: Access Control (MAC) Parameters, Physical Layers, and Management Parameters for 10 Gb/s Operation", Copyright © 2002, by IEEE. The IEEE disclaims any responsibility or liability resulting from the placement and use in the described manner.

Figures 6.4 and 6.5, along with Tables 6-1 to 6-9. *Infiband Architecture Specification, Vol. 1, Rel 1.1, Infiband Architecture Specification, Vol. 2, Rel 1.1*

The charts and tables referenced above from the Infiband Architecture Specification, Vol. 1, Rel 1.1 and Infiband Architecture

List of Figures

List of Tables

1

Introduction to Storage Networking

1.1 OVERVIEW

Storage networks provide shared access to storage by multiple computers and servers, thus increasing the efficiency of storage and the availability of stored data. Storage networks enable storage devices from different vendors, which may use different access protocols, to be logically 'pooled' for access and retrieval purposes. They permit information management functions such as backup and recovery, data mirroring, disaster recovery, and data migration to be performed quickly and efficiently, with a minimum of system overhead.

With the rapid increase in data storage requirements in the last decade, efficient management of stored data becomes a necessity for the enterprise. A recent industry study estimated the total size of the disk storage market to be almost 500,000 terabytes worldwide in 2002; this figure is expected to climb to 1.4 million terabytes by 2005. Many corporations now manage hundreds of terabytes of data in their information management divisions. However, the traditional 'islands of storage' management approach is vastly

Distributed Storage Networks   Thomas C. Jepsen
© 2003 John Wiley & Sons, Ltd   ISBN: 0-470-85020-5

inefficient; as much as 50% of storage capacity may be wasted or underutilized. The high cost of downtime creates a need for the increased reliability provided by distributed storage systems. Thus, the use of storage networks to manage access to data not only provides an increase in performance and survivability, but also generates real and immediate cost savings. The worldwide market for networked storage is anticipated to grow from US $2 billion in 1999 to over $25 billion by 2004. As business-to-business and business-to-consumer e-commerce matures, even greater demands for management of stored data will arise.

Increasingly, storage networks are being distributed over wide geographical areas to ensure data survivability and provide data synchronization over large distances. This book describes the evolution of data processing from a computer-centric model to a storage-centric model, and introduces the concept of a distributed storage-centric processing model. It describes common storage network functional components, such as fabric switches, storage directors, file managers, and gateways, and their roles in a distributed storage environment. It discusses distributed storage network applications, including storage integration, remote database synchronization, and backup/recovery functions. It provides a comparative view of Storage Area Network (SAN) and Network Attached Storage (NAS) functions and capabilities, and points out the advantages of each.

One of the primary obstacles to implementing a storage network cited by enterprise IT managers is a lack of knowledge about storage networking technology and the specific issues involved in extending a SAN or NAS over the MAN or WAN. This book addresses the 'terminology gap' between enterprise network planners and telecommunications engineers, who must understand the transport requirements of storage networks in order to implement distributed storage networks. The primary goal of this book is to provide IT managers, planners, and telecommunications professionals with the information they need in order to choose the technologies best suited for their particular environment.

1.1.1 Who Should Read This Book?

This book is aimed at the IT manager, the enterprise network planner, and the network design engineer, who are responsible for the planning and design of storage networks in an enterprise environment. It is also intended to enable telecommunications engineers to understand the transport requirements of storage networks. This book assumes a basic knowledge of storage networks and applications; the reader is assumed to have read and understood, for example, Barker and Massiglia, *Storage Area Network Essentials*. It is not intended to be a detailed implementation guide that would specify specific equipment settings or test procedures; rather, it is intended to enable high-level managers and planners make intelligent decisions about what sort of network is best suited for their needs.

1.1.2 Overview of Contents

This book focuses on three primary areas: (1) architectures for distributed storage networks; (2) storage protocols and their inherent distance limitations; and (3) management techniques for distributed storage networks. Each is summarized below.

The architectures section provides an historical overview of the evolution of storage network architectures. It describes the evolution of storage networks from simple point-to-point topologies to switched fabrics providing complete node-to-node connectivity. It discusses redundant, multi-tier, and backbone fabric architectures, and outlines the advantages of each. Example configurations are given for each architectural variant.

The protocols section details the protocols used for distributed storage applications. Common storage protocols, including the Small Computer Systems Interface (SCSI), Enterprise Systems Connection (ESCON™), FICON™, Gigabit Ethernet, and Fibre Channel are defined and discussed. The evolution from parallel bus-based protocols to serial fiber-optic-based protocols is presented. Distance limitations inherent in storage protocols are described, and techniques for extending storage network functions over the metropolitan area network (MAN) and wide area network (WAN) are discussed, including use of Asynchronous Transfer Mode (ATM) and wavelength division multiplexing (WDM). Emerging technologies for distributed storage networking, including InfiniBand™ and IP-based SAN solutions, are presented and described.

Storage management requirements, including security management, are analyzed in the management section. The Storage Networking Industry Association's Common Information Model (CIM) is used as the basis for describing a management architecture. Finally, the importance of planning and integration in formulating end-to-end storage solutions for the enterprise is emphasized.

1.2   EVOLUTION OF STORAGE NETWORKING

1.2.1   Mainframe Storage Networks

The mainframe computing environment developed in the 1960s provided the first conceptual model for storage architecture and management. In the mainframe-based architecture, a host processor uses a channel subsystem to communicate with external storage devices. The channel subsystem in turn addresses a control unit for each group of storage devices; a large mainframe computing environment might have several control units managing hundreds of tape and disk storage devices. (In the mainframe world, disk devices are referred to as *Direct Access Storage Devices*, or DASD.) A parallel bus/tag interface was initially used to provide connectivity between channels, control units, and storage devices; this copper-based bus limited both the bandwidth and distance of the I/O devices. The introduction of optical fiber and high-speed serial bus protocols such as *Enterprise Systems Connection* (ESCON) in the early 1990s reduced these limitations, and made it possible to extend storage device connectivity over geographically dispersed areas, sometimes referred to as *channel extension*.

1.2.2   Storage for Small Computer Systems

The introduction of first minicomputers, and then personal computers in the 1970s and 1980s, brought about large changes in computer

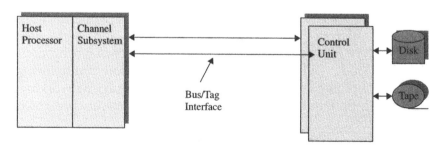

Figure 1.1   Mainframe Storage Network Architecture (1960s).

system architecture; the development of the open systems UNIX and Windows operating systems required new approaches to I/O operations and storage access. As computers became smaller and storage devices increased their capacity and bit density, disk storage was increasingly integrated into the computer architecture, using the Integrated Drive Electronics/AT Attachment (IDE/ATA) bus, as is done with the ordinary home personal computer. However, for applications requiring large amounts of storage, such as application servers, there was a requirement to add various types of external storage devices. The Small Computer Systems Interface (SCSI) bus and protocol were developed in the 1980s to meet this requirement. Like the mainframe bus/tag interface, however, the parallel copper-based SCSI bus architecture limited the distance at which external storage devices could be located. The Fibre Channel data transport protocol, developed in the early 1990s, solved the distance problem by extending the reach of storage connectivity to as much as 10 kilometers, and also provided the basis for solving another problem: the increasing complexity of managing large amounts of stored data.

1.2.3 Managing 'Islands of Storage'

In a traditional enterprise computing architecture, each computer is directly connected to its own storage devices, which it also manages. This approach creates 'islands of storage', which are not accessible by other computers (see Figure 1.2). It is difficult to manage storage efficiently, since one processor may run out of storage while another processor may have unused storage space that cannot be made available to the processor that requires it. Backup storage devices must be dedicated to each processor, even though they are typically used infrequently. The 'islands of storage' approach makes it difficult for applications running on separate systems (for example, mainframe applications and server-based applications) to share data. Also, adding new storage devices normally requires the computer system to be powered down, resulting in lost productivity.

Storage networks (see Figure 1.3) solve these problems by allowing multiple computers to access a set of storage devices, which are managed as a network. Storage efficiency increases, since the total storage capacity is accessible to each computer, eliminating

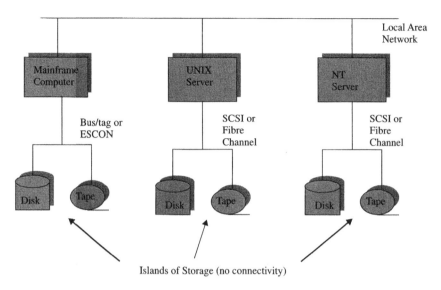

Figure 1.2 Traditional computer network architecture.

the possibility of a single processor exceeding its storage capacity while another processor has unused storage space. Backup storage devices are used more efficiently, since they are shared by all processors. Adding or deleting devices or units of storage capacity may be done on operational systems with no loss of function.

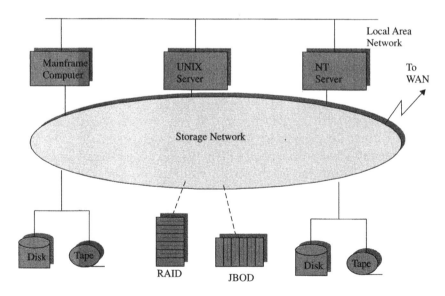

Figure 1.3 Computer network architecture with storage network.

1.3 TERMINOLOGY

1.3.1 What is a Storage Network?

Storage networks are special-purpose networks that transport data between storage devices, such as tape or disk, and computing devices, such as mainframes or servers. In this book, we use the term 'storage network' generically to refer to a group of networked, externally attached storage devices, together with their associated control and switching components, that are managed as a single entity. This definition is general enough to include mainframe storage networks, Storage Area Networks (SAN), and Network Attached Storage (NAS); as we will see, the distinctions among these architectures are gradually disappearing, and they share many common characteristics.

Storage networks transport data that is in an input/output block format recognizable to computer operating systems and storage devices. Storage networks use storage protocols, such as SCSI, ESCON, or Fibre Channel, which are optimized for high-speed, low-loss data transfer over copper wire or optical fiber. Storage networks may use a directly connected, switched, or arbitrated loop architecture.

1.3.1.1 How is a Storage Network Different from a Local Area Network?

Local Area Networks, or LANs, on the other hand, are used for computer-to-computer communication to support functions such as file transfer, remote procedure calls, and client/server applications. A LAN is generally limited to a single physical location, such as an office building or campus. LANs typically use the Ethernet protocol and run at speeds of 10, 100, or 1000 megabits per second over copper wire or optical fiber. LANs have broadcast and multicast capability and may have a bus or tree architecture.

1.3.1.2 How is a Storage Network Different from a Wide Area Network?

Wide Area Networks, or WANs, are used to transport data across a large area, for example across the entire country. A WAN may be operated as a public utility and provide transport services for a number of customers, or it may be privately operated. WANs typically use telecommunications transport protocols such as Asynchronous Transfer Mode (ATM), Synchronous Optical Network (SONET), or Dense Wavelength Division Multiplexing (DWDM) over optical fiber. WANs may employ a backbone or ring architecture.

1.3.2 What is a Storage Area Network?

A Storage Area Network, or SAN, is a storage network that provides shared access to storage by multiple computers and servers. SANs enable storage devices from different vendors and using different access protocols to be pooled for efficient management; they permit standard data management functions such as backup, recovery, mirroring, and data migration to be performed reliably and efficiently. SANs primarily use the Fibre Channel protocol to transfer data; however, SANs are able to include devices which use other protocols by employing bridges and gateway devices to perform protocol translation.

In its purest sense, the SAN topology is based on a switched architecture; a fabric switch is used to provide connectivity between a computing node and a storage node for the duration of a data transfer operation. However, the SAN architecture has evolved over time from simple point-to-point topologies to arbitrated loops to the present switched topology, so many SANs contain elements of these earlier topologies as well.

1.3.2.1 What is a Point-to-Point Topology?

As noted previously, the earliest use of Fibre Channel was in extending the range of SCSI-connected I/O devices. While SCSI buses may not be extended beyond 25 meters, and many are limited to 6 meters or less, use of Fibre Channel enables storage devices to be located as much as 10 kilometers away from the computing node. In this architecture, SCSI/Fibre Channel interworking is achieved by either using a hardware device, such as a *bridge*, to interwork the two protocols, or by using the Fibre Channel Protocol (FCP) to provide SCSI command set emulation. A *host bus adapter*, or HBA, is used to terminate the Fibre Channel on a storage or computing node.

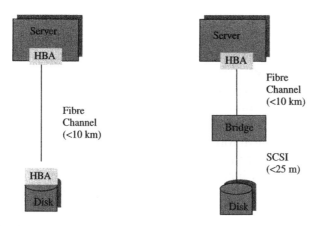

Figure 1.4   Point-to-point topology.

1.3.2.2   What is Arbitrated Loop Topology?

The Fibre Channel Arbitrated Loop (FC-AL) Topology represents the first step towards true storage area networking. The FC-AL protocol enables up to 127 nodes to be connected in a loop topology network; the output port of each node is connected to the input port of the next node in the loop. A connection may be established between any two ports on the loop at any time; arbitration logic is built into the protocol to determine which two ports will have priority access to the loop. Once a connection is established, the entire loop bandwidth is dedicated to data transfer between the two connected ports. The arbitration logic includes a fairness algorithm to prevent any two nodes from monopolizing access to the loop.

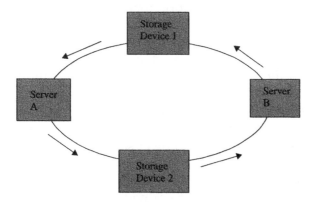

Figure 1.5   Arbitrated loop topology.

A refinement on the arbitrated loop topology is provided by adding a *hub* to the configuration (see Figure 1.6). In a true arbitrated loop topology, failure of a single node will cause the entire loop to become inoperative, since the entire bandwidth passes through each device. The hub contains circuitry to sense device failure, and permit data intended for other nodes to pass through if a node becomes inoperative. The addition of a hub in the middle of the configuration changes the physical topology from a loop to a star, while retaining the logical loop configuration. Use of a hub provides better cable manageability and increased reliability. Devices may be added or removed from the loop while it is operating if a hub is used.

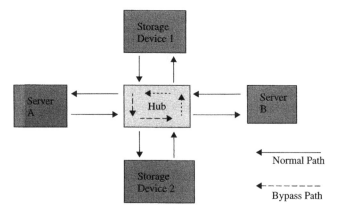

Figure 1.6   Arbitrated loop topology – hub configuration.

1.3.2.3   Switched Fabric Topology

A SAN utilizing switched fabric topology consists of computing nodes and storage nodes interconnected by means of a storage fabric (see Figure 1.7). A *fabric switch* enables any storage device to be connected to any computing device for the duration of a data transfer operation. A fabric switch can support multiple simultaneous full-bandwidth connections between storage and computing nodes. A *storage director* is a specialized type of fabric switch which provides enhanced management and reliability features, such as duplicated switch fabrics and power supplies. Use of the switched fabric also enables a common backup server to be connected to any of the storage devices for scheduled or manual backup purposes. A *gateway* may be employed to provide SAN/WAN interworking and protocol translation in distributed SAN applications.

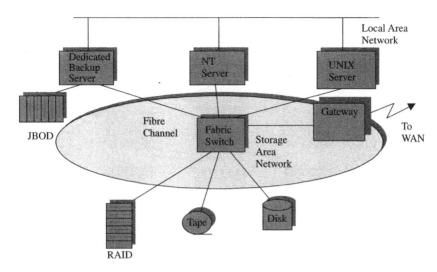

Figure 1.7 Switched fabric topology.

For greater reliability, a second fabric switch may be added to provide redundant paths to all components (see Figure 1.8). In the event that one fabric switch fails, the second switch allows operation to continue normally.

In both the single and redundant architectures, the supported configuration is limited to the number of ports available on a single fabric switch. Scaleability can be improved by using a two-tiered architecture, in which all computer nodes are attached to a host

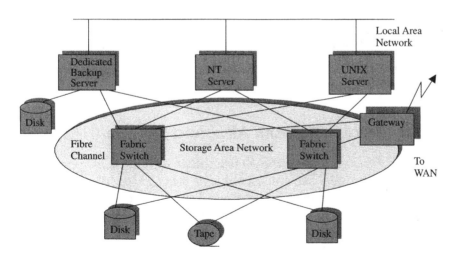

Figure 1.8 Redundant fabric switch configuration.

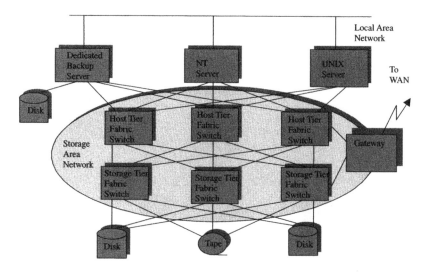

Figure 1.9   Two tier layered architecture.

tier consisting of multiple fabric switches, and all storage nodes are attached to a storage tier consisting of multiple fabric switches (see Figure 1.9). This may be expanded to as many switches as necessary. The path length from any computer to any storage device remains the same, regardless of the number of switches in each tier. However, since each fabric switch in each tier must connect to each switch in the other tier, many switch ports are consumed in providing connectivity.

Greater scaleability can be provided with a *backbone* architecture (see Figure 1.10). A backbone architecture uses core fabric switches to provide connectivity among groups of edge switches, or *sub-fabrics*. The backbone architecture is particularly well suited for distributed SAN use where the individual sub-fabrics are geographically dispersed over a large area.

1.3.3   What is Network Attached Storage (NAS)?

Network Attached Storage (NAS) is another technique for providing managed storage. NAS consists of a *file manager* (or 'filer') attached to a LAN which manages and provides access to stored data (see Figure 1.11). The NAS concept emerged from the informal practice of designating one computer node on a LAN as a pure file server, with no resident applications. The file management function was optimized to provide better performance and throughput for NAS.

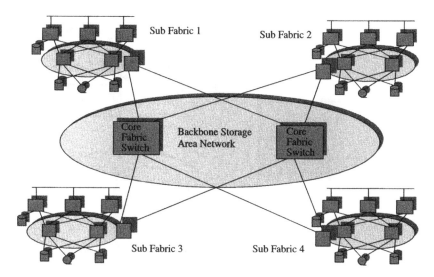

Figure 1.10 Core/edge backbone architecture.

1.3.3.1 How is NAS different from SAN?

NAS transfers file-structured data between a processor and LAN-attached storage, while a SAN transfers I/O blocks between processors and storage. NAS uses LAN protocols, such as Ethernet or Gigabit Ethernet, to transfer data.

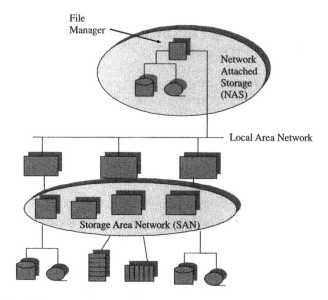

Figure 1.11 Network Attached Storage (NAS).

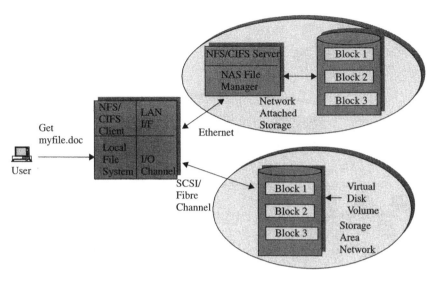

Figure 1.12 SAN versus NAS – the user viewpoint.

NAS uses a file sharing protocol to manage files. This is generally the Network File System, or NFS, in UNIX systems, and the Common Internet File System, or CIFS, in NT/Windows systems.

1.4 STORAGE CONCEPTS

1.4.1 How is Storage Shared Among Different Types of Processors?

True sharing of storage among different types of processors is difficult, since different operating systems use incompatible storage formats and access methods. There are three basic approaches to shared storage. One is to simply create separate partitions in storage for each type of operating system supported (e.g. UNIX, S/390, NT); however, in this approach, only one operating system is allowed to access the data in a given partition.

To share data among operating systems, data copy may be used. In this approach, data is extracted from one partition in flat file format, processed into the proper format, and loaded into the storage partition of another operating system. The software which performs this function is often referred to as a *data mover*.

In true data sharing, all data is stored in a generic storage format and a *virtualization layer* is used to enable the data to be

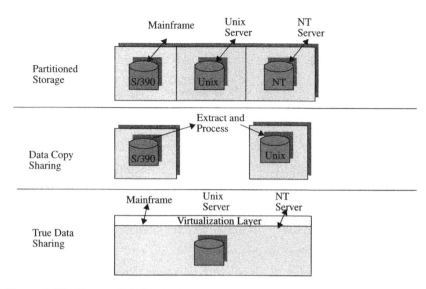

Figure 1.13 Types of data sharing.

accessed by multiple operating systems. The virtualization layer is able to emulate the access method and data transfer protocol of each type of operating system connected to it, and to translate between the operating system-specific protocol and the generic storage format employed internally. However, for true data sharing to be effective, it must provide file and record locking across all supported operating systems.

1.4.2 What is Storage Virtualization?

In *storage virtualization*, applications access data in 'virtual volumes' or 'virtual disks,' rather than accessing the physical devices containing the data directly. A virtual volume may consist of multiple physical disk units, or multiple 'slices' of storage from different disk units, which are managed as a single entity. Use of virtualization has many benefits from a management viewpoint; for example, it is possible to dynamically change the size of a virtual volume, move storage capacity from one volume to another, or install new physical devices, all without disrupting system operation. Virtualization may be performed by a software component, such as a Volume Manager, or by a hardware component, such as a RAID controller.

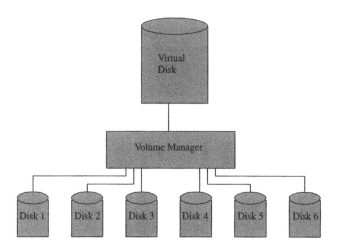

Figure 1.14   Storage virtualization.

1.4.3   What is a RAID?

A redundant array of independent (formerly 'inexpensive') disks, or
RAID, is a term used to describe a technology for managing a group
of disk units to provide increased performance, reliability, or both.
A RAID employs a form of storage virtualization; the application
accessing data sees a single virtual disk, while data is actually
written to or read from a group of physical disk devices managed
by a RAID controller using a technique called *striping*. In striping,
the RAID controller divides up the blocks of data that constitute
an I/O write request and a portion of the total number of blocks
(i.e. a stripe) is written to each physical disk. Conversely, the RAID
controller satisfies a read I/O request by reading blocks of data
from multiple physical disk devices simultaneously. This technique
improves performance by performing multiple disk read/write
operations concurrently rather than serially.

A stripe may be as small as a single sector (512 bytes) or as much as
several megabytes. For accessing large records or datasets for single
users, a small stripe gives better performance, since I/O thruput
is maximized if the data is spread across all available physical
devices. In multi-user environments, performance is improved if
the stripe size is set equal to a typical record size, since this permits
overlapping of I/O operations.

In addition to striping, RAID controllers may also employ
mirroring. Mirroring improves reliability by writing each block
redundantly to two different locations in physical disk storage.

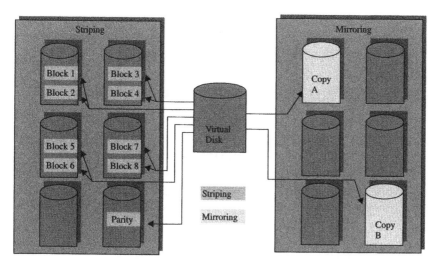

Figure 1.15 RAID architecture.

Many different combinations of striping and mirroring are possible to provide different levels of performance and reliability. Some of the common RAID types are as follows:

- RAID 0 – Striping but no mirroring. This provides the best performance, but is not fault-tolerant.
- RAID 1 – Mirroring but no striping. This provides redundancy for fault tolerance, but no performance improvement over a single disk.
- RAID 2 – Striping with error checking and correction (ECC) information stored on some disks.
- RAID 3 – Striping with ECC. One drive is dedicated to storing parity information (fixed parity). RAID 3 does not permit overlapped I/O. RAID 3 provides high availability at a lower cost than RAID 1.
- RAID 4 – Striping with large stripes and fixed parity. This allows a complete record to be written to a single drive; therefore the complete record can be read in a single read operation. This permits overlapping of read operations. However, write operations may not be overlapped, since the parity drive must be written.
- RAID 5 – Striping with parity distributed across multiple disks (floating parity). This allows overlapping of both read and write operations. Best for multi-user systems.

- RAID 10 – Striping and mirroring. RAID 10 is an array of stripes in which each stripe is a RAID 1 array of drives. Offers higher performance than RAID 1.

1.4.4   How is a RAID different from a JBOD?

Just a Bunch of Disks – Just a bunch of disks, or *JBOD*, is an acronym used to describe a management technique in which a group of hard disk units are managed as a single logical drive. Unlike RAID, JBOD does not provide performance or reliability improvements. JBOD is generally used to organize multiple disk drives of different capacities into a larger virtual disk. JBOD is also referred to as *spanning*.

1.5   SAN APPLICATIONS

SANs enable a number of data management functions to be automated in order to increase system reliability. *Backup* refers to the practice of periodically making copies of application data and transferring them to a storage device that is kept physically separate from the original copy, such as a tape cartridge or a RAID. If the original data is lost, it may be *restored* from the copy. Backup is generally not performed as a realtime function; that is, the data is not necessarily backed up at the time it is created, but rather at some regular scheduled time, based on a backup algorithm. Disk mirroring, on the other hand, writes data to multiple locations in storage as it is created or changed, and therefore can be thought of as a realtime function. Disk mirroring should therefore be implemented in such a way as to be transparent to the end user function, and should not affect system performance significantly.

Two levels of mirroring are in common use. *Synchronous mirroring* (or synchronous data replication) writes data to the mirror copy at the exact time it is created or changed and thus is a true realtime function. *Asynchronous mirroring* (or asynchronous data replication, or 'shadowing') logs changes as they occur, and then writes a group of changes to the mirror copy at some time interval; thus asynchronous mirroring is a 'near-realtime' function.

1.5.1   Backup

As noted earlier, SANs provide the ability to automate the backup process. In the 'islands of storage' architecture, each individual computer or server node must have a dedicated backup

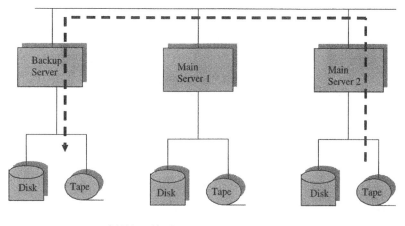

LAN-based backup uses server
processor cycles and LAN
bandwidth

Figure 1.16   LAN-based backup.

device, leading to inefficient use of resources. To improve backup
resource utilization, network designers first employed a *backup
server*, a separate server node attached to the same LAN as
the application servers, which managed backup for all application nodes in a centralized fashion. This configuration is referred
to as *LAN-based backup*. In this mode of operation, the backup
server is programmed to perform backup on data belonging to
each application server at specified intervals. When the scheduled backup time for an individual server occurs, the backup
server sends commands to the specified server, requesting it to
back up all or some portion of its backend storage. The backup
operation is performed by transferring the data through the application server, across the LAN, and through the backup server
to the dedicated backup storage. While this approach improves
resource utilization by centralizing the backup operation, it impacts
system performance through its use of application server processor cycles and LAN bandwidth to perform backup. As a
result, LAN-based backup is generally performed during non-
business hours when system performance will not be affected by
the operation.

1.5.1.1   LAN-Free Backup

Implementation of a SAN allows backup to be performed without
utilizing significant amounts of either LAN bandwidth or server

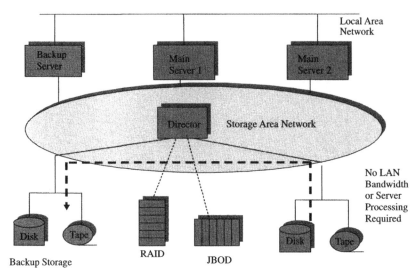

Figure 1.17   SAN-based backup.

processing cycles. In *LAN-free backup*, the LAN is used only for the purpose of sending backup commands to the individual servers. The servers then use the SAN fabric switch to connect the application storage to the backup storage to back the data up directly, eliminating the need to send data through the servers and over the LAN.

1.5.1.2   Server-Free Backup

A further refinement to the backup process is provided by *server-free backup*. In this configuration, scheduled backups are performed by moving data directly from the application backend storage to the backup storage without the involvement of the application server. Server-free backup may be performed by a separate SAN backup appliance, or by software resident in the storage director. It is sometimes referred to as *third party copy*. This approach provides full backup capability with a minimum of impact on the network and application servers.

1.5.2   Disk Mirroring

There are two general approaches to disk mirroring. In *processor centric mirroring*, the server or computer node is aware of the

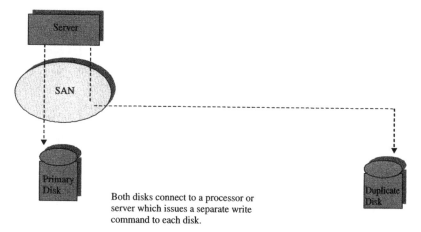

Both disks connect to a processor or
server which issues a separate write
command to each disk.

Figure 1.18 Processor-centric disk mirroring.

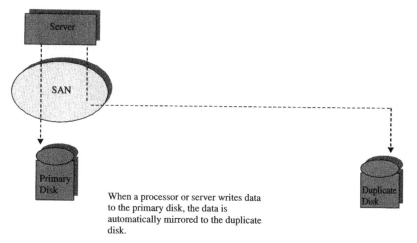

When a processor or server writes data
to the primary disk, the data is
automatically mirrored to the duplicate
disk.

Figure 1.19 Storage centric disk mirroring.

existence of a primary disk and a mirror disk, and simply issues
duplicate write commands to each to create mirror copies.

In *storage centric mirroring*, the server is aware only of the primary
disk, and the disk controller is responsible for copying the data
to the mirror disk. When data is written to the primary disk, it is
automatically copied to the mirror disk.

1.6 SUMMARY

The introduction of storage networks was largely driven by the
need to manage large quantities of stored data efficiently. The

need to synchronize databases at geographically separated locations, together with the development of storage protocols that could be extended over large distances, has led to the development of distributed storage networks to provide additional efficiency, reliability, and availability.

Mainframe computers provided the original model for storage networks. The evolution from copper-based bus/tag interfaces to fiber-based optical storage protocols made it possible for mainframe storage to be geographically distributed, and the parallel evolution from the SCSI bus architecture to Fibre Channel in the open systems environment led to new storage network approaches and architectures.

While Fibre Channel was first used to provide point-to-point connectivity over longer distances than SCSI buses could support, it also triggered the evolution of true storage area network, or SAN architectures, including the switched fabric and arbitrated loop, to manage storage of blocks of data. Using LAN-based servers to serve files to applications led to the evolution of Network Attached Storage, or NAS.

The need to manage storage efficiently has led to the development of new storage organizational concepts that are dependent on neither the operating system used or the physical track format of the storage device. Storage virtualization can be implemented in hardware by means of a redundant array of independent disks (RAID), or in software by a volume manager that manages a group of real storage devices as a virtual volume.

The use of storage networks enables many administrative functions to be performed efficiently. LAN-free backup eliminates the need to send large amounts of data across the LAN for backup purposes, and server-free, or third party copy backup, can be performed without any application server involvement. The use of processor-centric and storage-centric mirroring techniques enables duplication of stored data in real or near-real time.

2

Applications for Distributed Storage Networking

This chapter provides a rationale for creating geographically distributed storage networks, describes applications which utilize distributed storage networks for data storage, and differentiates applications which require 'near-realtime' and 'non-realtime' data access.

The introduction of serial fiber-based storage protocols such as ESCON and Fibre Channel greatly increased the distance over which blocks of data could be transferred between processors and storage devices. While bus-based protocols such as bus/tag and SCSI limited this distance to a few meters, ESCON and Fibre Channel enabled storage to be transported over distances as great as 10 kilometers – and even further, if the proper repeaters and protocol translators were used. This enabled the development of storage applications that were not limited to a specific geographical area, but rather could be distributed across a metropolitan area, or even a wide area, by using the proper networking techniques.

Applications of distributed storage networks include:

- high-performance storage consolidation,
- centralized management of server and storage assets,
- large data bases, date warehouses, and data marts,

Distributed Storage Networks   Thomas C. Jepsen
© 2003 John Wiley & Sons, Ltd   ISBN: 0-470-85020-5

- storage backup and recovery systems with LAN-free and server-free techniques,
- SAN implementations with robust storage management virtualization, hierarchical storage management, and storage resource management,
- NAS and SAN integration,
- high performance workgroups, data centers, and remote network implementations,
- campus backbones and WAN deployments,
- edge networks for data replication and scaleable performance (digital audio/video networks, webserver downloads),
- data migration from one physical site to another,
- comprehensive business continuity/disaster recovery solutions,
- remote operation of peripheral devices.

Extending a SAN over a large area requires the use of gateway devices or optical multiplexers to terminate the transport protocol and interface with the switching fabric (see Figure 2.1). Switching ports on the local fabric are connected to the gateway device, which provides connectivity through the WAN or MAN to a similar gateway in the remote fabric. This allows remotely located devices to be addressed just as though they were part of the local fabric.

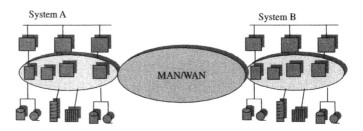

SAN functions can be extended across the Metro Area
Network (MAN) or Wide Area Network (WAN) by
using gateways or transport devices

Figure 2.1 Extending SAN functions across the MAN or WAN.

2.1 STORAGE INTEGRATION

Storage integration or *storage sharing* refers to the use of distributed storage networks to share disks and integrate storage across a wide geographical area. This approach is particularly useful in applications where the amount of data stored is so large that it would be infeasible (or uneconomical) to duplicate it. Some examples of applications that make use of distributed storage networks for storage sharing or integration include databases of genetic data for genome research, multimedia or video servers, and e-commerce applications where multiple servers update a common database.

In the shared storage configuration shown below (see Figure 2.2), each system has access to both its own storage and the storage of the other system. Many fabric switches have remote device mapping capability that makes a remote storage device appear to be part of the local SAN configuration. Thus, System A can access blocks of data on System B's storage devices as well as its own storage. Likewise, System B can access blocks of data on System A as well as its own storage. Users of either system would be unaware of the actual physical location of their data.

Shared access is not problematical if access is for read-only data. If data is to be written or modified, however, access to the data must be controlled so that only one user is modifying the data at any time, to prevent corruption. File systems and database managers typically employ a *locking mechanism* to ensure that only one user is attempting to update data at any time.

Distributed storage provides additional security for critical data as well. Randomizing the physical location of sensitive data makes it difficult for hackers or intruders to compromise system security.

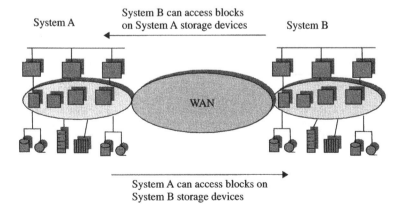

Figure 2.2 Distributed SAN for storage sharing and integration.

2.2 REMOTE BACKUP/RESTORAL

Remote backup/restoral refers to the use of distributed storage networks to provide non-realtime backup and restoral of user data from a remote location. Backup of data to a remote location is sometimes referred to as *electronic tape vaulting*. Traditionally, remote backup has been performed by writing data to tape at the primary site, and then transporting the tapes to the remote site by means of a truck or other vehicle. If data is lost or corrupted at the primary site, the tapes are retrieved from the remote storage site and brought to the primary site for recovery. (Data processing people sometimes refer to this method as CTAM, or 'Chevy Truck Access Method.') Most ordinary business and financial applications use some form of backup/restoral to provide increased reliability and availability of their business data.

Manual backup of system data is a time-consuming and sometimes disruptive process, since it requires that processing of certain datasets be halted during the backup period, and requires that personnel and equipment be dedicated to the backup process. The trend toward 24/7 uptime in data centers has greatly reduced the size and frequency of *backup windows*, or segments of time specifically allocated to perform backup operations, during which time application processing is suspended. Use of distributed storage networks to perform backup automatically to a remote site eliminates much of the overhead associated with manual backup. Data is simply backed up automatically across the MAN or WAN to tape or disk devices at the remote site, using a backup scheduling

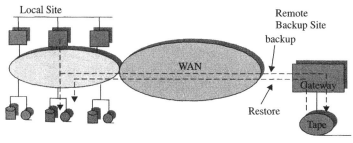

Data written to local storage is also written to tape at remote backup site. If data is lost, it can be restored from the remote site.

Figure 2.3 Remote backup/restore using distributed storage network.

algorithm. If data is lost at the primary site, it can be restored from the backup copy across the MAN/WAN network.[1]

2.3   DISK MIRRORING

Disk mirroring refers to the use of distributed storage networks to provide near-realtime copying of user data to multiple disks. Unlike backup, disk mirroring causes a redundant copy of the data to be made at time the transaction is committed and written to the local disk, rather than at a predefined backup time. Thus, mirroring provides greater availability of data than backup, but at the cost of duplicating storage capacity. Many applications in finance or banking require mission-critical data to be stored redundantly in a location that is physically separate from the primary site. Often the backup, or secondary, site is required to draw its power from a different power grid than the primary site, to ensure that loss of power at one site does not affect operations at the other. Remote disk mirroring may be either processor-centric or storage-centric. Special consideration must be take to ensure that the remote mirroring technique employed does not adversely affect system performance, and presents the user with the appearance of 'near-realtime' data access.

   Mirroring may be synchronous or asynchronous. A synchronous system mirrors every transaction as it is committed. The local write operation is not considered to be complete until the remote write has completed. This requires a data link capable of handling the full transfer bandwidth. If not, system performance will be noticeably degraded.

   Asynchronous mirroring is less dependent on the speed of the data link. Data on the remote system may lag behind data on the local system. The local system logs changes to data as they occur, and then periodically applies the logged changes to the remote system. The window for applying logs is typically between 5 minutes and 1 hour.

2.3.1   Processor Centric Remote Disk Mirroring

In processor-centric remote disk mirroring, the primary processor or server is aware of the existence of both the primary disk and the

---

[1] The use of tape devices for remote backup over extended distances involves some special considerations; this is discussed in Chapter 3.

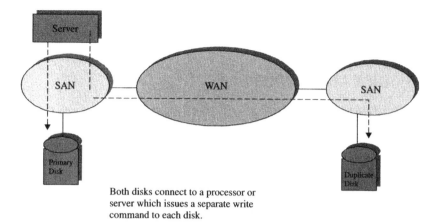

Both disks connect to a processor or
server which issues a separate write
command to each disk.

Figure 2.4   Processor-centric disk mirroring using remote mirror.

remote secondary disk. Separate write commands are sent to each
disk to write data to each individually, and separate responses are
received from each.

2.3.2   Storage Centric Remote Disk Mirroring

In storage-centric remote disk mirroring, the primary processor or
server is only aware of the primary, or local, disk. Copying data to
the remote mirror is done automatically by the controller for the
primary disk.

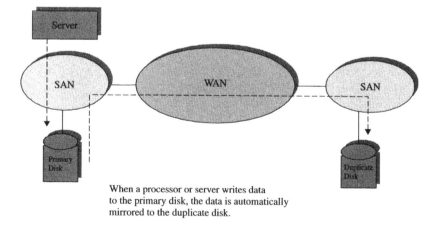

When a processor or server writes data
to the primary disk, the data is automatically
mirrored to the duplicate disk.

Figure 2.5   Storage Centric Remote Disk Mirroring.

2.3.3   'Split Mirror' Copy

Split mirror copy is a specialized form of disk mirroring that provides increased reliability and minimal impact on application performance. Split mirror copy uses a third mirror disk, often remotely located, to increase reliability and minimize the possibility of data loss. (Some implementations may use more than three mirrors, but the basic concept remains the same.) During normal operation, identical data is written to all three mirrors simultaneously; when it is necessary to make a copy, one of the mirrors is *split*, or removed from the configuration. Split mirror copy can be used to perform backups without the need for a backup window, or to create a copy of a database for emergency recovery purposes. Split mirror copy uses a combination of transaction logging and mirroring techniques to provide optimum performance and minimal disruption to running applications.

For applications that perform high-volume transaction processing, it is difficult to perform a copy operation at the precise time when all current transactions have completed and been written to disk, and no new transactions have begun; in other words, when the database contents are *consistent*. One way to achieve this is to simply stop the application from performing further processing while the backup is made; however, this greatly reduces performance. A better solution is to continue processing, suspend writes to the mirrors, and temporarily cache all changes. Read-only operations may be allowed to continue normally.

When it is necessary to make a backup copy or a duplicate database, the administrator suspends, or *quiesces*, the applications that normally write data to the mirrors, so that a copy can be made while the database is in a consistent state. One of the mirrors is then split, and a backup copy is made from its content. (Or, if a duplicate database is being created, the new database is activated, using the copied data.) This copy, often referred to as a *frozen image*, represents a 'snapshot' of the database contents at a specific point in time.

The split mirror is then returned to the mirrored configuration. Although suspending writes or quiescing the application guarantees consistency at the time the split is made, it is possible that additional changes have been written to the other two mirrors while the backup was being created from the third mirror. There are two basic ways to resynchronize the third mirror with the other

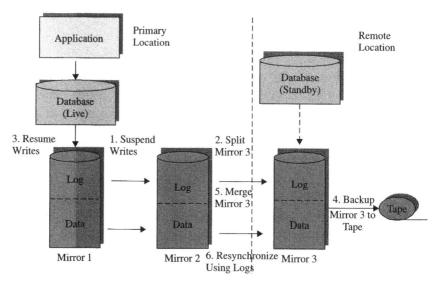

Figure 2.6 Split mirror copy using three mirrors.

two disks when it is merged back into the configuration. One is to simply overwrite all the data on the third disk with data from the other two; however, this is an inefficient use of I/O processing. A more efficient way is to use a transaction log to selectively update changed blocks on the third mirror. In this mode of operation, each mirror image contains a transaction log as well as stored data. The transaction log contains a record of all transactions that have been written to the mirror since the last resynchronization. It is possible to resynchronize the split mirror by simply 'playing back' all the changes recorded in the transaction logs of one of the other mirrors.

2.4 DATA MIGRATION

Storage networks may be used to efficiently move large volumes of data from one physical location to another when, for example, a company moves to a larger building. In the past, this was often an awkward process in which volumes of data had to be copied to tape and physically transported to the new location, often causing disruptions in day to day processing. Storage networks provide an elegant solution to this problem. Mirroring and/or backup techniques can be used to create a new copy of the data at the new location while processing continues as usual at the old location. At

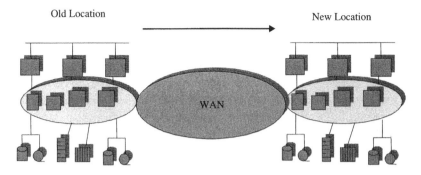

To reduce impact of re-location, stored data is
copied/moved to storage at new location.

Figure 2.7 Use of storage network for data migration.

a specified time, the copy at the old location is archived, or deleted, and the copy at the new location becomes the master copy. This technique has been utilized, for example, by telecommunications companies to move billing data from one processing center to another while maintaining ongoing operations.

2.5 BUSINESS CONTINUITY/DISASTER RECOVERY

Distributed storage networks play an important role in business continuity planning and in recovering from loss of data due to disasters. Business continuity strategies typically require that not

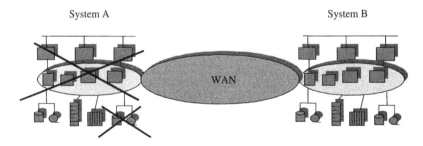

Two levels of disaster recovery:

1) If data is lost in System A, it can be recovered from System B
2) If System A is completely destroyed, processing can continue
   at System B

Figure 2.8 Distributed SAN for disaster recovery/business continuity.

only redundant storage, but also complete processing capabilities, be maintained at a remote location. This provides a multilevel business continuity and disaster recovery solution. If data is lost at the primary site, it can be recovered from the secondary site using standard backup/restoral or mirroring techniques. If processing capability is lost at the primary site, processing can continue at the recovery site. If either site becomes completely inoperative, the other site can continue full processing.

2.6 REMOTE OPERATION OF PERIPHERAL DEVICES

Storage protocols may be used to remotely operate peripheral devices, such as printers or check sorters, that are located at some distance from the server or processor. This may be done to allow peripherals to be located near the department that makes use of them, or to keep paper chaff and ink from entering a filtered air system. Remote peripheral operation can be performed using either SAN or mainframe storage architectures; in mainframe terminology, this function is referred to as *channel extension*. A financial services company might use this technique to remotely operate check readers and sorters in a remote processing center.

2.7 MAINFRAME/OPEN SYSTEMS CONNECTIVITY

Storage networks may be used to provide connectivity between mainframe systems and open systems running UNIX or NT/Windows operating systems. Applications making use of mainframe/open systems connectivity include:

- integration of e-commerce and mainframe-based applications,
- data warehousing,
- backup/recovery.

It is possible to move data between mainframe applications and open systems by using LAN bandwidth, or by creating a flat file and moving the data via file transfer protocol (ftp), but these approaches are slow and complex. A faster way is to make use of the bandwidth available in both the mainframe channel and the open systems storage network to transfer the data directly from storage

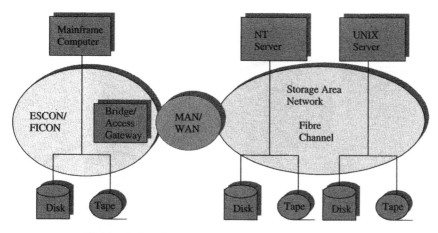

Enables sharing of storage among
mainframe, UNIX, and NT processors

Figure 2.9 Using a storage network for mainframe/open systems connectivity.

subsystem to storage subsystem. A gateway or bridge is normally used to translate between the ESCON or FICON storage protocol used in the mainframe channel subsystem and the SCSI or Fibre Channel used in the open systems storage network (Figure 2.9). The storage protocols can be extended across the WAN or MAN to provide remote connectivity.

2.8   NETWORK ATTACHED STORAGE (NAS)

Network Attached Storage (NAS) uses a file manager, located on a LAN, and a shared file access application, such as NFS or CIFS, to provide clients with shared access to stored files. The primary difference between NAS and SAN architecture lies in the fact that NAS serves file-structured data to clients while SANs serve block-structured data to application servers. However, this neat distinction is blurred somewhat by the fact that the NAS file manager must manage data at the block level in its own attached storage. The file manager contains metadata, in the form of directories and data structures, that maps file requests to blocks of data in disk storage. It follows from this that NAS can be seen as just another application that can benefit from SAN-based backend storage management, and this is precisely the function of a network appliance referred to as a *NAS head* (Figure 2.10). A NAS head is a

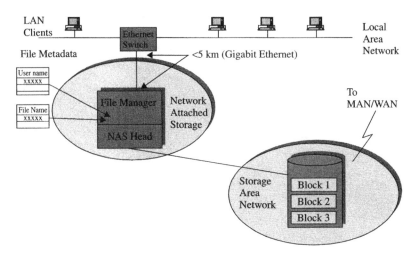

Figure 2.10 NAS head architecture.

file manager front end that serves files to its clients and attaches to a backend SAN for management of its block-structured data.

2.8.1   NAS File Sharing Protocol

NAS uses one of several standard file sharing protocols to enable shared access to files by multiple applications, and to support required functions, such as the ability to provide locking when more than one application is accessing a single file.

One common file sharing protocol is the Network File System, or NFS. NFS was first standardized by the IETF in 1989; the current version, NFS 4, is defined in RFC3010. NFS is widely used in UNIX environments and uses the Remote Procedure Call (RPC) mechanism to remotely open and serve files; NFS for NT/Windows environments is also available. When a client requests and is granted access to a file from the server, it obtains a lock on that file for a period of time referred to as a *lease*. A lock grants the owning client the right to modify the file, and to exclude other clients from modifying the same file. (Other clients may access the same file for read-only operations, but are not permitted to modify the file.) NFS may run over Unreliable Datagram Protocol (UDP) or Transmission Control Protocol (TCP); TCP is recommended for version 4.

Another file sharing protocol associated with NT/Windows environments is the Common Internet File Sharing protocol, or

CIFS. Many different versions of CIFS are in existence; the Storage Networking Industry Association has issued a CIFS Technical Reference to promote standardization (CIFS, 2002). CIFS provides shared file services to clients over a network; it is based on the Server Message Block (SMB) protocol used by many personal computers and workstations. Like NFS, CIFS provides shared file access and the ability to lock a file to prevent other users from modifying it. CIFS may run on top of NETBIOS, or directly on top of TCP.

2.8.2 Distributing NAS Applications

NAS applications can be distributed over a wide geographical area in two ways. The use of switched Gigabit Ethernet enables NAS file managers to be as much as 5 km distant from the production LAN without the need for repeaters. This would enable, for example, a NAS file manager or head to be co-located with remotely located backend storage for storage consolidation purposes.

For the NAS head configuration, the backend SAN could be distributed across multiple sites, using any of the architectures described for multi-site SANs.

2.9 SUMMARY

The development of storage protocols that operate over extended distances has made it possible for a wide variety of distributed storage applications to be developed that improve the efficiency and reliability of storage-based applications. Distributed storage applications improve efficiency by enabling data stored in multiple physical locations to be consolidated and accessed by any network server in a transparent fashion. Remote backup and mirroring improve the reliability of the system by creating redundant copies of critical data, and improve the efficiency by eliminating backup downtime and manual backup operations. Business continuity and disaster recovery capabilities enable enterprises to recover quickly and transparently from system failure or data loss. Storage protocols enable data to be transferred from mainframe applications to open systems applications rapidly and transparently. NAS applications provide shared file access for clients using standard LAN-based technology.

3

Distance Considerations for Storage Networks

Most storage protocols were initially designed to support a range of a few meters, and were not intended to be extended beyond the room in which the processor or server was located. As storage capacity requirements increased and requirements for distributed storage arose, some distance-based limitations became apparent. This led to the design of more advanced protocols that could operate efficiently over long distances, and the use of optical fiber for high-bandwidth data transport. This section discusses distance considerations for storage protocols at the physical, protocol, and application levels.

3.1 PHYSICAL LAYER

Over time, storage protocols have evolved from parallel bus transfers using copper wire to high-speed serial protocols over optical fiber. This evolution in physical media is discussed below.

3.1.1 Parallel Bus Limitations

Storage protocols originally utilized parallel copper wire bus architectures in which commands and control information were sent

Distributed Storage Networks   Thomas C. Jepsen
© 2003 John Wiley & Sons, Ltd   ISBN: 0-470-85020-5

over dedicated lines, and data bytes were written and read over data buses that were one or more bytes in width. Both the mainframe bus/tag interface (see Figure 3.1) and the SCSI bus (see Figure 3.2) follow this model. Increases in the storage capacity of disk devices and improvements in access latencies led to demands for improvements in the data transfer rate. This demand was met by both (a) increasing the width of the data bus to return more bytes per transfer, and (b) increasing the clock rate for data.

As the bandwidth of the bus increases, certain effects become noticeable which limit the effective length of the bus. One is *clock skew*, or *cable skew*. As the clock rate increases, bus signals become shorter in duration, and the propagation delay of the bus becomes significant. Small differences in the length of the individual wires in a cable may cause signals that left one device's drivers at identical times to arrive at another device's receivers at different times. Adding to this effect is the fact that individual line driver and receiver components do not necessarily have the same threshold and response characteristics, increasing the probability of timing errors.

Another length-limiting factor for copper buses is their transmission characteristic. A bus effectively functions as a transmission line, and exhibits transmission line behavior. To prevent signal reflections, the end of a transmission line must be terminated with a terminator of the proper impedance. However, variations in individual

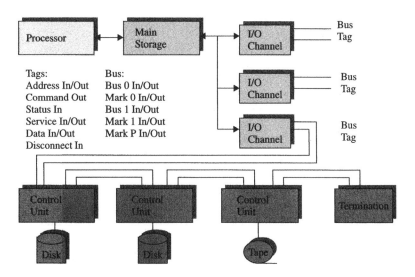

Figure 3.1 Bus/tag architecture.

components such as connectors, receivers, and terminators may cause impedance mismatches or *bus discontinuities* which in turn generate reflections. If the reflected signals have sufficient amplitude, and are delayed sufficiently from the original signal by propagation delay, they may be mistakenly interpreted as valid signals and create errors.

Adding to both of these is the effect of noise on the line. Signals induced into the bus by nearby electromagnetic devices can cause unpredictable effects. This can, however, be mitigated to some extent by the use of shielded cable and connectors. Together, the effects of clock skew, signal reflections, and line noise limit the maximum length of a single ended SCSI bus to 6 meters, and therefore it is most commonly used only to connect devices within a frame or cabinet assembly. (Note: some versions of the SCSI protocol have even shorter maximum lengths; for example, Fast SCSI is limited to 3 meters, and Ultra SCSI is limited to 1.5 meters. For more information on these variants, see Section 5.1, SCSI Protocol.)

The use of differential mode signals can improve the noise immunity. In differential mode, each signal consists of two lines, designated +SIGNAL and −SIGNAL, each of which is the logical inversion of the other. The SCSI standard defines a differential mode physical interface which enables the bus to be extended to a maximum of 25 meters for applications which require running cables outside the cabinet. However, it has the disadvantage

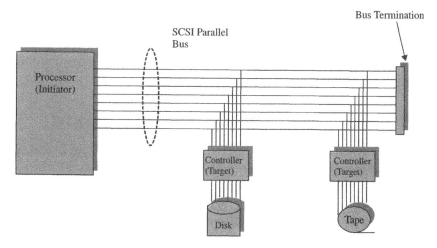

Figure 3.2 SCSI bus topology.

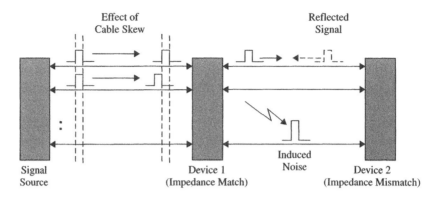

Figure 3.3 Parallel bus signal impairments.

of requiring many more wires in the cable, and a different (and incompatible) connector.

3.1.2   Optical Networking Considerations

As fiber optic technology was developed in the late 1980s and early 1990s, researchers saw a way to both increase the data transport rate of storage protocols and to remove the limitations on distance imposed by the parallel bus architecture. The answer to both problems was to exploit the nearly infinite bandwidth capabilities of optical fiber to develop storage data transfer protocols that transmitted data bits serially as bursts of photons. Enterprise Systems Connection, or ESCON, was developed by IBM in 1991 as a replacement for the bus/tag interface, and Fibre Channel, standardized by ANSI in 1994 as a generic data transport protocol, was quickly adopted for use as a storage protocol that could remove the distance limitations inherent in SCSI.

3.1.2.1   Optical Fiber Technology for Storage Protocols

There are two basic types of optical fiber in use in networks today: Single Mode Fiber (SMF) and MultiMode Fiber (MMF). Single mode fiber allows light to travel along only one path, or mode, through the center of the fiber. Single mode fiber generally has a core diameter of 8 or 9 mm, and is able to transmit high bandwidth over long distances. Single mode fiber is used for virtually all WAN and MAN networks.

Multimode fiber allows multiple modes of transmission to exist in the fiber. This is due to the fact that light propagates not only by traveling in a straight line down the center, but also by being reflected off the boundary of the core and the cladding. Multimode fiber has two standard core sizes, 62.5 and 50 mm. (Multimode fiber is sometimes specified by both the core and the cladding diameters, for example 62.5/125 mm.) Because of the dispersion effects caused by having multiple modes of transmission, multimode fiber does not provide the same levels of bandwidth or range capability as single mode fiber; however, due to its low cost, it is frequently used in LANs and short-haul applications.

Both SMF and MMF are used for storage networking applications. SMF is generally preferable, due to its superior bandwidth and transmission range capabilities. However, MMF may yield satisfactory results over shorter distances if attention is paid to its transmission characteristics. For example, existing MMF cabling within a building may be used to provide connectivity between storage devices in data centers and long-haul SMF terminated in a telecom closet.

Optical fiber may be lit by either laser or light emitting diode (LED) sources. Although they are cheaper than lasers, LEDs do not perform well at higher data rates, and lasers are generally used for higher bit rate transmission. Three wavelength regions are in common use for transmission; short wavelengths around 850 nanometers (nm); longer wavelengths centered around 1310 nm to provide minimum dispersion; and long wavelengths centered around 1550 nm to provide minimum attenuation. Table 3.1 lists

Table 3.1   Common optical fiber types and applications

Type	Dimensions (mm)	Use/Application	Applicable standards
MMF	50/125	Campus LAN; laser-driven	ISO/IEC 11801 TIA/EIA-568
MMF	62.5/125	FDDI/Ethernet/Token Ring LAN; LED-driven	TIA/EIA-568A
SMF	5–9	Standard Single Mode; dispersion optimized for 1300–1324 nm	IEC 60793-2 ITU-T G.652
SMF	5–9	Non-Zero Dispersion Shifted Fiber, dispersion optimized for 1530–1565 nm (C-band), 1565–1625 nm (L-Band)	IEC 60793-2 ITU-T G.655

common types of optical fiber deployed in LAN, MAN, and WAN networks today.

3.1.2.2 Attenuation and Loss Budgets

The maximum distance that light can travel in optical media is limited by three factors – the strength of the signal injected at the near end, the attenuation of the medium at the light frequency, and the sensitivity of the receiver at the far end. Engineering an optical link is a two-step process. First, a *loss budget* is calculated, which specifies the maximum allowable loss in the link, given a minimum input power and a specified receiver sensitivity for a given signal to noise level (see Figure 3.4). The loss budget is normally specified in dB. These parameters can be found in the specifications for the individual protocols. Then the attenuation for the optical fiber is calculated for the required distance. If the attenuation is less than the allowable loss given by the loss budget, then the link will function correctly.

Attenuation for optical fiber media is generally logarithmic over large distances, and has been specified in the industry standards for optical fiber. Attenuation is greater at short wavelengths (850 nm) than at longer wavelengths (1300 and 1550 nm). Therefore it is possible to specify maximum unrepeatered distances for storage protocols based on loss budgets and media attenuation; Table 3.2 shows loss budgets and maximum distances for common storage protocols.

Loss Budget = Minimum Transmitted Power–Minimum Receiver Sensitivity

Figure 3.4 Computing loss budgets for optical links.

3.1.2.3 Differential Mode Delay

One phenomenon which limits both bandwidth and distance for multimode fiber is *Differential Mode Delay* (DMD). DMD occurs when laser sources are used with multimode fiber. Lasers tend to generate a few transmission modes with approximately equal power; since different modes take different paths through the fiber,

Table 3.2 Loss budget for common optical storage protocols

Protocol	Fiber type	Loss budget	Maximum distance
ESCON	SMF	14 dB	20 km
ESCON	MMF (62.5 mm)	8 dB	2–3 km
ESCON	MMF (50 mm)	8 dB	2 km
FICON	SMF	7 dB	10 km
FICON (using offset coupler)	MMF (62.5 and 50 mm)	5 dB	550 m
Fibre Channel	SMF	14 dB	10 km
Fibre Channel	MMF	6 dB	1.5 km
Gigabit Ethernet 1000BaseLX	SMF	4.6 dB	5 km
Gigabit Ethernet 1000BaseSX	MMF (62.5 mm)	2.6 dB	220–275 m
Gigabit Ethernet 1000BaseLX (using offset coupler)	MMF (62.5 mm)	2.4 dB	550 m
Gigabit Ethernet 1000BaseSX	MMF (50 mm)	3.6 dB	550 m
Gigabit Ethernet 1000BaseLX (using offset coupler)	MMF (50 mm)	2.4 dB	550 m

they will arrive at the far end at different times. This condition is referred to as *underfilled launch*. The effect of this is to spread out the pulse in time; if the distance is great enough, the signal becomes degraded and is unreadable (see Figure 3.5).

There are several ways to minimize the effect. One is to use an offset coupler. This consists of a short length of single mode fiber connecting to the transmitting laser, and a special coupling which enables the signal to be injected into the multimode fiber at a point away from its center. The effect is to distribute the modes evenly, so that they tend to arrive at the other end at approximately the same time.

3.1.2.4 Chromatic Dispersion

Digital signals carried over optical fiber actually consist of multiple wavelengths, rather than just a single frequency. Since different wavelengths travel through the optical media at different velocities, pulses tend to 'spread out,' particularly at longer wavelengths and higher data rates. This effect is referred to as *chromatic dispersion,*

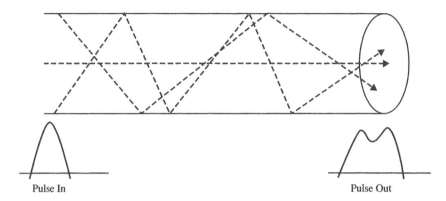

Pulse In   Pulse Out

Figure 3.5 Differential Mode Delay (DMD).

and telecommunications engineers will recognize it as simply the optical version of the Heaviside effect which occurs in analog telephony. While there is no optical equivalent of a 'loading coil' to minimize the phenomenon, a new type of optical fiber, referred to as *Non-Zero Dispersion Shifted Fiber* (NZDSF), provides a constant amount of chromatic dispersion across the frequency spectrum.

3.1.2.5 Wavelength Division Multiplexing (WDM)

To transmit data over longer distances than allowed for in the loss budget, the signal must be regenerated or repeatered. Frequencies in the 1310 nm region normally require electrical regeneration. Therefore each optical fiber carrying a single 1310 nm Signal must be terminated and its signal converted to electrical signals. The electrical signals are then amplified and used to drive a laser which converts the signal to optical pulses again.

For signals in the 1550 nm region, however, it is possible to use optical amplifiers to regenerate the signal without the necessity of converting it to an electrical signal. One such optical amplifier is the Erbium Doped Fiber Amplifier (EDFA). Use of optical amplifiers makes *Wavelength Division Multiplexing* (WDM), a practical technology for mid- and long-range transport of optical signals. In WDM, a group of wavelengths around the 1550 nm region are combined onto a single mode fiber and transmitted to the far end as a group. The use of optical amplifiers makes it possible to regenerate the signals without the need for Optical-to-Electrical-to-Optical (OEO) conversion.

Refinements in the technology have made it possible to carry ever-increasing numbers of channels on a single optical fiber. While

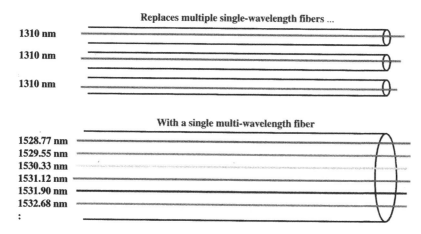

Figure 3.6   Use of wavelength division multiplexing.

the earlier WDM implementations typically supported 8 or 16 channels, it is now common to support as many as 32 channels, and some commercially available products support over 170 channels. WDM with improved channel density is generally referred to as Dense Wavelength Division Multiplexing (DWDM).

Storage protocols can make efficient use of WDM technology for long range applications. If multiple ESCON or Fibre Channel links must be installed from one city to another to support a distributed storage application, it would be costly and inefficient to run a separate optical fiber for each link. Instead, each ESCON or Fibre Channel link can be converted to a single WDM wavelength, and all the wavelengths run over a single optical fiber. By using EDFA amplification, the protocols can be transmitted over much greater distances than their native-mode loss budgets would allow.

3.2   PROTOCOL CONSIDERATIONS

While use of optical fiber technology can extend the range of storage protocols at the physical level, other factors must be taken into account at the protocol level. Storage protocols are 'stop and wait' protocols that were originally designed to operate over distances of a few meters at most, and propagation delays can have a significant effect on performance.

As an example, assume a disk mirroring operation using a remote site that is 50 km from the primary site. Disk write access latency for both sites might be in the vicinity of 3 milliseconds. Mirroring to the remote site requires factoring in the propagation delay of the fiber optic link, which is about 10 microseconds per kilometer, and the number of command and data acknowledgments required by the protocol, since storage protocols require multiple data and command acknowledgments per data transfer. If the protocol used requires six commands and acknowledgments per transfer, then the total time required to perform the disk mirroring operation would be 3 ms (local write) + 10 us × 50 km × 6 acknowledgments = 3 ms (propagation time) + 3 ms (remote write) = 9 ms (total time required for mirror operation). Thus, the performance of the mirroring operation is affected not only by the distance, but also by the protocol operation.

3.2.1   Command Execution

Storage protocol data transfer functions normally consist of three phases: a *command* phase, a *data transfer* phase, and a *status* phase (see Figure 3.7). In the command phase, a command is issued to the storage device by the controller or initiator. This might be a positioning command, a read command, or a write command. In the data transfer phase, the data is transferred to or from the device, depending on the operation performed. In the status phase, information is returned to the controller/initiator on the success or failure of the operation. If the transfer failed for some reason, additional error information is returned in this phase.

Many storage protocols require an acknowledgment to be returned to the initiator/controller after each command is issued to the storage device. This adds processing overhead due to both the round trip delay of the command and response, and the command execution delay at the remote end. This can have a large impact on

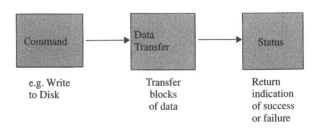

Figure 3.7 Storage protocol data transfer functions.

performance over large distances. It reduces the maximum number of input/output operations which may be performed per second, and in severe cases may cause I/O operations to time out.

The solution to the problem is to use a non-synchronous command execution protocol that does not require individual responses to each command before proceeding to the next operation. An example of this is the use of channel command word (CCW) pipelining in FICON™ (see Figure 3.8). The ESCON protocol requires an individual acknowledgment for each CCW sent to the device controller. FICON, on the other hand, allows one acknowledgment to be returned for multiple CCWs, signifying completion of the entire data transfer operation.

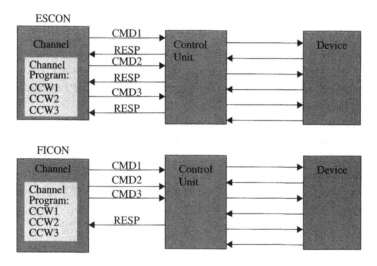

Figure 3.8 CCW pipelining in FICON.

3.2.2 Data Acknowledgments

Each data frame or packet that is transferred between the controller/initiator and the storage device must be acknowledged. Frame acknowledgments are required by the operating system or channel program to ensure that resources, such as buffers, are being allocated fairly among competing applications. If frame sizes are small, and propagation time is significant, however, frame acknowledgments may consume more I/O service time than actual data transfer. This can result in a phenomenon known as *data droop*

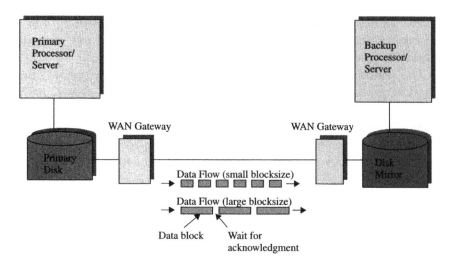

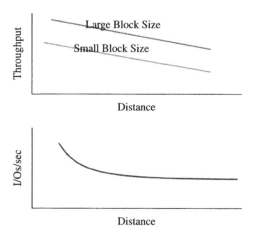

Figure 3.9 Effect of data droop in SAN/WAN applications.

over large distances, due to the latency required for frame/packet acknowledgment.

To avoid this effect, frame/packet sizes should be as large as possible when doing I/O over large distances. Fibre Channel permits *data streaming*, in which multiple frames are sent in one I/O exchange requiring only one acknowledgment. Figure 3.10 shows the effect that data droop has on throughput and I/O performance as distance increases.

Figure 3.10 Effect of data droop on I/O performance.

3.2.3 Remote Tape Backup over Extended Distances

The use of tape drives for remote backup and remote vaulting presents special considerations when extended distances are involved. Before data can be written to or read from the tape, the drive must be running at the correct speed. For a write, this means that the data must be available from the network when the tape reaches the proper operating speed. If the network latency is variable, this can present problems, because the data may not be available when the tape drive is ready to write it. Data and command acknowledgments, as described above, may also cause problems over long distances. Tape drives are sequential devices, and must complete each I/O block before the next can be written. Sending of acknowledgments introduces additional latency that can adversely affect performance over long distances. These problems can be minimized by using buffering and pipelining. Buffering ensures that a complete I/O block is available for write before the write operation begins, and pipelining allows synchronous commands to be pre-acknowledged before the buffered data is actually written to tape.

3.3 CACHING

Caching occurs at many different levels in a typical computing system. Caching may take place at the application, the operating system, the storage network and at the storage controller. RAID typically uses caching to improve the performance of write operations and the "hit ratio" of read operations. The type and number of caching operations performed may affect performance and data reliability of storage networks over an extended distance. Many storage network architectures use caching in multiple areas; this can have an effect on network performance and data reliability.

Caching may be *write-through* or *write-back*. Write-through caching writes data back to storage immediately when it is changed. This provides higher reliability by reducing the probability of transaction journal inconsistency, but creates more traffic and protocol overhead through the network. Database management systems often use write-through cache to ensure transactional consistency. Write-back caching stores a group of changes in cache memory and then writes them back to storage at a specified interval. This improves performance by reducing the number of network accesses required, but creates the possibility that transaction inconsistencies will occur due to losing track of write order. Synchronous mirroring is analogous to write-through caching; asynchronous mirroring is analogous to write-back caching.

3.4 SUMMARY

The need for improved transfer capacity and extended range led to the development of optical-fiber-based storage protocols in the 1990s. The use of high-speed serial protocols over fiber optics eliminated the distance-limiting effects of parallel bus impairments such as clock skew, impedance mismatch, and reflections, and made it possible to extend the distance between storage devices and servers. Fiber-based storage protocols can be extended to distances as great as 20 km in native mode, and even further if wavelength division multiplexers or repeaters are used (Figure 3.11). This distance extension capability in turn enabled the creation of cost-efficient architectures for storage consolidation, remote backup and mirroring, and business continuity.

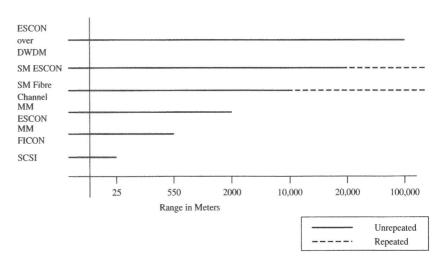

Figure 3.11 Distance limitations for common storage protocols (native mode).

4

Architectures for Distributed Storage Networking

As shown in the previous chapter the distance limitations of each protocol must be taken into account when designing a distributed storage network. SCSI has the shortest range, and is primarily suited for connecting devices within a frame or cabinet. Differential mode SCSI, however, may be extended out of the cabinet to connect devices within the same computer room. Native mode ESCON and Fibre Channel may be used to extend storage connectivity throughout a building, or across a business park or campus, up to a maximum of 10–20 km without the use of repeaters.

For Metropolitan Area Networks (MANs) covering a distance <100 km, repeaters or wavelength division multiplexing may be used to extend the range of ESCON, Fibre Channel, or Gigabit Ethernet. For longer distances, transport via Asynchronous Transfer Mode (ATM) or Time Division Multiplexing (TDM) over Synchronous Optical Network (SONET) is commonly used. Other long-distance options include long-haul Dense Wavelength Division Multiplexing (DWDM) and Internet Protocol (IP) techniques, such as IP SCSI (iSCSI) or Fibre Channel over IP (FCIP).

Distributed Storage Networks   Thomas C. Jepsen
© 2003 John Wiley & Sons, Ltd   ISBN: 0-470-85020-5

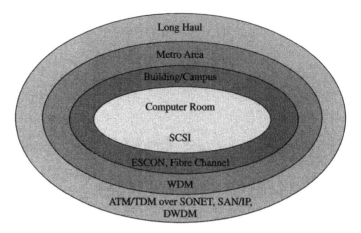

Figure 4.1 Distance versus protocol for storage protocols.

Figure 4.1 provides a comparative view of storage protocols and the environments for which they are best suited. The following sections describe architectures for each of these environments.

4.1 STORAGE NETWORKING IN THE BUSINESS PARK

Storage networks may be distributed within the business park or campus for a variety of reasons. It is common for a business enterprise or educational institution to occupy space in a number of buildings, and it may be most economical to locate storage for all of the sites in a single location. Alternatively, storage may be distributed among multiple sites, and backup capabilities may be located in a central location.

Native mode ESCON or Fibre Channel links may be used to provide storage connectivity within buildings or across a business park or campus without the need for additional equipment, as long as the distance is <10 km (20 km for ESCON). Remotely located SCSI devices may also be connected by using ESCON/Fibre Channel and a protocol bridge.

Gigabit Ethernet may be extended over distances <5 km, and is increasingly being used to extend high-bandwidth LANs and provide NAS-based storage networking in a campus or business park environment.

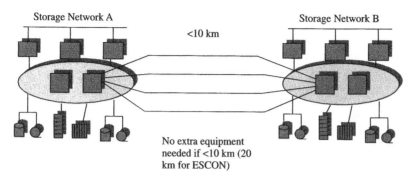

Figure 4.2   Using native mode ESCON or Fibre Channel to provide storage connectivity in the business park (<10 km).

Normally, the fiber optic network within a building complex, business park, or campus is privately maintained by the business or institution making use of the network.

4.2   STORAGE NETWORKING IN THE METRO NETWORK

The term Metropolitan Area Network (MAN) is generally used to describe network connectivity over an urban area; distances between end points are assumed to be 100 km or less. MANs are commonly used to link together business or educational sites within a single metropolitan area. Storage networks may be linked over MANs to provide business continuity, or to synchronize multiple databases.

4.2.1   ESCON/Fibre Channel in the MAN Using Link Extenders

The range of native mode ESCON or Fibre Channel links may be extended to approximately 100 km by using *repeaters* or *link extenders*. These are devices which regenerate the signal at the physical layer. A separate repeater or link extender is required for each link. Depending on the distance and device capabilities, multiple link extenders may be required.

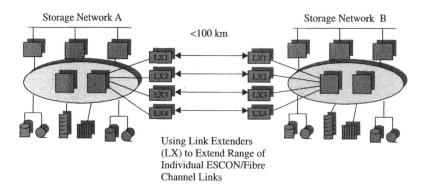

Figure 4.3 Extending ESCON/Fibre Channel links in the MAN using link extenders.

4.2.2 ESCON/Fibre Channel/GigE in the MAN Using Point-to-Point WDM

Alternatively, multiple ESCON, Fibre Channel, and Gigabit Ethernet links can be multiplexed onto a single optical fiber for point-to-point transport across MAN distances using Wavelength Division Multiplexing (WDM). Each link is transported across the MAN using a separate wavelength on the WDM fiber. Distances of up to 50 km are commonly covered using this technique; some WDM systems support distances as great as 100 km. WDM equipment for enterprise access typically supports anywhere from 8–32 channels, with each channel consisting of a single ESCON, Fibre Channel, or Gigabit Ethernet link.

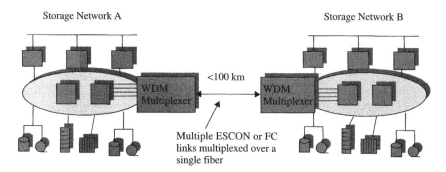

Figure 4.4 Extending ESCON/Fibre Channel links in the MAN using point-to-point WDM.

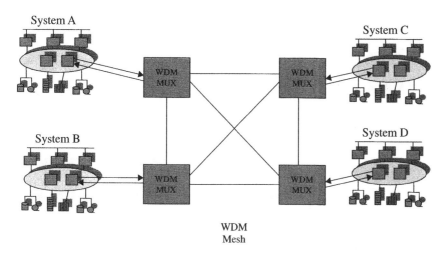

Figure 4.5   Extending ESCON/Fibre Channel links in the MAN using mesh WDM.

Additional connectivity, load sharing, or redundancy can be provided by using a mesh configuration among multiple sites (Figure 4.5). A mesh configuration provides multiple site-to site paths, enabling load sharing or failover in case of link failure.

4.2.3   ESCON/Fibre Channel in the MAN Using a WDM Ring Configuration

ESCON and Fibre Channel links may also be transported over WDM using a ring configuration. In this configuration, individual links are added and dropped at each location around the ring. The ring also provides additional reliability by providing an alternate path in case of failure of the primary path.

Storage connectivity across the MAN may be provided and maintained by the business or institution using the network, or by a public or private carrier. In the link extender or point-to-point WDM scenario, the business or institution may purchase or lease 'dark fiber' from a telecommunications service provider, and provide the necessary equipment to 'light' the fiber. The ring configuration is more complex to install and maintain and is generally provided as a high-reliability service offering by a public carrier.

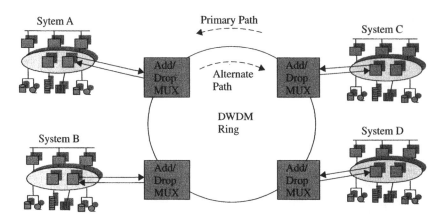

Figure 4.6 Extending ESCON/Fibre Channel links in the MAN using a WDM ring configuration.

4.3 STORAGE NETWORKING IN THE WIDE AREA NETWORK

Storage networks may be connected over the WAN to provide remote database synchronization, to provide disaster recovery/business continuity solutions, or to enable wide area storage sharing.

For distances >100 km, the storage protocol is normally terminated and the data transported to the remote site using Asynchronous Transfer Mode (ATM) or Time Division Multiplexing (TDM) over SONET. For ATM transport, the storage protocol data frames are converted to ATM cells, and transported over the physical layer transport, which may be SONET or DWDM. Similarly, for TDM transport, the data frames are inserted into the SONET payload. At the remote end, the frames are removed from the transport and the storage protocol is regenerated. Compression techniques may also be used to provide more efficient use of transport bandwidth.

If storage over IP technology is employed, such as iSCSI or FCIP, the data frames are converted to IP packets, and transported over the Internet or private network using TCP/IP transport protocol. The use of IP as a storage protocol provides virtually unlimited distance at a relatively low cost. Recently, applications have been developed using asynchronous mirroring over iSCSI that have permitted databases in North America to be mirrored to databases in Europe.

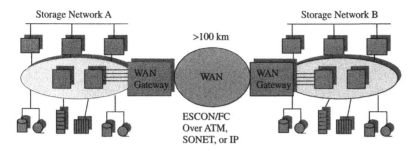

Figure 4.7 Extending ESCON/Fibre Channel links across the WAN.

WAN transport services are normally provided by a public telecommunications carrier. IP based solutions may use the Internet, or a private network.

4.4 SUMMARY

When designing a distributed storage network, the distance limitations of storage protocols must be taken into account. Storage networks are typically designed to be geographically distributed over a business park environment, a metropolitan area, or a wide area, each with specific protocol requirements. Figure 4.8 shows options for extending storage protocols in enterprise, MAN and WAN environments.

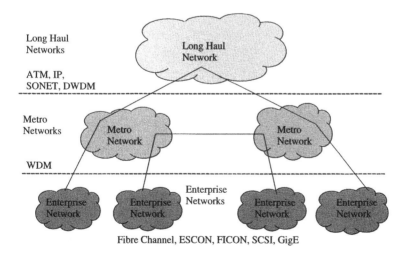

Figure 4.8 Storage protocols in enterprise, MAN, and WAN environments.

5

Protocols for Distributed Storage Networking

This chapter provides a detailed overview of the common storage protocols employed in storage networks. While not all-inclusive, this section is intended to provide a comparison of the capabilities and features found in each protocol, and to indicate its relative suitability for various storage applications. For implementation details, such as timings and state diagrams, the reader is referred to the standards for each protocol. Table 5.1 provides a quick comparison of the protocols discussed, and lists the key features of each.

5.1 SMALL COMPUTER SYSTEMS INTERFACE (SCSI)

The Small Computer Systems Interface (SCSI) was originally developed in the 1980s to provide a standard device interface bus for small computers to enable devices such as tape and disk drives to be attached. Standardization was driven not only by the emergence of small computer systems, but also by the demands of manufacturers of storage peripherals for a vendor-independent logical device interface.

Standardization was begin in 1982 with the formation of the X3T9.2 standards group by the American National Standards

Distributed Storage Networks   Thomas C. Jepsen
© 2003 John Wiley & Sons, Ltd   ISBN: 0-470-85020-5

Table 5.1 Storage protocols – a quick comparison

Parameter	SCSI SPI	ESCON	FICON	Fibre Channel	Gigabit Ethernet
Application	Open Systems I/O Bus	Mainframe Storage Connectivity	Mainframe Storage Connectivity	Open Systems Storage Connectivity	LAN/MAN transport protocol
Media Type	Single-ended or Differential Copper	Optical Fiber	Optical Fiber	Copper or Fiber	Copper or Fiber
Topology	Shared Bus	Point-to-point, switched	Point-to-point, switched	Point-to-point, switched, arbitrated loop	CSMA/CD LAN, switched point-to-point
Parallel/Serial	Parallel	serial	serial	serial	serial
Transfer Width	8, 16, or 32 bits	8 bits	32 bits	32 bits	8 bits
Supported Devices	up to 32	4096 (point to point); >1,000,000 (switched)	64 k	2^{24} devices/fabric (theoretical max.); 127 per arbitrated loop	2^{48} devices (theoretical max.)
Bandwidth	5–320 MB/sec	200 Mb/s	1 Gb/s	133, 266, 532 Mb/s; 1, 2, 4, 10 Gb/s	1 Gb/s, 10 Gb/s
Blocksize	Operating system dependent	1035 byte packet	128 k frame transfer buffer	2112 byte packet	1500 byte packet
Bit Error Rate	10^{-9}	10^{-15}	10^{-12}	10^{-12}	10^{-12}
Connection Based?	Yes	Yes	Yes	Connection-based or Connectionless	Yes
Max. Distance	6 meters (single-ended) 25 meters (differential bus)	3 KM. (MMF) 20 km. (SMF) w/o repeaters	10 km w/o repeaters	10 km. w/o repeaters	5 km.
Section	5.1	5.2	5.3	5.4	5.5

Institute, or ANSI. The first specification, now referred to as SCSI-1, was released in 1986 as X3.131-1986, and defined an interface that supported tape and disk devices.

5.1.1 Applications

SCSI is now used to attach a wide variety of devices to servers and computers, including tape, disk, CD-ROM, DVD, RAID, and scanners. SCSI performs block-size data transfers between storage devices and computer applications. The block size is operating system dependent; typical values are 512, 1024, and 2048 bytes.

5.1.2 Standards

The original specification for SCSI, SCSI-1, was released by ANSI as X3.131-1986 in 1986. SCSI-2, released as X3.131–1994 in 1994, added additional device support, support of wider buses and faster transfer rates, and backward compatibility with SCSI-1.

Work on SCSI-3 begin in 1996, and is currently ongoing within the T10 Technical Committee of the International Committee on Information Technology Standards (INCITS).[1] SCSI-3 adds faster clock rates (Ultra2 SCSI, Ultra3 SCSI) and support of a low voltage differential (LVD) bus; it also supports a serial ('Firewire') protocol using IEEE1394, and 1 Gb/s Fibre Channel protocol. As the original specification had become too cumbersome to manage as a single document, a layered approach was adopted by the T10 Committee in which separate specifications were created which defined individual device-specific command sets and physical interfaces. Each document is identified by an acronym and a number specifying its 'generation'. While many of the work items have been completed, and their specifications released, others are still work in progress. Some of the major specifications and their identifying acronyms are:

- SAM – SCSI Architecture Model
- SBC – SCSI Block Commands (disk drives)
- RBC – Reduced Block Commands (disk drives)

---

[1] INCITS T10 Technical Committee, http://www.t10.org.

- SSC – Stream Commands (tape drives)
- SMC – Media Changer Commands
- MMC – Multimedia Commands (CD-ROM, DVD)
- SCC – Controller Commands (RAID)
- SES – Enclosure Services (SES)
- OSD – Object-Based Storage Devices
- MSC – Management Server Commands
- SPC – Primary Commands (all devices)
- SPI – SCSI Parallel Interface
- SBP – Serial Bus Protocol
- FCP – Fibre Channel Protocol
- SSA – Serial Storage Architecture
- SRP – SCSI RDMA Protocol
- SAS – Serial Attached SCSI

Figure 5.1 shows the specification roadmap for SCSI, and lists the ANSI INCITS numbers for specifications that have been released.

The need to continually provide new features and performance levels, together with the need to provide backward compatibility with existing storage configurations, has led to the existence (and co-existence) of a bewildering plethora of different flavors of SCSI. The primary types currently in use are:

- *SCSI-1:* uses an 8-bit bus; supports data rates of up to 4 MB/s. Allows attachment of tape and disk drives. Specified by X3.131-1986.
- *SCSI-2:* adds support of additional devices; includes Fast SCSI, Wide SCSI. Uses 50-pin connector (or optional 68-pin connector). Specified by X3.131-1994.
- *Wide SCSI:* provides support of 16- or 32-bit transfers (2 cables). Uses 68-pin connector.
- *Fast SCSI:* uses 8-bit data bus, but doubles the clock rate to support data rates of 10 MB/s.
- *Fast Wide SCSI:* uses a 16-bit bus (2 cables) and supports data rates of 20 MB/s.
- *Ultra SCSI:* uses an 8-bit bus and supports data rates of 20 MB/s using synchronous data transfer.

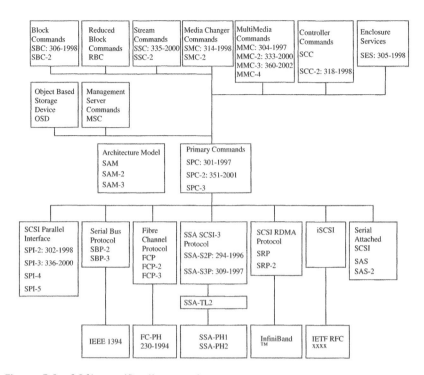

Figure 5.1 SCSI specification roadmap.

- *SCSI-3:* uses a 16-bit bus (single cable) and supports data rates of 40 MB/s. Also called Ultra Wide SCSI.
- *Ultra2 SCSI:* uses an 8-bit bus and supports data transfer rates of up to 40 MB/s using synchronous data transfer and Low Voltage Differential (LVD) bus.
- *Wide Ultra2 SCSI:* uses a 16-bit bus and supports data rates of up to 80 MB/s using synchronous data transfer and LVD.
- *Ultra3 SCSI:* uses double transition clocking and LVD to support data rates of up to 160 MB/s.
- *Ultra 320 SCSI:* uses double transfer speed, pre-compensation, and LVD to support data rates of up to 320 MB/s.

5.1.3   Network Topology – SCSI Parallel Interface (SPI)

The 8-bit (narrow) SCSI bus consists of nine signal lines, a parity line, and an 8-bit data bus. The 16-bit wide SCSI option expands the data bus to 16 lines, and adds another parity line. The 32-bit

Table 5.2 SCSI bus signals and definitions

Signal line	Meaning	Definition
SEL	Select	Used by Initiator to select Target, or by Target to reselect Initiator
BSY	Busy	Asserted to indicate bus is busy
C/D	Control/Data	0 – Data; 1 – Control
I/O	Input/Output	Driven by Target to set direction of transfer; also indicates Selection/Reselection. 0 – Initiator to Target; 1 – Target to Initiator
MSG	Message	Driven by Target during Message phase
REQ	Request	Driven by Target to request REQ/ACK data transfer handshake on the primary bus
ACK	Acknowledge	Driven by Initiator to acknowledge REQ/ACK data transfer handshake on the primary bus
ATN	Attention	Driven by Initiator to indicate Initiator has message for target
RST	Reset	Hard Reset
DB(P)	Data Bus (Parity)	Odd parity if at least one bit is active on DB(0–31), DB(P), DB(P1), DB(P2), DB(P3)
DB(7)–DB(0)	Data Bus (0–7)	DB(7) is MSB; also highest priority during arbitration
DB(P1)	Data Bus (Parity 1)	Odd parity if at least one bit is active on DB(8–31), DB(P1), DB(P2), DB(P3)
DB(15)–DB(8)	Data Bus (8–15)	Data bus expansion for 16 bit bus. DB(15) is MSB
ACKQ	Acknowledge Q	Driven by Initiator to acknowledge REQ/ACK data transfer handshake on the secondary bus
REQQ	Request Q	Driven by Target to request REQ/ACK data transfer handshake on the secondary bus
DB(P2)	Data Bus (Parity 2)	Odd parity if at least one bit is active on DB(16–31), DB(P2), DB(P3)
DB(31)–DB(16)	Data Bus (16–31)	Data bus expansion for 32 bit bus. DB(23) and DB(31) are MSBs
DB(P3)	Data Bus (Parity 3)	Odd parity if at least one bit is active on DB(16–31), DB(P2), DB(P3)

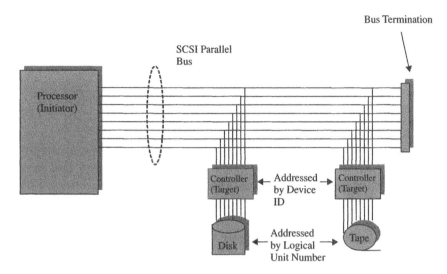

Figure 5.2 SCSI network topology.

wide SCSI option expands the data bus to 32 lines, and adds two additional parity bits. Table 5.2 lists all bus signals and their definitions.

The SCSI network topology (see Figure 5.2) permits the connection of 8, 16, or 32 devices, depending on bus width. Each device may be either an *initiator* or a *target*. The initiator is normally the host processor, and targets are generally storage devices. An initiator initiates a bus operation, and a target performs the operation. The SCSI bus protocol permits peer-to-peer data transfer between an initiator and a target; only one transfer may be in progress at any one time. An arbitration process is used to determine which device may have control of the bus at any time.

5.1.4 Addressing

The maximum number of devices which may be addressed on the SCSI bus is determined by the bus width. For the standard 8-bit (narrow) SCSI, bus, a maximum of eight devices may be addressed. The 16-bit and 32-bit wide SCSI buses allow a maximum of 16 and 32 devices to be addressed respectively. Each device on the SCSI bus has a device ID, which is a value from 0–31.

For the 8-bit bus, the highest numbered device ID (7) has the highest priority. Priority becomes somewhat complexified with the addition of the wide buses; byte 1 has the highest priority, followed by bytes 2, 3, and 4, in that order. Within each byte, the highest number has the highest priority. Device Ids in order of priority, from highest to lowest, are as follows:

7, 6, 5, 4, 3, 2, 1, 0, 15, 14, 13, 12, 11, 10, 9, 8,

23, 22, 21, 20, 19, 18, 17, 16, 31, 30, 29, 28, 27, 26, 25, 24.

Priority settings may be *speed-driven* or *load-driven*. Speed-driven priority gives the highest priority to the host adapter. The next highest priority is given to time-critical devices such as streaming tape or writeable CD-ROM, and the lowest priority is given to the fastest devices, such as disk drives. This arrangement prevents the fastest devices from monopolizing bus access. Load-driven priority gives the highest priority to time-critical devices, and the lowest priority to the host adapter, with disk devices in between.

Each device ID has one or more Logical Unit Numbers, or LUNs, associated with it. The device ID corresponds to the device controller, and the LUN corresponds to the actual storage unit. For most storage devices, there is one LUN for each device ID, designated as LUN0; however, some storage devices, such as multidisk CD-ROM changers, may support multiple storage units.

To discover the devices connected to the bus, an initiator sends an INQUIRY command to each possible device ID. If a device ID is present on the bus, it responds to the command; if not, the command times out.

5.1.5   Bus Protocol

The SCSI bus is a time-shared bus. For devices to transfer information, one of the devices has to gain control of the bus. This occurs during the bus arbitration and selection phases. Once the device has gained control of the bus, it may initiate data transfer with another device. Only one pair of devices may perform data transfer operations at a time. Once the operation is complete, the bus is returned to the Bus Free state, and another device may arbitrate for control of the bus.

5.1.5.1   Bus Arbitration and Selection Phases

Bus arbitration and selection begins with the bus in the Bus Free state. The Bus Free state is indicated by the SEL and BSY signals being false for a period of time referred to as the *bus settle delay* (400 ns). This delay is necessary to determine that no transients are present on the lines. A device attempts to gain control of the bus by asserting BSY and placing its device ID on the data bus. This is done by asserting the data bus bit corresponding to the device ID; Device ID 7, for example, will set DB(7) true. The device then waits for one arbitration delay (2.4 microseconds), and checks the data bus to see if a higher-priority device has requested the bus. If no higher priority device has requested the bus, then the device asserts the SEL signal to signal that it has gained control of the bus. Any lower-priority device attempting to gain control of the bus has now lost the arbitration, and must return its BSY and Device ID to the false state.

After a *bus clear delay* (800 ns) and a bus settle delay, the bus enters the selection phase. If the device that won the arbitration phase is an initiator, it now sets I/O false and places both its device ID and the device ID of the target it wishes to transfer data to/from on the data bus. It also asserts ATN to indicate that a Message Out phase will follow selection. The initiator waits two *deskew* delays (8–45 ns, depending on bus speed) and releases BSY. After a bus settle delay, it waits for a response from the target. When the target sees its device ID and SEL asserted, it responds by asserting BSY. When the initiator detects the response from the target, it waits two deskew delays and releases the SEL signal. At this time, the target may assert the REQ signal to indicate it is ready for information transfer.

If the device that won the arbitration is a target, it may enter the reselection phase. Reselection occurs when an information transfer operation previously started by an initiator was suspended by the target. For example, if the operation was a read, and the target had to perform a seek operation to locate the requested data, it would suspend the information transfer while performing the seek. The target asserts I/O and places both its device ID and the device ID of the initiator it wishes to transfer data to/from on the data bus. The target waits two deskew delays and releases BSY. After a bus settle delay, it waits for a response from the initiator. The initiator determines that it has been reselected when SEL and I/O are asserted and its device ID bit is set. It then looks at the data bus to determine the reselecting target, and asserts BSY to signal reselection. After the target detects BSY, it also asserts BSY, waits two deskew delays, and releases SEL.

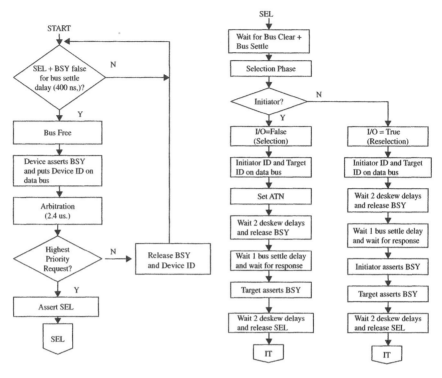

Figure 5.3 Bus arbitration and selection phases.

5.1.5.2 Information Transfer Phase

The Information Transfer Phase consists of four sub-phases: command, data, status, and message. The C/D, I/O, and Msg signals are used to differentiate these subphases. Table 5.3 lists possible values for these signals and their function.

Table 5.3 Information transfer phase signals and functions

MSG	C/D	I/O	Function	Direction
0	0	0	Data Out	Initiator to Target
0	0	1	Data In	Target to Initiator
0	1	0	Command	Initiator to Target
0	1	1	Status	Target to Initiator
1	0	0	(reserved)	
1	0	1	(reserved)	
1	1	0	Msg Out	Initiator to Target
1	1	1	Msg In	Target to Initiator

5.1.5.3 Asynchronous Data Transfer

Asynchronous Data Transfer is used for all Information Transfer Phase functions, including command, status, data, and message transfer. (Note that the data phase may optionally use synchronous data transfer instead; see below for details.) Each REQ/ACK handshake transfers 8, 16, or 32 bits, depending on the negotiated transfer width. The 8-bit and 16-bit primary data buses use the REQ and ACK signals for the handshake; the upper bytes of the 32-bit wide data bus (the secondary bus) use the REQQ and ACKQ signals, as the timing is slightly different. In the following description, REQ and ACK refer to both generically.

The target controls the direction of data transfer by setting the I/O signal. If the I/O signal is false, data transfer is from initiator to target (Data Out); if I/O is true, data transfer is from target to initiator (Data In).

If transfer is from target to initiator (I/O = true), the target first sets the proper values on DB(P) and DB(7–0) for 8-bit transfers, DB(15–0), DB(P), DB(P1) for 16-bit transfers, or DB(31–0), DB(P), DB(P1), DB(P2), DB(P3) for 32-bit transfers, and asserts REQ. The initiator reads the data bus while REQ is true, and signals that the data is accepted by asserting ACK. When the target sees the ACK, it releases the data bus and sets REQ to false.

If transfer is from initiator to target (I/O = false) the target requests data by asserting REQ. The initiator sets the proper values on DB(P) and DB(7–0) for 8-bit transfers, DB(15–0), DB(P), DB(P1) for 16-bit transfers, or DB(31–0), DB(P), DB(P1), DB(P2), DB(P3) for 32-bit transfers, and asserts ACK. The values on the data bus remain valid as long as REQ is asserted by the target. When the target sees ACK set to true, it reads the values on the data bus and sets REQ to false. When the initiator sees REQ set to false, it releases the data bus and sets ACK to false.

5.1.5.4 Typical State Progression during Information Transfer Phase

Many different state transitions are possible during the Information Transfer Phase; however, a frequently used state progression would be as follows:

- Message Out Phase.
- Command Phase.

- Data In/Data Out Phase.
- Status Phase.
- Message In Phase.

This typical state progression is described below.

5.1.5.5 Message Out Phase

The Message Out Phase allows the target to request that a message be sent from the initiator to the target. The target asserts MSG and C/D, and sets I/O to false to indicate Message Out.

The Message Out phase is normally entered after selection. The first message sent from the initiator to the target during a normal information transfer phase is an IDENTIFY message. The IDENTIFY message establishes a logical connection between the initiator and a specified LUN within the target. The IDENTIFY message may be followed immediately by a SYNCHRONOUS DATA TRANS-FER REQUEST message to negotiate a synchronous data transfer between two devices, and/or a WIDE DATA TRANSFER REQUEST to request a 16-bit or 32-bit data transfer.

5.1.5.6 Command Phase

The Command Phase allows the target to request command infor-mation from the Initiator. The target asserts C/D and sets MSG and I/O to false to indicate Command phase during the REQ/ACK handshake.

A command is communicated by sending a command descriptor block to the target. Commands are device-specific; typical com-mands include READ and WRITE commands for each device type. A READ command would be followed by a Data In data transfer in the data phase; a WRITE command would be followed by a Data Out transfer.

5.1.5.7 Data In/Data Out Phase (Asynchronous
Data Transfer)

Data In allows the target to request that data be sent to the initiator from the target. The target asserts I/O and sets MSG and C/D to false to indicate Data In during the REQ/ACK handshake.

Data Out allows the target to request that data be sent from the initiator to the target. The target sets MSG, C/D and I/O to false to indicate Data Out during the REQ/ACK handshake.

If asynchronous data transfer is being used, data is transferred 8, 16, or 32 bits at a time using a REQ/ACK handshake, as described above under 'Asynchronous Data Transfer.' The sender waits until an ACK is received before sending the next transfer.

5.1.5.8   Data In/Data Out Phase (Synchronous Data Transfer)

Data In/Data Out signal conditions for MSG, C/D, and I/O are the same as for asynchronous data transfer.

If the initiator and target have agreed to transfer data synchronously, multiple bytes may be transferred between the initiator and the target using a REQ/ACK offset. The REQ/ACK offset specifies the maximum number of REQ pulses that may be sent by the target before an ACK is returned by the initiator. Data transfer completes successfully when the numbers of REQs and ACKs are equal.

If I/O is true (transfer data to initiator) the target first sets DB(P) and DB(7–0) for 8-bit transfers, DB(15–0), DB(P), DB(P1) for 16-bit transfers, or DB(31–0), DB(P), DB(P1), DB(P2), DB(P3) for 32-bit transfers, to their desired values and then asserts REQ. REQ is asserted for a minimum of an assertion period (8–80 ns, depending on bus speed). The initiator reads the values on the data bus and sets ACK. REQ is then set to false, and the values on the data bus may be changed or released.

If I/O is false (transfer to the target) the initiator transfers one bus width for each REQ received. After receiving the leading edge of a REQ pulse, the initiator sets DB(P) and DB(7–0) for 8-bit transfers, DB(15–0), DB(P), DB(P1) for 16-bit transfers, or DB(31–0), DB(P), DB(P1), DB(P2), DB(P3) for 32-bit transfers, to the desired values and asserts ACK. The initiator asserts ACK for a minimum of an assertion period. The target reads the values on the data bus. The initiator may then set ACK to false.

5.1.5.9   Status In Phase

The Status In phase allows the target to request that status information be sent from the target to the initiator. The target asserts C/D and I/O and sets MSG to false to indicate status phase during the REQ/ACK handshake.

Table 5.4 Byte transfer order for 8, 16, and 32-bit data transfer widths

Transfer number	Secondary bus		Primary bus		Data transfer width
	31–24	23–16	15–8	7–0	
1				W	8 bit
2				X	
3				Y	
4				Z	
1			X	W	16 bit
2			Z	Y	
1	Z	Y	X	W	32 bit

A status byte is sent from the target to the initiator during the Status In phase at the completion of each command. A status of GOOD indicates that the target has successfully completed the command.

5.1.5.10 Message In Phase

The Message In phase allows the target to request that messages be sent from the target to the initiator. The target asserts MSG, C/D, and I/O during the REQ/ACK handshake to indicate Message In phase.

If command execution has terminated normally, the message sent from the target to the initiator will be a COMMAND COMPLETE message. After sending the COMMAND COMPLETE message, the target returns to the Bus Free state by setting BSY to false.

5.1.6 Physical Layer

The SCSI bus may be implemented using Single-Ended (SE) logic or differential mode. Two different versions of the differential mode bus have been specified; a High Voltage Differential (HVD) bus and a Low Voltage Differential (LVD) bus; the LVD bus allows interoperability with SE devices. The bit error rate of the SCSI bus is typically in the order of 1×10^{-9}.

The initiators must supply power for the terminators. An extra line, TERMPWR is included in the bus to power the terminators. For the wide SCSI option, a second terminator power line, TERMPWRQ, is included and must be powered by the initiators.

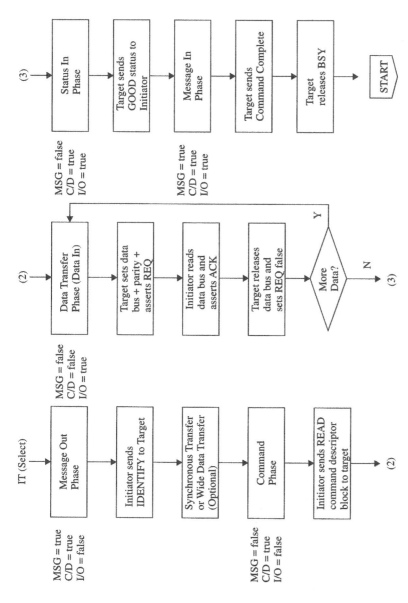

Figure 5.4   SCSI Information transfer phase–typical READ operation.

Three connector types are currently specified. The A connector supports the 8-bit (narrow) primary bus. The P connector supports the 16-bit (wide) primary bus. The Q connector supports the secondary bus for the 32-bit (wide) option.

5.1.6.1   Single Ended Bus (SE)

The single-ended bus configuration uses open-collector or tri-state logic to drive signal lines. The bus must be terminated at each end. The termination may consist of a 330 ohm resistor to ground and a 220 ohm resistor to +5 volts, or, alternatively, the termination may be an active voltage regulator device with a characteristic impedance of between 100 and 132 ohms. (See ANSI X3.131-1994 for details.)

5.1.6.2   High Voltage Differential (HVD)

The High Voltage Differential (HVD) mode bus provides better noise immunity and permits operation over longer distances than the SE. It consists of a pair of wires for each signal, designated SIGNAL+ and SIGNAL-. Each signal is the logical inverse of the other.

5.1.6.3   Low Voltage Differential (LVD)

The Low Voltage Differential (LVD) bus is used with Ultra2 and Ultra3 SCSI. It uses lower voltage logic levels than the HVD; due to its lower power dissipation, it can be packaged in inexpensive LSI devices. Like the HVD, each signal consists of a pair of wires designated SIGNAL+ and SIGNAL-. Each signal is the logical inverse of the other. The LVD bus allows SE devices and LVD devices to interoperate on the same bus.

5.1.7 SCSI Summary

SCSI in its multiple variations and permutations, remains a widely used protocol for adding peripherals to small computer systems, and for in-the-frame connectivity of storage arrays. In spite of its distance limitations, it is a relatively low overhead storage protocol which offers high performance if properly configured.

Table 5.5 Maximum specified length for SCSI buses

Bus type	Number of attached devices	Maximum distance (meters)					Notes
		SCSI-1	SCSI-2/Fast SCSI	Ultra SCSI	Ultra2 SCSI	Ultra3/Ultra320 SCSI	
SE	1–4	6	3	3			
	5–8	6	3	1.5			
	9–16	6	3				Additional length restrictions may apply for >16 devices
HVD	Point-to-point	25	25	25	25		
	Multi Drop	25	25	25	12		
LVD	Point-to-point	25	25	25	25	25	
LVD	Multi Drop	12	12	12	12	12	

However, in the future, it is likely that the SCSI Parallel Interface (SPI) will be largely replaced by serial protocols, including Fibre Channel Protocol (FCP) and the Serial Bus Protocol (SBP). For storage network applications, use of the FCP FC-4 layer permits the SCSI command protocol to be used over a high-speed fiber link, and removes the distance limitations of the copper bus. For general purpose computing, SBP over IEEE 1394 enables external peripheral connectivity. Development of the iSCSI protocol by the IETF adapts SCSI for use in an IP storage environment.

5.2 ENTERPRISE SYSTEMS CONNECTION (ESCON)

Enterprise Systems Connection, or ESCON^{TM}, is a serial optical fiber-based protocol for connecting mainframe computers to storage subsystems. It was introduced by IBM Corporation in 1991 to extend the bandwidth and range of its channel interfaces by replacing the parallel copper-based bus/tag interface previously used.

5.2.1 Applications

ESCON is used to provide high-bandwidth switched or point-to-point connectivity between mainframe computer channel subsystems and control units at rates of up to 200 Mb/s. It enables remote connection of storage devices at distances of up to 20 km without the use of repeaters.

5.2.2 Standards

ESCON was originally developed as a proprietary storage protocol by IBM Corporation for use in their computer systems. An open systems version of ESCON, the Single-Byte Command Codes Sets Connection (SBCON) Architecture, was standardized by ANSI in 1997 and documented in X3.296, *Single-Byte Command Codes Sets Connection (SBCON) Architecture*. ESCON and SBCON are nearly identical in terms of functionality and architecture; the terms are used interchangeably in the remainder of this section.

5.2.3 Network Topology

ESCON and SBCON are intended to provide high-bandwidth, low error-rate connectivity over extended distances between mainframe host channel subsystems and storage control units and devices. ESCON is also an important component of the Sysplex® architecture, which permits synchronous parallel processing among distributed mainframe computers.

Figure 5.5 shows a typical storage network using ESCON or SBCON. The basic components of the storage network are the channel subsystem, an optional switch or director, a control unit, the controlled storage devices, and the ESCON/SBCON links that connect the channel subsystem to the control units. The channel subsystem directs the transfer of information between I/O devices and processor main storage, and provides the common controls for the attachment of different I/O devices by means of one or more channel paths. The channel subsystem may consist of one or more logical *channel images* which share the same physical facilities and channel paths. In a *point-to-point* configuration, bidirectional ESCON/SBCON links connect host processor channel subsystems directly to control units or control unit images. In a *switched* configuration, bidirectional switched connectivity to control units or control unit images is provided by an ESCON/SBCON switch or director. A *control unit* provides the logical capability to control and

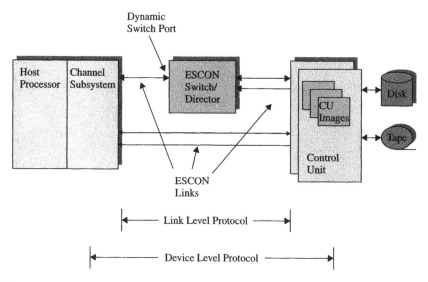

Figure 5.5   ESCON/SBCON network architecture.

operate one or more I/O devices, and adapts the characteristics of each individual I/O device to the link interface provided by the channel. The control unit subsystem may consist of one or more *control unit images*, which share the same physical facilities and links. ESCON/SBCON consists of both a link level protocol, which controls link operations, and a device level protocol, which performs the actual I/O operations on the storage devices.

A specific application of the ESCON protocol is in providing storage connectivity for the Geographically Dispersed Parallel Sysplex computing system. Figure 5.6 shows a typical configuration for parallel processing using a sysplex configuration. The GDPS may be used for multisite disaster recovery or business continuity purposes over distances of up to 40 km; it consists of host processors, coupling facilities, sysplex timers, and disk storage at each site. The coupling facility provides data caching, locking and queueing for the processors, and allows multiple processors to communicate with one another and with locally stored data. The coupling facilities are connected to one another using fiber optic links referred to as *HiPerLinks*.™ The processing power of the Sysplex configuration can be increased by adding additional processors.

Since the processors operate synchronously, a common reference timer must be provided. The configuration shown in Figure 5.6 uses two reference timers for additional reliability and redundancy. The

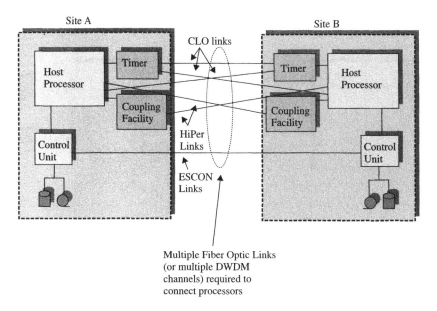

Figure 5.6 ESCON parallel processing configuration.

reference timers are connected by means of Control Link Oscillator (CLO) fiber optic links.

ESCON/SBCON links are used to provide connectivity to disk storage at each site, and to provide site-to-site storage interconnectivity. Support of the Sysplex configuration requires many intersite links; therefore use of WDM for multiplexing multiple links onto a single fiber is desirable.

5.2.4 Addressing

ESCON/SBCON supports different addressing capabilities for point-to-point and switched modes; each is described below.

5.2.4.1 Point-to-Point Configuration

In point-to-point mode, each ESCON/SBCON link is capable of addressing up to 16 control unit images. Each control unit or control unit image is capable of supporting up to 256 attached storage devices. Therefore, in point-to-point mode, a maximum configuration consists of 4096 addressable storage devices (16 CU images × 256 storage devices).

5.2.4.2 Switched Configuration

An ESCON/SBCON switch or director may support as many as 254 switch ports. One switch port is normally reserved for the switch or director control unit; therefore the theoretical maximum configuration of a switched ESCON/SBCON configuration is 1,036,288 addressable storage devices (253 switch ports × 16 CU images × 256 storage devices), assuming a single channel.

The purpose of the switch is to connect two ports together for the duration of the connection. All frames originating at one of the ports will be transferred to the other port and vice-versa; connections are bidirectional. Connections may be static or dynamic. Static connections are semi-permanent connections set up using the switch/director control unit; dynamic connections are set up on a frame-by-frame basis, based on addressing information contained in the frames. Multiple connections may exist simultaneously in the switch.

Each frame contains a Start Of Frame (SOF) delimiter, which indicates if a dynamic connection is requested. Each frame also contains an End Of Frame (EOF) delimiter which indicates if an existing dynamic connection shall be terminated. A dynamic connection will continue until an EOF delimiter requesting termination is received.

5.2.5 Link and Device Level Functions

To perform data transfer, a link-level facility is used to create a logical path between a channel and a control unit. A device-level protocol is used to perform data transfer and other system functions. Each is described below.

5.2.5.1 Link Level Protocol

A link-level facility is used to provide link management functions, including initialization, offline, connection recovery, and link failure operations, and management of logical paths. Link-level management functions use monolog communication if no connection exists, or dialog communication if a connection has been set up as described above.

Logical paths must be established between channels and control units before device-level operations can be performed. Logical paths are created during channel and control unit initialization procedures. A logical path is identified by the combination of an 8-bit link address assigned to the channel, a 4-bit logical address assigned to the channel image, an 8-bit link address assigned to the control unit, and a 4-bit logical address assigned to the control unit image.

Link level operations use link control frames. A link control frame consists of a fixed-length link header, a variable-length information field, and a fixed-length link trailer. Some link-level operations do not require an information field, in which case the link control frame consists of only a header and a trailer. Figure 5.7 shows the format of a link control frame.

Figure 5.8 shows the format of a link control frame header. The link header begins with a SOF delimiter. It is an *ordered set* of transmission characters that cannot occur in an error-free frame. The SOF is not counted as part of the 5 bytes in the header. There are two types of SOF delimiters: the *connect SOF delimiter*, which initiates a dynamic connection, and a *passive SOF delimiter*, which does not initiate a connection.

The SOF delimiter is followed by a destination address field. The destination address field consists of an 8-bit destination link

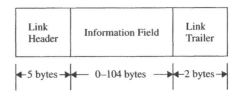

Figure 5.7 Link control frame format.

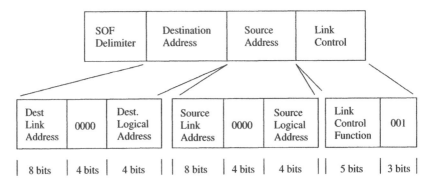

Figure 5.8 Link control frame header format.

address and a 4-bit destination logical address, with 4 zero bits in between. The destination address field is followed by a source address field. Similar to the destination address field, the source address field consists of an 8-bit source link address and a 4-bit source logical address, with 4 zero bits in between.

The last field in the link header is the link control field. It consists of a 5-bit link control function field, followed by a three-bit field containing the value '001'. The link control function field specifies the function of the link control frame. Table 5.6 lists valid link control function field values and their meaning.

The link control frame trailer consists of a 16-bit cyclical redundancy check (CRC) field. The CRC field is used by the receiving link level facility to detect errors that may have occurred during

Table 5.6 Link control function field values and their meaning

Link control function field value Bit 0 1 2 3 4	Link control function
0 0 0 0 0	Test Initialization Result (TIR)
0 0 0 0 1	Test Initialization (TIN)
0 0 0 1 0	Link Level Reject (LRJ)
0 0 0 1 1	Port Reject (PRJ)
0 0 1 0 0	Link Level Busy (LBY)
0 0 1 0 1	Port Busy (PBY)
0 0 1 1 0	(reserved)
0 0 1 1 1	(reserved)
0 1 0 0 0	Establish Logical Path (ELP)
0 1 0 0 1	Remove Logical Path (RLP)
0 1 0 1 0	Logical Path Established (LPE)
0 1 0 1 1	Logical Path Removed (LPR)
0 1 1 0 0	Link Level Acknowledgment (ACK)
0 1 1 0 1	State Change Notification (SCN)
0 1 1 1 0	Acquire Link Address (ALA)
0 1 1 1 1	(reserved)
1 0 0 0 0	Identifier Response (IDR)
1 0 0 0 1	Request Node Identifier (RID)
1 0 0 1 0	Link Incident Notification (LIN)
1 0 0 1 1	Request Incident Record (RIR)
1 0 1 0 0	Link Incident Data (LID)
1 0 1 0 1 Through 1 1 1 1 1	(reserved)

transmission. The header source address, destination address, and link control fields, and the information field, are included in the generated CRC. The CRC uses the generation polynomial $X^{16} + X^{12} + X^5 + 1$ as defined by ISO/IEC 9314-2.

The link control frame ends with an EOF delimiter. It is an ordered set of transmission characters that cannot occur in an error-free frame. The EOF delimiter also signals to the receiver that the preceding two bytes consist of the CRC field for the frame. There are two types of EOF delimiter: the disconnect-EOF delimiter, which is used to initiate removal of a dynamic connection, and a passive-EOF delimiter, which performs no action.

Link control frames are used to establish logical paths between channel images and control unit images. A channel sends Establish Logical Path (ELP) link control frames to each of the control unit images in its configuration definition to establish a logical path to each. This may occur when the channel is initialized, when the configuration changes, or when the channel is notified that a previously established logical path no longer exists. The source address in the link control header field gives the link and logical address of the channel image initiating the logical path establishment. The destination address gives the link and logical address of the control unit image with which the channel is establishing the path. The link control field contains the value 01000 to specify that the frame is an ELP frame.

The information field of the ELP frame contains eight bytes. The first byte specifies the number of unacknowledged data requests that can be outstanding, beyond one. The other seven bytes specify the *pacing parameters* for each Device Information Block (DIB) size permitted by the channel. This consists of a value specifying the number of pairs of idle characters that may be inserted between device frames for certain operations.

If the logical path is successfully established, the control unit image returns a Logical Path Established (LPE) link control frame in response. If for some reason the logical path cannot be established (e.g. if the control unit image does not support the DIB sizes requested by the ELP link control frame), then the control unit returns a Logical Path Removed (LPR) link control frame containing the appropriate reason code.

The link level protocol includes functions for error detection and notification, and connection recovery procedures. If the channel detects a link failure or degraded mode operation, it initiates

appropriate recovery procedures. If the control unit detects a condition that indicates that a link failure has occurred, or that a link is
operating in degraded mode, it sends a Link Incident Notification
(LIN) link control frame to the channel, using any functional link.

5.2.5.2   Device Level Protocol

Device level protocols allow transfer of information related to a
single I/O operation, transfer of status related to a control unit or
I/O device, and recovery when errors are detected by the channel
or control unit. Types of information transferred by device level
protocols include commands, status, control information, and the
actual data transferred between storage devices and the channel.

Device level protocol information is transferred between a channel and a control unit using device frames. A device frame consists
of a fixed-length link header, a variable-length information field,
and a fixed-length link trailer. The information field may be subdivided into a device header and a device information block.
Figure 5.9 shows the format of a device frame.

Figure 5.10 shows the format of a device frame link header. The
format is the same as for the link control header except for the

Link Header	Device Header	Device Information Block	Link Trailer
5 bytes		5–1028 bytes	2 bytes

Figure 5.9   Device frame format.

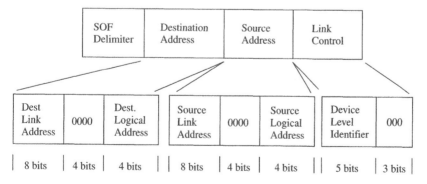

Figure 5.10   Device frame link header format.

device level identifier, which is set to all zeroes to indicate use of SBCON interface architecture, and the last three bits which are set to all zeroes to indicate that this is a device frame.

The Device Header comprises the first four bytes of the information field of a device frame. The device header consists of three subfields: a one-byte information field identifier (IFI), a two-byte device address, and a one-byte Device Header Flag (DHF) field. Figure 5.11 shows the format of the device header.

Bits 0–2 and bit 5 of the IFI are reserved and set to zeroes. Bit 3, the Address-Specific (AS) bit, indicates that the device frame is associated with the I/O device specified by the device address in byte 3 of the device header, if it is set to 1. If it is set to 0, the device address is not used. For command frames and data frames, AS must be set to 1; for status frames and device control frames, AS may be 1 or 0. Bit 4, the supplemental-status (ES) bit, is used to control the transfer of supplemental status. For a command frame, a data frame, and a device control frame sent by the control unit, the ES bit must be set to 0; for a status frame or a device control frame sent by the channel, the ES bit may be 1 or 0. Bits 6 and 7 of the IFI (T2 and T1) specify the device frame type. Device frames may be data, control, status, or device control frames.

A data frame may be sent by either a channel or a control unit. A command frame may only be sent by a channel. A status frame may only be sent by a control unit. A device control frame may be sent by either a channel or a control unit.

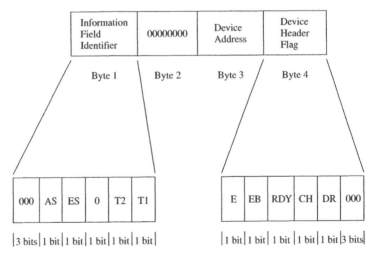

Figure 5.11 Device header format.

The device address field consists of 16 bits following the IFI. The first eight bits are set to all zeroes. The second 8 bits are used to specify a device address in the range 0–255.

The DHF field is a 1-byte field immediately following the device address field. Bit 0, the End (E) bit, indicates a transfer of data (or a request for data) which exactly satisfies the remaining count for the current Channel Control Word (CCW) being executed when set to 1. For a command frame, a data frame, or a device control frame, the E bit may be set to 1 or 0. For a status frame, the E bit must be set to 0. Bit 1, the End Block (EB) bit, is used by the control unit to notify the channel of a disconnection. The EB bit may be set to 1 or 0 for a device control frame; for all other frames, it is set to 0. Bit 2, the Ready (RDY) bit, is used to indicate that (1) the operation is considered in progress at the channel or control unit, (2) the sender of data is ready to transfer data, (3) the sender of data is ready to accept a new data request, or (4) the channel grants a requested connection. For command and status frames, the RDY bit is set to 0; for data and device control frames, the RDY bit may be set to 1 or 0. Bit 3, the Chaining (CH) bit, is used to indicate that the channel intends to initiate or continue a data or command chaining operation. The CH bit is set to 0 for status and data frames, and may be set to 1 or 0 for command and device control frames. Bit 4, the Data Request (DR) bit, is used by the recipient of data during a data transfer operation to request a specific amount of data. The DR bit is set to 0 for status and data frames, and may be set to 1 or 0 for command and device control frames.

Table 5.7 summarizes device header fields and their meanings; Table 5.8 lists valid device frame types.

The Device Information Block (DIB) is a variable-length field that immediately follows the device header. The format of the DIB is different for each type of device frame. Figure 5.12 shows the DIB format for data, command, status, and device control frames.

The size of the DIB depends on the device frame type and function. The DIB for a data frame may be 1–1024 bytes in length. The DIB for a command or device control frame is 4 bytes in length. The DIB for a status frame is normally 4 bytes in length; when supplemental status is included, it may be 5–36 bytes in length.

The data frame DIB is used to transfer data between the channel and the control unit during an I/O operation. The exact length is set by the DIB parameters of the ELP frame when the logical path is established, and may be 16, 32, 64, 128, 256, 512, or 1024 bytes.

Table 5.7 Device header fields and their meanings

Type of Device Frame	IFI								Device Header Flags							
	0	1	2	3	4	5	6	7	0	1	2	3	4	5	6	7
	0	0	0	AS	ES	0	T2	T1	E	EBY	RD	CH	DR	0	0	0
Data	0	0	0	1	0	0	0	0	X	z	X	z	z	z	z	z
Command	0	0	0	1	U	0	0	1	X	z	z	X	X	z	z	z
Status	0	0	0	X	X	0	1	0	z	z	z	z	z	z	z	z
Control	0	0	0	X	X	0	1	1	X	X	X	X	X	z	z	z

Legend:
U – Set to 0 by the channel; unpredictable results if 1
X – May be set to 0 or 1
z – Set to 0 by the sender and ignored by the recipient
0 – Set to 0
1 – Set to 1

Table 5.8 Valid device frame types

T2	T1	Device frame type	Device information block
0	0	Data	Data
0	1	Command	Flags, CCW Command, Count
1	0	Status	Flags, Status, Count, Supplemental Status
1	1	Control	Control Function and Parameters

The command frame DIB is used to transfer the current channel command word (CCW) from the channel to the control unit. A command frame is used to initiate an I/O operation with an I/O device, and, if command chaining is being performed, is used to update the CCW information at the control unit. The command frame DIB contains a command flag byte, a command byte, and a 16 bit count field. The flag field contains data (CD) and command (CC) chaining bits and a data chaining update (DU) flag. The command byte contains one of the 7 basic I/O commands, plus device-specific modifiers. Command byte contents are shown in Table 5.9. The 16-bit count field contains the byte count for the current CCW, and is an unsigned value from 0–65,535.

The status frame DIB is used to return status to a channel from a control unit. A status frame may be returned to any device frame that initiates a connection. Once a connection is established, a status frame may be sent as a result of a command frame, or during data

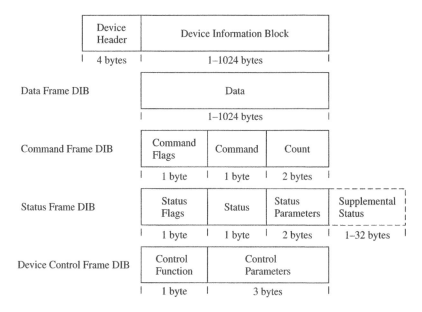

Figure 5.12   DIB format for data, command, status and device control frames.

Table 5.9   Command frame command byte contents

Command	Bit position							
	0	1	2	3	4	5	6	7
(reserved)	M	M	M	M	0	0	0	0
Sense	M	M	M	M	0	1	0	0
(reserved)	M	M	M	M	1	0	0	0
Read Backward	M	M	M	M	1	1	0	0
Write	M	M	M	M	M	M	0	1
Read	M	M	M	M	M	M	1	0
Control	M	M	M	M	M	M	1	1

M = device-specific modifier

transfer. A status frame may be sent with the AS bit set to 0 or 1, depending on whether the status being returned is for the control unit or a device. If the ES bit is set to 1, 1 to 32 bytes of supplemental status are also returned. The status frame DIB consists of a 1-byte status flag field, a 1-byte status byte, and a 16-bit status parameter field. Table 5.10 lists the contents of the status byte.

A device control frame DIB consists of a 1-byte control function field and a 3-byte control parameter field. Control functions are listed in Table 5.11. Their actual usage is partly determined by the

Table 5.10 Status byte format and meaning

Bit	Description	Meaning
0	Attention	Generated when asynchronous condition occurs in control unit or I/O device
1	Status Modifier	Generated by I/O device when (1) device cannot provide current status, (2) control unit is busy, (3) normal command sequence must be modified, (4) command retry must be initiated
2	Control Unit End	Control unit is available for use by another operation
3	Busy	I/O operation cannot be executed because (1) a previous I/O operation or chain of I/O operations is being executed, (2) stacked or pending status conditions exist, and pending status is being returned in response to a command, (3) control unit or device is shared with another I/O channel and is not currently available, (4) device is performing internal function
4	Channel End	Presented when the data transfer portion of an I/O operation is completed
5	Device End	Presented to the channel when (1) completion of an I/O operation is indicated by the I/O device, (2) I/O device has transitioned from busy to not-busy status, (3) I/O device has transitions from not-ready to ready, (4) control unit or I/O device has recognized that an asynchronous condition has occurred
6	Unit Check	Control unit or I/O device has detected an unusual condition that is detailed by sense information
7	Unit Exception	Control unit or I/O device has detected an unusual condition that must be reported to the upper layer protocol

device header flag bit settings. The control parameter field contains additional information related to the specified control function, and its format and usage are also determined by the device header flag bit settings. Table 5.12 shows the mapping of device header IFI and flag bits to control functions.

Device level operations are initiated by a Start I/O command from the host processor to the channel. The channel begins execution of a channel program by executing the first Channel Command Word (CCW), and sending a command frame to the control unit specified by the I/O address. If no connection exists to the specified control

Table 5.11   Control functions

Control function field value					Control function
Bit 0	1	2	3	4	
0	0	0	0	0	Multipurpose
0	0	0	1	0	Command Response
0	0	1	0	0	Stack Status
0	0	1	1	0	Cancel
0	1	0	0	0	System Reset
0	1	0	1	0	Selective Reset
0	1	1	0	0	Request Connection
0	1	1	1	0	Request Status
1	0	0	0	0	Device Level Exception
1	0	1	0	0	Status Accepted
1	0	1	1	0	Device Level Acknowledgment
1	1	0	0	0	
Through					(vendor specific)
1	1	1	1	1	

unit, the command will use a dynamic SOF to initiate a connection. The first command of the channel program will have the CH bit set to 0.

If the specified control unit is busy, it will return a status frame to the channel with the status modifier bit and busy bits set. Figure 5.13 shows initiation of an I/O operation.

Commands may be *immediate* commands or *non-immediate* commands. Immediate commands are typically completed as a single operation, such as a request for status; non-immediate commands require multiple operations, such as transfer of multiple data frames.

If the first command is an immediate command, the control unit responds by sending a status frame with the channel end bit set. It may also set the device end bit, depending on the operation performed. If the status frame has the supplementary Status Available (SA) bit set, it indicates that supplementary status is available. The channel may then request that supplementary status be sent to it by sending a request status frame with the ES bit set.

If no device end was contained in the status frame, the channel indicates acceptance of the status by returning a status accepted frame. If chaining is required, the status accepted frame has the CH bit set to 1; if not, the status accepted frame has the CH bit set to

Table 5.12 Device header IFI/flag bit and control functions

Control function	IFI								DHF								From	Control parameter field
	0	1	2	3 (AS)	4 (ES)	5	6 (T2)	7 (T1)	0 (EB)	1 (EB)	2 (RDY)	3 (CH)	4 (DR)	5	6	7		
Multipurpose:																		
Accept Command Response	0	0	0	1	N	0	1	1	N	1	1	N	N	N	N	N	CH	N
Accept Connection	0	0	0	X	U	0	1	1	N	1	1	N	N	N	N	N	CH	N
Deny Connection	0	0	0	X	N	0	1	1	N	1	0	N	N	N	N	N	CH	N
Rescind Connection	0	0	0	X	N	0	1	1	N	1	N	N	1	N	N	N	CU	N
Data Request	0	0	0	1	N	0	1	1	W	N	N	N	1	N	N	N	CC	Note 1
Command Response	0	0	0	1	N	0	1	1	X	N	N	N	X	N	N	N	CU	Note 2
Stack Status	0	0	0	X	N	0	1	1	N	N	N	N	N	N	N	N	CH	N
Cancel	0	0	0	1	N	0	1	1	N	N	N	N	N	N	N	N	CH	N
System Reset	0	0	0	0	N	0	1	1	N	N	N	N	N	N	N	N	CH	N
Selective Reset	0	0	0	1	N	0	1	1	N	N	N	N	N	N	N	N	CH	Note 3
Request Connection	0	0	0	X	N	0	1	1	N	N	N	N	N	N	N	N	CU	N
Request Status	0	0	0	V	X	0	1	1	N	N	N	N	N	N	N	N	CH	N

Table 5.12 Device header IFI/flag bit and control functions (cont.)

Control function	IFI								DHF								From	Control parameter field
	0	1	2	3	4	5	6	7	0	1	2	3	4	5	6	7		
				AS	ES		T2	T1	EB	RDY		CH	DR					
Device Level Exception																		
Address Exception	0	0	0	1	z	0	1	1	z	z	z	z	z	z	z	z	CU	Note 4
Status Accepted	0	0	0	X	z	0	1	1	z	z	z	X	z	z	z	z	CH	z
Device Level Acknowledgment	0	0	0	X	z	0	1	1	z	z	z	z	z	z	z	z	CU	z

Note 1: Includes data count in control parameter field.

Note 2: Includes DIB size control in bits 5, 6 and 7 of the control function field. For write operations, includes data request count and pacing count in control-parameter field. For read operations, includes NDR-R count in control parameter field.

Note 3: Includes modifier bits in control parameter field.

Note 4: For write operations, includes data request count and pacing count in control parameter field. For read operations, includes exception code in control parameter field.

CC: Either channel or control unit sends frame

CH: Channel sends frame

CU: Control Unit sends frame

U: Bit is set to 0; otherwise, unpredictable results

V: Bit is set to 1; otherwise, unpredictable results

W: Bit is set to 1 if CCW count is satisfied by this data request; otherwise, this bit is set to 0.

X: Bit is set to 1 or 0 as appropriate.

z: Bit is always set to 0 by sender and ignored by recipient.

0: Bit is always set to 0 and checked for 0.

1: Bit is always set to 1 and checked for 1.

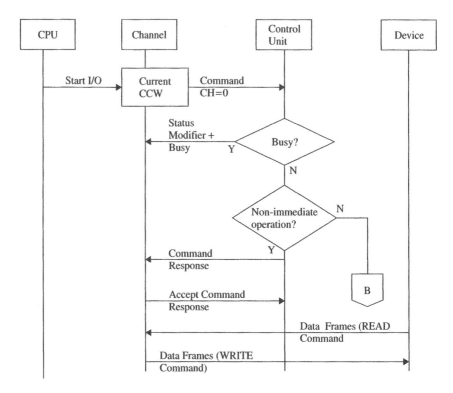

Figure 5.13 Initiation of I/O operation – non-immediate command.

0. If device end was included in the status frame, and chaining is required, then the next command frame is sent with the CH bit set to 1. Figure 5.14 shows I/O initiation for an immediate command.

For succeeding immediate commands, the control unit signals acceptance of the command by returning status of channel end. Execution of the command, however, may begin as soon as it is received and all error checking has been done. Since execution may occur before the status is sent, the I/O operation may be completed before the status is sent, and device end may be returned along with channel end.

If the first command is a non-immediate command, the control unit responds with a command response frame. The channel indicates that the I/O operation is in progress by responding with an accept command response. A write operation may begin immediately after the accept command response has been sent. A read operation may begin after the control unit receives the accept command response.

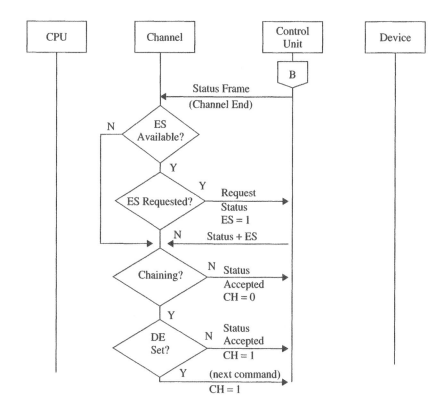

Figure 5.14   I/O initiation for immediate command.

For succeeding non-immediate commands, the control unit indicates acceptance of the command by sending a command response frame to the channel. Execution, however, may proceed as soon as the command is received and error checking has been done. If the operation is a read, the control unit may begin to transfer data immediately after sending the command response frame. If the operation is a write, the channel may begin to transfer the data requested by the I/O device, provided that the DR bit was set to 1 in the command response frame.

For data transfer operations, the amount of data transferred is determined by either the CCW count or the amount of data required by the I/O device for the current command (if less than CCW count). The recipient of the data should have the count provided with the current CCW. If the operation is a write, the control unit should receive the count in a command frame. The recipient of the data initiates data transfer. Data transfer is initiated by the channel if the operation is a read; it is initiated by the control unit if the operation is a write. Data transfer is initiated by setting the Data Request (DR) bit. If the operation is a read, the DR bit is set in the first command frame for the first request made for the current CCW. If the operation is a write, the DR bit is set in the command response for the first request made for the current CCW. If the command response for a write command for the current CCW had a DR bit set to 0, the DR bit may be set to 1 for a data request frame. The DR bit may also be set to 1 for subsequent data request frames for the current CCW, for both read and write operations.

Multiple data requests may be required if the first data request is less than the total data required for the current CCW; additional data requests use the data request frame (if chaining is not in effect). All data frames must be of the DIB size in effect for the I/O operation, except for the last transfer, which may be smaller. The E bit is set to 1 in the data frame which exactly completes the CCW count. The NDR field for the logical path specifies one less than the number of data requests that may be outstanding; for example, an NDR of 0 specifies that 1 data request may be outstanding at any time. A data request is outstanding from the time it is sent until a data frame is received with a RDY bit set and there are no previous outstanding requests for that CCW.

If successive CCWs are executed for a single I/O operation, data chaining may be used. When each CCW becomes the current CCW, a command frame is used to transfer the chain-data flag, the count, and other flags associated with this CCW to the control unit to inform it that data chaining is in effect for this CCW. Data chaining only occurs during an I/O operation, and only when the Chain-Data (CD) bit was set to 1 in the previous command frame. When data chaining takes place at the channel, the CH bit of the device header flag and the DU bit of the command flag field are both set to 1 to identify the command frame as being associated with data chaining. When the control unit receives a command frame with CH and DU set to 1, the chaining condition is set, and the previous command frame had the CD bit set to 1, then the command flags and count from the current command frame are accepted and become the current flags and count.

When a data frame is received with the E bit set to 1, and the quantity of data received equals the data requested and the count for the CCW, data chaining is expected. The next frame received should be either the command frame containing the flags and count for the next CCW, or a device control frame that terminates the I/O operation.

I/O operations may be ended by either the channel or the control unit. If the I/O operation completes normally, the control unit terminates the operation by sending status to the channel. If an abnormal condition occurs, the channel may terminate the I/O operation by sending a cancel, selective reset, or system reset control frame to the control unit. For normal ending, the control unit sends channel end status, and may also include device end status. If device end status is not included with the channel end status, it may be sent later by the control unit. If the control unit has disconnected, it may be necessary for the control unit to send a request connection control frame to the channel to request connection. An accept connection with a dynamic SOF will be returned to establish a connection in order to transfer the device end status.

The control unit initiates ending of non-immediate I/O operations with channel end/device end status when one of the following conditions occurs and there are no errors:

- The quantity of data transferred exactly equals the total count associated with the current command and exactly equals the amount of data required by the I/O device.
- The quantity of data transferred exactly equals the total count associated with the current command but does not equal the amount of data required by the I/O device.
- The quantity of data transferred is less than the total count associated with the current command but exactly equals the amount of data required by the I/O device.

If the quantity of data transferred is less than or equal to the total count associated with the current command but greater than the amount of data required by the I/O device, the control unit initiates ending of the I/O operation with channel end/device end and unit check status.

For an immediate operation, the control unit initiates ending of an I/O operation with channel end/device end status with the transfer count valid (XV) status flag set to 0 and the transfer count in the status parameter field set to 0.

Figure 5.15 shows several different normally ending I/O operations and the status returned to the channel.

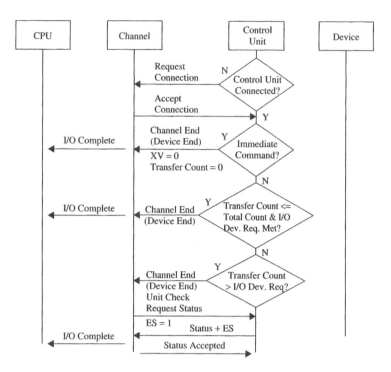

Figure 5.15 Ending I/O operations.

5.2.6 Physical Layer

The ESCON/SBCON physical layer uses 8B/10B encoding and ordered sets to provide physical layer messaging and frame delineation. A 1300 nm optical interface is supported. Each is described below.

5.2.6.1 ESCON/SBCON Transmission Coding

ESCON/SBCON uses 8B/10B line coding, in which each 8 bits of data to be transmitted is encoded into a 10-bit transmission character, which is sent serially over the fiber link. Due to the 25% overhead of 8B/10B encoding, the ESCON data rate of 160 Mb/s requires a transport bit rate of 200 Mb/s. At the receiving end, each transmission character is decoded into the original 8 bits of data. In addition to the transmission characters which may be decoded into the 256 possible 8-bit combinations, there are additional transmission characters, referred to as *special characters*, which are used for purposes which require them to be distinct from frame contents. Special characters include ordered sets, sequences, and the idle sequence. Functions performed using special characters include:

- Idle function
- Not-Operational Sequence (Ordered Set)
- Connect Start of Frame (SOF) delimiter
- Passive Start of Frame (SOF) delimiter
- Abort delimiter
- Disconnect End of Frame (EOF) delimiter
- Passive End of Frame (EOF) delimiter
- Unconditional Disconnect (UD) Sequence (Ordered Set)
- Unconditional Disconnect Response Sequence (Ordered Set)
- Offline Sequence (Ordered Set).

The beginning of a frames is indicated by the initial SOF delimiter ordered set, and the ending of a frame is indicated by the EOF delimiter ordered set. A special character referred to as the *idle character* is used to perform the idle function. Idle characters may be inserted between frames to perform pacing functions, and are used as part of the Not-Operational, Unconditional Disconnect, Unconditional Disconnect Response, and Offline sequences.

Each eight bits of data and each special character actually has two possible encodings, referred to as *Running Disparity Minus* (RD-) and *Running Disparity Plus* (RD+). At transmission time, the transmitter will select one or the other encoding. Which encoding is chosen is based on the relative number of ones and zeroes in the transmission character. This is done in order to maintain the *DC balance*, or ratio of ones to zeroes, in the bit stream.

5.2.6.2 ESCON/SBCON Optical Link Specifications

The ESCON/SBCON physical interface consists of an optical transmitter and receiver at each end of an ESCON/SBCON link. The ESCON/SBCON link consists of a pair of optical fibers, one for each direction of transmission. Short jumper cables are often used to connect units to a trunk cable for long-distance applications. Table 5.13 gives link loss budgets and distance limitations for unrepeated ESCON/SBCON links at 1300 nm wavelength.

Table 5.13 Link loss budgets and distance limitations for ESCON/SBCON links (1300 nm)

Fiber type and size	Loss budget (dB)	Maximum distance	Notes
50 um. MMF	8.0	2.0 km	800 Mhz-km minimum trunk modal bandwidth
62.5 um. MMF	8.0	2.0 km	500 Mhz-km minimum trunk modal bandwidth
62.5 um. MMF	8.0	2.0–3.0 km	800 Mhz-km minimum trunk modal bandwidth
9–10 um. SMF	14.0	20 km	

Table 5.14 Multimode output optical interface signal

Parameter	Min	Max	Unit
Average Power[1,2]	−20.5	−15	dBm
Center Wavelength	1280	1380	nm.
Spectral Width (Full Width, Half Maximum)		175	nm.
Rise Time (T_r) 20–80%[1,3]		1.7	ns.
Fall Time (Tf) 80–20%[1,3]		1.7	ns.
Eye Window[1]	3.4		ns.
Extinction Ratio[1,4]	8		dB
T_r, T_f at Optical Path Output[3,5]		2.8	ns.
Optical Output Jitter[6]		0.8	ns.

1. Based on any valid 8B10B code pattern. The length of the jumper cable between the output interface and the instrumentation is 3 meters.
2. The output power should be greater than −29 dBm through a worst case link as specified in Table 5.13. Higher order mode loss (HOML) is the difference in link loss measured using the device transmitter as compared to the loss measured with a source conditioned to achieve an equilibrium mode distribution in the fiber. The transmitter shall compensate for an excess HOML occurring in the link (e.g. HOML in excess of 1 dB for a 62.5 um link).
3. The minimum frequency response bandwidth range of the optical waveform detector shall be 100 KHz to 1 GHz.
4. Measurement shall be made with a DC-coupled optical waveform detector that has a minimum bandwidth of 600 MHz and whose gain flatness and linearity over the range of optical power being measured provide an accurate measurement of the high and low optical power levels.
5. The maximum rise or fall time (from chromatic dispersion, modal dispersion, etc.) at the output of a worst-case link as specified in Table 5.13. The 0% and 100% levels are set where the optical signal has at least 10 ns. to settle. The spectral width of the transmitter shall be controlled to meet this specification.
6. The optical output jitter includes both deterministic and random jitter. It is defined as the peak to peak time-histogram oscilloscope value (minimum of 3000 samples) using a 2^7-1 pseudorandom pattern or worst-case 8B10B code pattern.

5.2.6.3   Multimode Interface Specifications

Table 5.14 defines output characteristics for the ESCON/SBCON optical signal. The parameters in this table are based on the requirement that the bit error rate not exceed 10^{-15}, including operation at the minimum interface power level. The use of a noncoherent light source, such as an LED, is required.

Table 5.15 lists specifications for the multimode input optical interface signal. To assist in fault isolation, the input interface activates a loss of signal (LOL) state when the optical data cannot be detected. The optical power threshold to activate the LOL state, the LOL optical power hysteresis, and the reaction time for the LOL state change to occur are also specified.

Table 5.15   Multimode input optical interface signal

Parameter	Min	Max	Unit
Saturation Level[1]	−14.0		dBm
Sensitivity[1,2]		−29	dBm
Acquisition Time[3]		100	ms.
LOL Threshold[4]	−45	−36	dBm
LOL Hysteresis[4,5]	0.5		Db
Reaction Time for LOL State Change	3	500	us.

1. Based on any valid 8B10B code pattern measured at, or extrapolated to, 10^{-15} BER measured at center of eye. This specification shall be met with worst-case conditions as described in Table 5.13 for the fiber optic link and Table 5.14 for the output interface. This value allows for 0.5 dB retiming penalty.
2. A minimum receiver output eye opening of 1.4 ns at 10^{-12} should be achieved with a penalty not exceeding 1 dB.
3. The time to reach synchronization after removal of the condition that caused the loss of synchronization. The pattern sent for synchronization is either the idle character or an alternation of idle and data characters.
4. In direction of decreasing power:
If power >-36 dBm, LOL state is inactive; If power <-45 dBm, LOL state is active. In direction of increasing power:
If power <-44.5 dBm, LOL state is active; if power is >-35.5 dBm, LOL state is inactive.
5. Required to avoid random transitions between LOL being active and inactive when input power is near threshold level.

5.2.6.4   Single Mode Interface Specifications

Table 5.16 gives specifications for the single mode output optical interface signal. The parameters in this table are based on the requirement that the bit error rate not exceed 10^{-15}, including operation at the minimum interface power level.

Table 5.16   Single mode output optical interface signal

Parameter	Min	Max	Unit
Average Power into SMF[1]	−8.0	−4.0	dBm
Center Wavelength[1]	1261	1360	nm.
Rise Time (T_r) 20–80%[1,2]		1.5	ns.
Fall Time (Tf) 80–20%[1,2]		1.5	ns.
Eye Window[1]	3.5		ns.
Extinction Ratio[1,3]	8.2		dB
Relative Intensity Noise (RIN_{12})[4]		−112	dB/Hz
AC Optical Path Penalty[5]		1.5	dB
Optical Output Jitter[6]		0.8	ns.

1. Based on any valid 8B10B code pattern. The measurement is made using a 4 meter single mode duplex jumper cable and includes only the power in the fundamental mode of the single mode fiber.
2. The minimum frequency response bandwidth range of the optical waveform detector shall be 100 KHz to 1 GHz.
3. Measurement shall be made with a DC-coupled optical waveform detector that has a minimum bandwidth of 600 MHz and whose gain flatness and linearity over the range of optical power being measured provide an accurate measurement of the high and low optical power levels.
4. The Relative Intensity Noise is measured with a 12 dB optical return loss into the output interface.
5. The maximum degradation in input interface sensitivity (from jitter, mode hopping, intersymbol interference, etc.) that can occur using a worst-case link as specified in Table 5.13. The spectral width of the transmitter shall be controlled to meet this specification.
6. The optical output jitter includes both deterministic and random jitter. It is defined as the peak to peak time-histogram oscilloscope value (minimum of 3000 samples) using a 2^7-1 pseudorandom pattern or worst-case 8B10B code pattern.

Table 5.17 lists specifications for the single mode input optical interface signal. To assist in fault isolation, the input interface activates a loss of signal (LOL) state when the optical data cannot be detected. The optical power threshold to activate the LOL state, the LOL optical power hysteresis, and the reaction time for the LOL state change to occur are also specified.

5.2.7   Summary

ESCON/SBCON was the first optical storage protocol, and is still widely deployed in mainframe environments. It inherited the basic channel program execution protocol from the earlier bus/tag interface; however, it substitutes a connection setup sequence for the selection sequence used in the parallel bus/tag interface. Many features of ESCON and SBCON, including the use of 8B/10B encoding,

Table 5.17   Single mode input optical interface signal

Parameter	Min	Max	Unit
Saturation Level[1]	−3.0		dBm
Sensitivity[1]		−28	dBm
Return Loss[2]	12.5		
Acquisition Time[3]		100	ms.
LOL Threshold	−40	−31	dBm
LOL Hysteresis[4]	1.5		dB
Reaction Time for LOL State Change	.25	5000	ps.

1. Based on any valid 8B10B code pattern measured at, or extrapolated to, 10^{-15} BER. This specification shall be met with worst-case conditions as described in Table 5.13 for the fiber optic link and Table 5.16 for the output interface.
2. The measurement is made using a 4 meter single mode duplex jumper cable and includes only the power in the fundamental mode of the single mode fiber.
3. The time to reach synchronization after removal of the condition that caused the loss of synchronization. The pattern sent for synchronization is either the idle character or an alternation of idle and data characters.
4. Required to avoid random transitions between LOL being active and inactive when input power is near threshold level.

ordered sets, and switched topologies, can be found in later storage protocols as well.

Limitations of ESCON/SBCON include a relatively low transport rate of 200 Mb/s, a synchronous command protocol that reduces I/O performance over extended distances, and lack of a credit-based flow control mechanism. All these have been addressed by more recently developed protocols, including FICON and Fibre Channel.

5.3   FIBER CONNECTION (FICON)

5.3.1   Applications

Fiber Connection, or FICON™, is a high-speed, high-performance storage protocol specifically designed to provide improved I/O performance for mainframe computer networks over long distances. It provides higher bandwidth, improved I/O handling capability, and larger frame sizes than ESCON while still supporting the same channel architecture. FICON may be used on fiber optic links at distances of up to 10 km.

5.3.2 Standards

FICON was developed by IBM Corporation in the late 1990s and released in 1998. It was intended to enable I/O channels to keep pace with improvements in processor speed and capacity. FICON is based on the Fibre Channel standards, with an FC-4 layer optimized for gigabit-level enterprise storage applications.

5.3.3 Network Topology

FICON may be used to provide native-mode channel-to-control unit storage connectivity, or it may be used in existing ESCON configurations by employing a protocol translation device such as a bridge. Up to eight ESCON links may be time-division-multiplexed onto a single 1.062 Gb/s FICON link at 50% utilization. Figure 5.16 shows FICON used in bridged, point-to-point, and switched configurations.

FICON provides improvements in maximum system configuration relative to ESCON. While ESCON supports only 16 control unit images, FICON supports a maximum of 256. FICON also

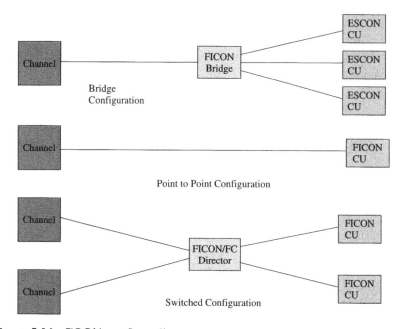

Figure 5.16 FICON configurations.

increases the total number of supported devices per control unit from 4096 to 64 k.

FICON provides improved bandwidth and throughput relative to ESCON. While ESCON supports a maximum unidirectional bandwidth of 17 MB/s, FICON is capable of supporting bidirectional transfers at 100 MB/s.

5.3.4 Command Protocol

FICON uses asynchronous command execution to improve command execution performance. ESCON, on the other hand, uses synchronous command execution, in which each command requires an acknowledgment to be returned to the channel before execution can proceed.

FICON allows Channel Command Words (CCWs) to be *pipelined*. In this mode of execution, multiple CCWs may be executed without returning status or acknowledgment for each command. One status is returned for the entire set of commands executed. Use of CCW pipelining increases the maximum number of I/Os per second from 400–500 for ESCON to as much as 4k–5k for FICON, depending on blocksize. Figure 5.17 shows an example of CCW pipelining.

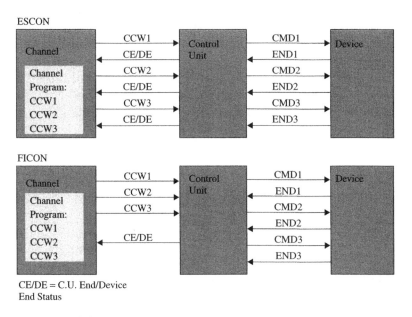

CE/DE = C.U. End/Device
End Status

Figure 5.17 FICON CCW pipelining.

5.3.5   Data Framing

Data transfer performance on ESCON links is limited by the small maximum data frame size (1035 bytes) and the need for data frame acknowledgments. ESCON links begin to show some performance degradation at distances of around 9 km due to data transfer effects. By using large data transfer frames and thereby reducing the need for multiple acknowledgments, FICON links are able to maintain performance at distances of up to 100 km (using large data transfer sizes).

5.3.6   Physical Layer

FICON uses 8B/10B line coding, in which each 8 bits of data to be transmitted is encoded into a 10-bit transmission character, which is sent serially over the fiber link. At the receiving end, each transmission character is decoded into the original 8 bits of data. In addition to the transmission characters which may be decoded into the 256 possible 8-bit combinations, there are additional transmission characters, referred to as *special characters*, which are used for purposes which require them to be distinct from frame contents. Groups of special characters, called *ordered sets*, are used as frame delimiters, primitive signals, and primitive sequences.

FICON allows use of long-wavelength lasers on multimode fiber optic cable using a mode-conditioning patch cable. This allows existing installed multimode fiber to be used over short and intermediate (<550 meters) distances.

Table 5.18   Link loss budgets and distance limitations for FICON optical links

Bandwidth@ wavelength	Fiber Type and Size	Loss Budget (dB)	Maximum Distance	Modal Bandwidth (MMF)
1062@1310 nm	50 um MMF	5	550 m	400 MHz-km; using mode conditioning patch cable
1062@1310 nm	62.5 um MMF	5	550 m	500 MHz-km; using mode conditioning patch cable
1062@1310 nm	9 um SMF	7	10 km	

Table 5.19   FICON single mode output optical interface specifications

Parameter	Units	Minimum	Nominal	Maximum
Average Power[1]	dBm	−8.5		−4
Center Wavelength[1]	nm.	1280	1310	1355
Spectral Width (RMS)[2]	nm.			1.7
20–80 Rise Time[1,3]				0.26
20–80 Fall Time[1,3]				0.26
Extinction Ratio[1,4]	dB	11		
Relative Intensity Noise (RIN)	dB/Hz			−120

1. Launched into single-mode fiber, based on any valid 8B/10B code pattern, measured using a four-meter single-mode duplex jumper cable. Includes only power in the fundamental mode of the single-mode optical fiber.
2. Spectral width may be increased on the basis of center wavelength and distance tradeoffs; link budget analysis is required for such a change.
3. Minimum frequency response bandwidth range of the optical waveform detector is 800 kHz to 3 GHz.
4. Measurement can be made with a dc-coupled optical waveform detector of 800 MHz minimum bandwidth and whose gain flatness and linearity over the range of measured optical power provide an accurate measurement of the high and low optical power levels.

Table 5.20   FICON input single mode optical interface specifications

Parameter	Units	Minimum	Maximum
Saturation Level	dBm	−3	−22
Sensitivity	dBm	−22	
Return Loss	dB	12	

5.3.6.1   FICON Single Mode Output Optical Interface

Table 5.19 gives specifications for the FICON single mode output optical interface.

5.3.6.2   FICON Single Mode Input Optical Interface

Table 5.20 gives specifications for the FICON single mode input optical interface.

5.3.7   Summary

Since its introduction in 1998, FICON has been used primarily in high-performance processing and distance extension applications that require high bandwidth and improved I/O performance; it has displaced ESCON in about 15% of mainframe storage networks. A 2 Gb/s version of FICON is scheduled to be released in 2003.

5.4 FIBRE CHANNEL (FC)

Fibre Channel (FC) is a high speed serial data transfer protocol that forms the basis for the Storage Area Network (SAN) architecture. While Fibre Channel originally was developed as a general purpose data protocol, it has been used almost exclusively as a storage protocol.

5.4.1 Applications

Fibre Channel is commonly used to connect Unix and NT servers to storage networks using a variety of network topologies, at distances of up to 10 km without the need for repeaters. Its distinguishing features include a *nameserver* capability, which enables lookup of any node on a Fibre Channel network using a World Wide Name, and a *zoning* capability, which partitions switch ports into port groups for resource allocation and security purposes. Fibre Channel also provides multiple classes of service and a credit-based flow control function to provide reliable data transport under heavy load conditions.

5.4.2 Standards

Development of the Fibre Channel was begun in 1988 by the ANSI X3 standards group, and continues under the INCITS T11 Technical Committee. The primary standard, ANSI X3.230–1994, Fibre Channel – Physical and Signaling Interface (FC-PH), was originally released in 1994. The original specification defined optical interfaces that ran at 133, 266, and 532 Mb/s, and 1.062 Gb/s, as well as a short-haul copper interface. (The non-obvious reason for the obscure bit rates is that they correspond to byte rates of 12.5, 25, 50 and 100 Mbyte/second, respectively.) Since then, a 2 Gb/s optical interface has been standardized, and 4 and 10 Gb/s interfaces are currently under development.

Work is currently in progress on the ANSI/INCITS Fibre Channel Framing and Signaling (FC-FS) Specification. The FC-FS Specification updates and modifies many portions of the original FC-PH specification. Major differences between the FC-PH and FC-FS specifications are noted in the following text.

5.4.3   Network Topology

Fibre Channel network topology has evolved from its earliest use as a simple point to point link extender technology for SCSI-based storage devices to a shared-bandwidth arbitrated loop model, and finally to a switched model allowing multiple port to port connections that provides the basis for the SAN architecture. Each network topology is discussed below.

5.4.3.1   Point-to-Point Topology

In the point-to-point topology, Fibre Channel links are used to connect servers directly to storage devices. Each link consists of two optical fibers, one for each direction of transmission, to provide bidirectional data transfer. Point-to-point connection is frequently used to extend the range of SCSI-connected devices; a bridge is used to convert the Fibre Channel to SCSI protocol at the remote end. Figure 1.4 shows examples of point-to-point connection using Fibre Channel.

5.4.3.2   Arbitrated Loop Topology

The arbitrated loop (FC-AL) topology enables up to 127 nodes to operate on a shared-bandwidth loop. In a true loop configuration, each node is connected to one fiber in the incoming direction and one fiber in the outgoing direction. Only one pair of nodes is allowed to communicate at any time; an arbitration algorithm is used to determine which pair of nodes is given access to the bus if there is contention. If the communicating nodes are not adjacent, the data being sent from one node to the other simply passes through the intermediate nodes. The two communicating nodes are able to perform simultaneous bidirectional data transfer for the duration of the bus access by utilizing both ring directions.

   The FC-AL architecture is referred to as a *blocking* architecture, since only two ports may communicate at any time. However, the architecture may be *meshed* or *non-meshed*. In a non-meshed architecture, there is exactly one path between ports. In a meshed architecture, multiple paths may be available.

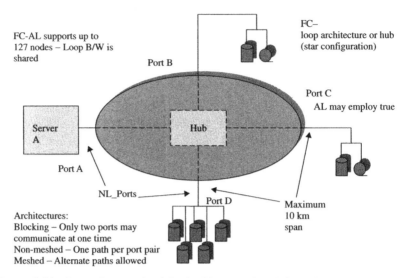

Figure 5.18 Fibre Channel arbitrated loop network topology.

There are several variations on the basic FC-AL architecture. A hub may be used in place of the loop. In this configuration, each node communicates with a central hub by means of a fiber pair. The hub provides a logical loop configuration, but changes the physical configuration to a 'star.' The hub configuration provides additional reliability by making it possible to bypass nodes which are faulted or out of service. Hubs typically support 8, 16, or 32 ports.

The logical ports on each server or storage device in the FC-AL configuration are referred to as Node Loop Ports (NL_Ports). Each port is assigned a priority based on its physical address, similar to the use of Device Ids in SCSI. However, to ensure that lower priority ports are able to gain access to the loop, an access window is used. When a port has arbitrated for the loop and won access, it is not allowed to arbitrate for the loop again until it has transmitted at least one idle signal, to enable other ports to arbitrate for the loop.

5.4.3.3 Switched Topology

In the switched topology, a Fibre Channel fabric switch is used to connect servers to storage for the duration of a data transfer. The interface cards used to support Fibre Channel interfaces on servers, processors, and storage devices are called *Host Bus Adaptors* (HBAs). The logical ports represented by the HBAs are referred to as Node Ports (or N_Ports) for addressing and configuration purposes. The switch ports to which they connect are referred to as Fabric Ports (or

F_Ports). The purpose of the fabric switch is to provide connectivity from any one F-Port on the switch to any other F_Port on the switch for the purpose of connecting a server's N_Port to a storage N_Port for the duration of a data connection. Each N_Port terminates two optical fibers, one for each direction of transmission.

5.4.3.4   Mixed Loop/Fabric Configurations

Switched Fibre Channel networks and FC-AL networks can inter-operate as a mixed loop/fabric network topology. In this topology, some nodes are connected to an arbitrated loop, and others are connected to a fabric switch. Interconnection between the two architectures is provided by means of an L_Port, which connects to a switched fabric F_Port and provides arbitrated access to the arbitrated loop. By using profiles, it is possible to set up 'virtual subnetworks' within the mixed loop/fabric configuration to restrict node access. Membership in a *public loop profile* group enables switched or loop nodes to communicate with other loop or fabric ports; membership in a *private loop profile* enables loop devices to communicate only with other loop nodes. Figure 5.20 shows a mixed fabric/loop configuration.

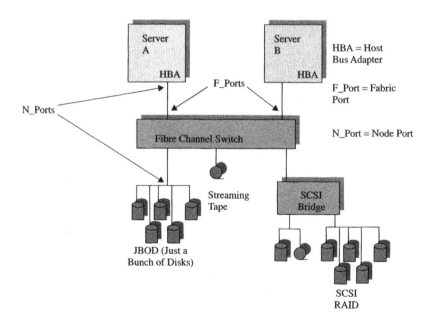

Figure 5.19   Fibre Channel switched network topology.

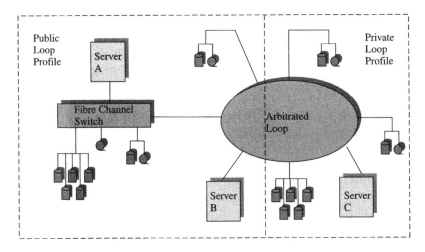

Figure 5.20   Mixed fabric/loop configuration.

5.4.4 Protocol Overview

The following paragraphs describe addressing, zoning, classes of service, flow control, and protocol architecture of the Fibre Channel protocol.

5.4.4.1 Addressing

The Fibre Channel storage network architecture provides integrated services, such as name service, discovery service, and port management. Hosts and storage subsystems can query well-known servers to discover network configuration, node name/port mapping, and other network management functions. Each server providing these services has a well-known address corresponding to the N_Port providing the service. These addresses are recognized by the fabric, which is capable of routing requests to these servers. Nameserver queries are handled as normal N_Port-to-N_Port transactions, as described below.

The name server translates between world wide names and fabric addresses. A *World Wide Name* (WWN) is a 64-bit unsigned name identifier which, as the name suggests, is unique in the world. A Fibre Channel device may use the nameserver query capability to discover the fabric address of an N_Port by specifying its WWN. In addition to the query capability, the nameserver provides a dynamic notification service. If a device has subscribed to this service, it is notified whenever N_Ports are added to or removed from the configuration.

5.4.4.2   Zoning

The Fibre Channel protocol allows 'virtual subnetworks' to be set up within the fabric for a variety of operational, administrative, and security purposes; this is referred to as *zoning*. This enables system administrators to create groups of ports or addresses that are allowed to communicate with one another. The nameserver is aware of zoning, and query responses will only provide information on ports or addresses that are in the same zone as the requestor. Some common reasons for implementing zones are as follows:

* *Operating system compatibility.* Different operating systems have different storage formats and locking capabilities. One way to manage a multi-operating system storage network using Fibre Channel is to create different zones for each server operating system (e.g. NT, UNIX, OS/390) and its associated storage.
* *Creating a backup group.* A zone can be created which includes a set of disk drives and a backup device such as a tape drive or RAID unit to enable the disk data to be backed up. A new backup group can be created by simply creating a new zone with the backup device and different disk drives.
* *Security.* To prevent unauthorized access to critical data, a zone can be set up which limits access to stored data to only those servers which have a legitimate reason to access it.

There are two general types of zoning. Hardware zoning allows device-level zoning in which certain servers are allowed to access specific storage devices. Software zoning enables zones to be created using WWNs and port names.

5.4.4.3   Classes of Service

Fibre Channel provides multiple classes of service for different data transfer operations and service levels.

* *Class 1:* Class 1 service provides connection-oriented circuit-switched data transfer. This class of service provides a dedicated

full-bandwidth connection between the two communicating entities. A connection must be established by the fabric switch(es) before data transfer can begin. This class of service guarantees in-order delivery of data. It is used for applications which require high levels of reliability and availability, such as scientific applications and large data block transfers.

- *Class 2:* Class 2 service provides shared-bandwidth connections between communicating entities and individual frame acknowledgments. Frames from different sources are multiplexed together and switched on an individual basis in the fabric, based on destination. This class of service is used for common data center operations, such as tape backup and mass storage.

- *Class 3:* Class 3 service provides datagram transmission over shared-bandwidth connections. Individual frames are not acknowledged. Class 3 service is normally used for TCP/IP networking and FC_AL loop operation.

- *Class 4:* Class 4 service is connection-oriented and based on a virtual circuit model. It provides delivery confirmation with bandwidth and latency guarantees.

- *Class 6:* Class 6 service provides reliable multicast service, based on Class 1.

- *Intermixed:* Intermixed service is a hybrid service offering which allows interleaving of class 2 or class 3 frames during an established class 1 connection. Since dedicated bandwidth will be wasted if no data is available for a class 1 connection, intermixed service improves the bandwidth utilization of class 1 connections by filling in the 'empty slots' with lower-priority data.

Operation of Classes 1, 2 and 3 are discussed below. Classes 4 and 6 are currently under development as part of INCITS Project 1331D.[2]

5.4.4.4 Flow Control and Classes of Service

The Fibre Channel protocol includes a flow control mechanism to pace the flow of frames between N_Ports, and between N_Ports and the fabric, to prevent buffer overflow at the receiver. Flow control

---

[2] For current status of FC class 4 and class 6 development, see Fibre Channel Framing and Signaling (FC-FS), Rev 1.90, INCITS Project 1331D, April 2003, ftp://ftp.t11.org/t11/pub/fc/fs/03-173v1.pdf (work in progress)

may be *end-to-end* between N_Ports, or it may be *buffer-to-buffer* between N_Ports and fabric ports. Class 1 and Class 2 connections may use end-to-end flow control, while Class 2 and Class 3 connections use buffer-to-buffer flow control. In both cases, two counts are maintained at each transmitting port: (1) a credit value, indicating the number of receive buffers allocated for this connection or exchange; and (2) a credit count corresponding to the number of outstanding unacknowledged frames which have been transmitted. The credit count is incremented for each frame transmitted, and decremented for each frame acknowledgement received. The credit count must be greater than 0 and less than the credit value. Figure 5.21 shows both end-to-end and buffer-to-buffer flow control.

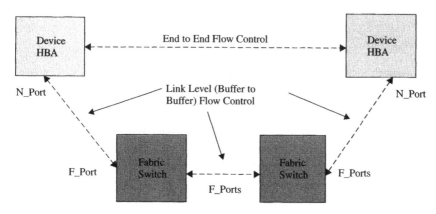

Figure 5.21   Fibre Channel flow control mechanisms.

5.4.4.5 Fibre Channel Protocol Architecture

The Fibre Channel protocol uses a multilayered architecture that provides well-defined interfaces and uses service primitives to perform layer-to-layer transactions. Figure 5.22 shows the architectural layers in the Fibre Channel protocol model and explains the purpose of each.

The FC-4 *Upper Layer Protocols* layer supports interworking with a variety of network and storage channel protocols. Command and data formats for each protocol are mapped to the appropriate Fibre Channel link control or data frame format. The FC-3 *Common Services* layer provides port-related services common to two or more ports in a node. The FC-2 *Signaling Protocol* layer is the transport

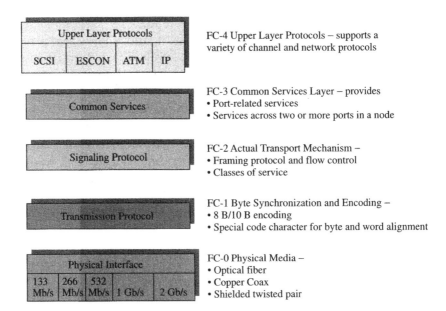

Figure 5.22 Fibre Channel protocol architecture.

mechanism which provides framing, flow control, and classes of service. The FC-1 *Transmission Protocol* provides byte synchronization and 8B/10B transmission encoding/decoding, and special codes for byte and word alignment. The FC-0 *Physical Interface* provides interworking with the actual physical transmission media, including optical fiber, coaxial cable, and twisted pair wiring.

The arbitration logic used in the FC-AL protocol is considered to operate at 'FC-1.5' level, i.e. midway between FC-1 and FC-2.

5.4.5 FC-2 Functions: Links, Frames, Sequences and Exchanges

The following paragraphs describe Fibre Channel link initialization, frame format, and the use of sequences and exchanges in the Fibre Channel protocol.

5.4.5.1 Links and Link Initialization

A link is a hardware facility which manages the transmission and reception of data. A link control facility exists in each N_Port and

F_Port. Before data can be transferred, a link must be initialized. Link initialization is required when a port is powered on, when it is in an offline state, or has been reset. After a link has been initialized, link control frames or data frames may be sent. Link control facilities are capable of detecting error conditions, such as loss of signal or loss of synchronization. When this occurs, the link enters a link failure state.

5.4.5.2 Frames

A frame is the basic unit of information transfer in Fibre Channel. A frame begins with a start of frame delimiter, and ends with an end of frame delimiter. Figure 5.23 shows the format and content of a Fibre Channel frame.

The Start of Frame (SOF) delimiter is an ordered set that immediately precedes the frame content. Different SOF delimiters are defined for the first and succeeding frames of a sequence, and for the individual classes of service (see Section 5.4.6.1 for details).

The Frame Header is the first field in the frame content and immediately follows the SOF. The frame header contains control information for routing frames between N_Ports and managing

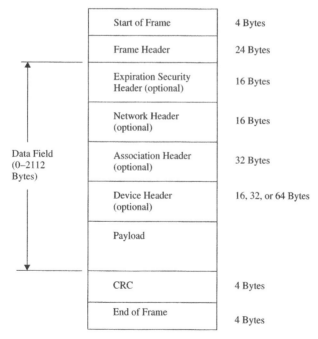

Figure 5.23 Fibre channel frame format.

exchanges and sequences (see below). It is used to control link operations, control device protocol transfers, and detect missing or out-of-order frames. The frame header field includes a source identifier (S_ID), a destination identifier (D_ID), a sequence identifier (SEQ_ID), an originator exchange identifier (OX_ID), and a responder exchange identifier (RX_ID), as well as other fields. The S_ID is a 3-byte field that identifies the N_Port or F_Port within the source entity that is transmitting the frame. The D_ID is a 3-byte field that identifies the N_Port or F_Port within the destination entity that is the recipient of the frame. The SEQ_ID is assigned by the sequence initiator to uniquely identify the sequence; the responder uses the same SEQ_ID in its response. The originator assigns each new exchange an OX_ID unique to the originator or originator/responder pair and places it in the frame header of each frame in the exchange. The responder assigns an RX_ID unique to the responder or originator/responder pair to the exchange and communicates it to the originator.

The frame header also contains a 3-byte F_CTL field that keeps track of current exchange and sequence status.

Four optional header fields follow the frame header. The expiration security header contains an expiration timer value. If the expiration security header is used, a frame will be discarded if it is received at a time later than the timeout specified in the expiration timer value.[3]

The network header is used for routing between Fibre Channel fabrics with different address spaces, or between Fibre Channel networks and non-Fibre Channel networks. The network header contains name identifiers for Network_Source_Addresses and Network_Destination_Addresses.

The association header is used to locate an Exchange Status Block during an exchange or to identify a process or group of processes within a node associated with an exchange.

Use of the device header is application-specific, based on the value in the type field.

The payload contains the data to be transferred. The payload consists of 4-byte words aligned on word boundaries. Two types of payload may be defined by the R_CTL field in the frame header.

---

[3] Fibre Channel Framing and Signaling (FC-FS) Rev. 1.90 does not support the expiration security header. Instead, it supports an Encapsulating Security Payload Header (ESP_Header) and ESP_Trailer which are used to encapsulate an encrypted payload as defined in IETF RFC2406.

An FT_0 (link control) payload consists of 0 bytes; an FT_1 (data frame) payload consists of 0–2112 bytes.

The Cyclical Redundancy Check (CRC) field is used to verify the integrity of the frame header and the data field; it does not include the SOF or EOF delimiters. The Fibre Channel CRC uses the following 32-bit polynomial:

$$X^{32} + X^{26} + X^{23} + X^{22} + X^{16} + X^{12} + X^{11} + X^{10}$$
$$+ X^8 + X^7 + X^5 + X^4 + X^2 + X + 1$$

The End Of Frame (EOF) delimiter is an ordered set that immediately follows the CRC. Different EOF formats are used to indicate (1) valid frame content, (2) invalid frame content, and (3) frame content corrupted. Different EOF delimiters are also used for the different classes of service.

There are two general types of frames: *data frames* and *link control frames*. Data frames transport user data and initiate link operations. Link control frames provide acknowledgments and indicate error or busy conditions.

5.4.5.3   Sequences and Exchanges

Control and data transactions are performed using sequences and exchanges. A sequence is made up of one or more related data frames, transmitted unidirectionally, and their link control frame responses, if applicable. An exchange is made up of multiple sequences which may flow in one direction, or both directions, between the originator and the responder. Figure 5.24 shows the relationship between frames, sequences, and exchanges.

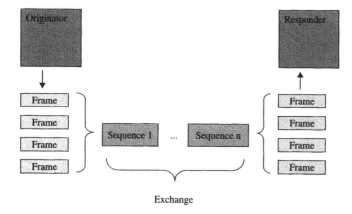

Figure 5.24   Fibre Channel frames, sequences and exchanges.

5.4.5.4 Fabric Login Protocol

Before an upper layer protocol can use Fibre Channel for data transfer, the operating environment has to be established. To do this, each N_Port must first login to the fabric, and then login to all other N_Ports with which it intends to exchange data. The login process sets the service parameters, end-to-end flow control credits, and/or buffer-to-buffer credits for the N_Port.

To login to the fabric, the N_Port must use the FLOGI link service sequence. Fabric login is performed during the initialization process. Fabric login establishes the presence of the fabric, provides the N_Port with service parameters for the fabric, provides the fabric with N_Port identification parameters in the form of a 64 bit N_Port_Name and a Node_Name, and establishes buffer-to-buffer credit. Figure 5.25 shows the format of the data frame payload for the FLOGI/PLOGI sequence used for both fabric and N_Port logins.

Common Service Parameters are the parameters that are common to all supported service classes. For fabric login, these parameters include FC-PH version, buffer-to-buffer credit, receive data field size, and resource allocation timeout (R_A_TOV). *Port Name* identifies the N_Port for purposes unrelated to network addressing, such as diagnostics. *Node Name* similarly identifies the node for purposes unrelated to network addressing, such as diagnostics. *Class Service Parameters* must be supplied for each supported class of service. Class service parameters for fabric login include class validity (whether or not each class is supported on this N_Port), whether or not intermix and stacked connect requests are allowed for Class 1, and if sequential in-order delivery is enforced for classes 2 and 3. *Vendor Version Level* enables vendor-specific version information to be specified for an N_Port.

Normal response to a fabric login is an Accept (ACC) link service reply sequence indicating that fabric login has completed and N_Port login may proceed. If the response indicates that no fabric exists, a point-to-point N_Port login may proceed.

16 Bytes	8 Bytes	8 Bytes	16 Bytes	16 Bytes	16 Bytes	16 Bytes	16 Bytes
Common Service Parameters	Port Name	Node/ Fabric Name	Class 1 Service Parameters	Class 2 Service Parameters	Class 3 service Parameters	Reserved	Vendor Version Level

Figure 5.25 FLOGI/PLOGI payload used for login.

The N-Port receives a 24-bit fabric address as part of the fabric login process. The fabric address consists of three parts: an 8-bit Domain ID, an 8-bit Area ID, and an 8-bit Port ID. The Domain ID is a value in the range 1–239 which refers to the fabric switch element. The Area ID refers to a group of ports administered by the switch, and the Port ID is the unique value assigned to this N_Port. This information is then used as the source identifier (S_ID) for frames sent by this N_Port

5.4.5.5   N_Port Login Protocol

After an N_Port has logged into the fabric, it must login with the other N_Ports with which it will communicate. This is done so that each N_Port can learn the service parameters of the other ports with which it will communicate, set the end-to-end credit for the destination N_Port, and set buffer-to-buffer credit for point-to-point topologies. All N_Ports which support Class 1, 2, or 3 service must login with all other ports. N_Port login protocol uses the PLOGI link service sequence (see Figure 5.24) with parameters that are specific to N_Port login.

Common service parameters are similar to fabric login, with the addition of buffer-to-buffer credit and error detect timeout (E_D_TOV) for point-to-point topology, and parameters relating to concurrent sequences and relative offset. Class service parameters which must be specified for N_Port login include acknowledgment requirements and end-to-end credits for Class 1 and Class 2.

Three different acknowledgment mechanisms are supported. ACK_1 provides an acknowledgment for each frame received. ACK_N provides an acknowledgment for every N frames received.[4] ACK_0 provides an acknowledgment for every sequence received.

Receipt of ACK_1 or ACK_N provides flow control pacing for end-to-end credit. For buffer-to-buffer flow control, receipt of Receiver Ready (R_RDY) provides pacing.

Normal response to a N_Port login is an Accept (ACC) link service reply sequence indicating that N_Port login has completed successfully. For Class 2 and Class 3 service, successful reception of a frame causes an R_RDY response to be returned to the sender. For Class 1 or Class 2 service, an acknowledgment (ACK) is returned for both the PLOGI and ACC sequences. Figure 5.26 shows a normal N_Port login process and messages for all three service classes.

---

[4] Fibre Channel Framing and Signaling (FC-FS) Rev 1.90 does not support ACK_N.

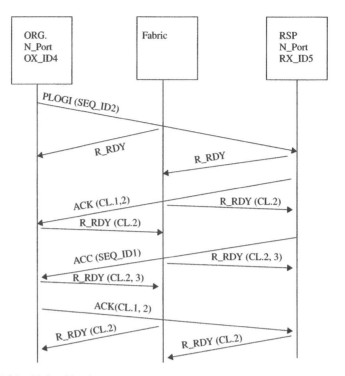

Figure 5.26 N_Port login process.

5.4.5.6 Timers

Two timer values are assigned in the login process which determine the fabric's response to error conditions, missing frames, or delayed frames. Error detect timeout (E_D_TOV) is used as the timeout value for detecting an error condition. During data frame transmission, E_D_TOV represents the timeout for a data frame to be delivered, the destination port to transmit a Link Response, and the Link Response to be delivered to the sequence initiator. Each N_Port receives a value for E_D_TOV as part of the Common Service Parameters received during fabric login The default value for E_D_TOV is 10 seconds.[5] E_D_TOV sets an upper bound for the completion of the following actions:

- Transmission of consecutive data frames within a single sequence.
- Re-transmission of a class 2 data frame in response to an F_BSY or P_BSY.

---

[5] Fibre Channel Framing and Signaling (FC-FS) Rev 1.90 changes the default from 10 seconds to 2 seconds.

- Transmission of ACK frames from the point in time that the event occurred that initiated the acknowledgment.

Expiration of E_D_TOV is used to initiate a link timeout or sequence timeout.

Resource Allocation Timeout (R_A_TOV) is used to ensure that no frames from failed exchanges remain in the fabric when an error has been detected, and to determine when allocated resources may be reused. For switched topology, R_A_TOV is equal to the E_D_TOV plus two times the maximum time that a frame may be delayed within the fabric and still be delivered. Each N_Port receives a value for R_A_TOV as part of the Common Service Parameters received during fabric login. For point-to-point topology, R_A_TOV is equal to twice the value of E_D_TOV. The default value of R_A_TOV is 120 seconds.[6]

5.4.5.7   Data Transport

Class 1 Service

Class 1 service provides a dedicated connection and guaranteed bandwidth between two N_Ports. Before data transfer can occur, a connection must be established. To request a connection, the requesting N_Port must send a frame with an SOF Connect Class 1 (SOFc1) to the destination N_Port, and must receive an ACK from it signifying connection acceptance, before the connection exists. If the fabric is unable to establish a dedicated connection, it returns a busy or reject frame with a reason code; otherwise, it must allocate a circuit for the connection. One round-trip delay for connection request and acknowledgment must take place before data transfer may begin; therefore, Class 1 service is best suited for large data transfers where the connection setup latency is small compared to the total transfer time.

Once a connection is established, it is dedicated for use by the requesting and destination N_Ports, and no other data frames may use it. The maximum size of the data field for each data frame is determined by the receive data field size set for the destination N_Port. Each data frame sent from one N_Port to the other will be acknowledged by (1) an ACK_1 response for an individual frame: (2) an ACK_N response for N frames: or (3) an ACK_0 for a complete sequence.

---

[6] Fibre Channel Framing and Signaling (FC-FS) Rev 1.90 changes the default from 120 seconds to 10 seconds.

The acknowledgment also provides end-to-end flow control. The credit counter, EE_Credit_CNT, is set to 0 after N_Port login. It is set to 1 when the frame containing the connect request SOF is sent. It is incremented by 1 for each succeeding data frame sent. The EE_Credit_CNT is decremented by 1 for each ACK_1 received, or by N for each ACK_N received.

Stacked connection requests may be allowed for Class 1 connections, if this capability was enabled during fabric login. Stacked connection requests occur when an N_Port requests a connection with a destination N_Port that is currently busy. If stacked connection requests are enabled, the request will be queued in the fabric until the destination device terminates its present connection and is free to establish a new connection.

The data frame F_CTL field contains flags for the first sequence, the last sequence, and the last data frame. These flags are returned in the corresponding ACK. The end of exchange is signaled to the sequence recipient by the last sequence and last data frame flags in F_CTL. The connection is terminated by a disconnect-terminate EOF (EOFdt) in the last ACK returned to the originator. Figure 5.27 shows flow of data frames and acknowledgments for Class 1 service.

Class 2 Service

Class 2 service uses frame switching to multiplex frames from multiple originating N_Ports onto shared-bandwidth paths to destination N_Ports. The fabric switch examines the destination address of each frame and forwards it to the specified destination. End-to-end flow control is provided between the originating and destination N_Ports, and between each N_Port and the fabric. Acknowledgments are provided for either individual frames or groups of frames. Messaging is also provided to indicate if a frame has been busied or rejected by either the destination N_Port or the fabric. Figure 5.28 shows frame flow among multiple devices for class 2 service.

The use of multiplexing allows efficient use of link and fabric bandwidth. Class 2 data transfer does not require in-order delivery of frames; however, this can be optionally specified by the N_Port as part of fabric login.

Class 2 data transfer is initiated by an originating N_Port sending an initiate Class 2 SOF (SOFi2) to the destination N_Port. The fabric F_Port returns an R_RDY to the originator, and the destination N_Port returns an R_RDY to the fabric; note that the R_RDY

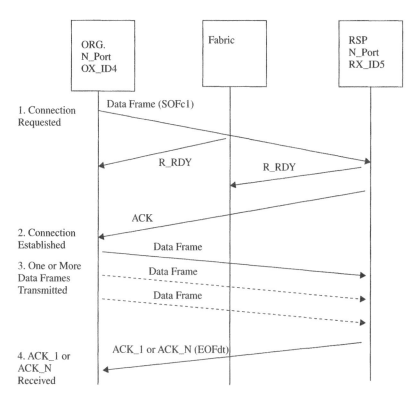

Figure 5.27 Class 1 data transfer operation.

primitive signal does not pass through the fabric. The destination also returns an ACK, which is responded with R_RDY by both the fabric and the source N_Port. The source begins to send data frames to the destination; each frame or group of frames is acknowledged.

The data frame F_CTL field contains flags for the first sequence, the last sequence, and the last data frame. These flags are returned in the corresponding ACK. The sequence initiator signals end of sequence to the sequence recipient by the last sequence and last data frame flags in F_CTL; however, the recipient does not consider the sequence completed until all data frames have been received. The connection is terminated by a terminate EOF (EOFt) in the last ACK returned to the originator. Figure 5.29 shows data frame and acknowledgment flow for Class 2 service.

Class 3 Service

Class 3 service is a connectionless service based on frame switching. It is a datagram service which does not provide confirmation of

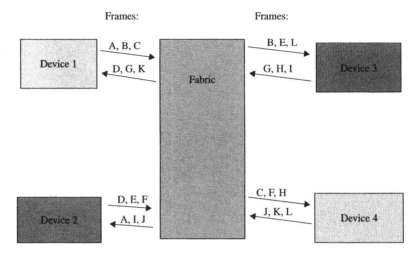

Figure 5.28 Class 2 service frame flow.

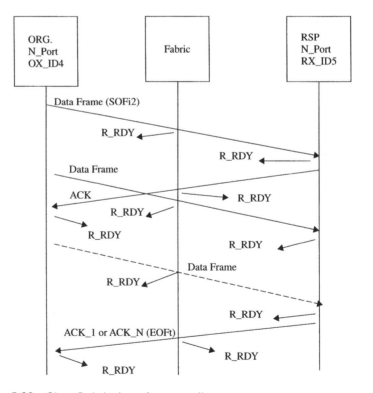

Figure 5.29 Class 2 data transfer operation.

delivery/nondelivery of frames. (It is assumed that upper level protocols will manage data integrity.) Class 3 does not provide acknowledgements, or indications that a frame has been busied or rejected.

The fabric may discard Class 3 service frames if congestion is experienced. Recovery of missing frames requires retransmission of the sequence from which the frames are missing. Although Class 3 service does not provide reliable data transport, it has low protocol overhead due to the absence of connection setup time and acknowledgment round-trip delays.

A sequence is initiated by the originator with a data frame containing a Class 3 initiate SOF (SOFi3). A R_RDY response is returned by the fabric and the destination upon receipt of the data frame and each succeeding data frame. The initiator indicates end of sequence by setting the last frame bit in F_CTL and putting a terminate EOF (EOFt) in the frame. Figure 5.30 shows data frame flow for Class 3 service.

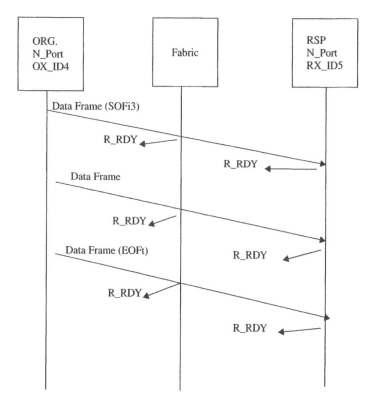

Figure 5.30   Class 3 data transfer operation.

5.4.6   FC1 Functions: Transmission Coding

Fibre Channel uses 8B/10B line coding, in which each 8 bits of data
to be transmitted is encoded into a 10-bit transmission character,
which is sent serially over the fiber link. At the receiving end,
each transmission character is decoded into the original 8 bits
of data. In addition to the transmission characters, which may
be decoded into the 256 possible 8-bit combinations, there are
additional transmission characters, referred to as *special characters*,
which are used for purposes which require them to be distinct
from frame contents. Groups of special characters, called *ordered
sets*, are used as frame delimiters, primitive signals, and primitive
sequences. Each is defined below.

5.4.6.1   Frame Delimiters

The beginning of a frame is indicated by the initial Start Of Frame
(SOF) delimiter ordered set, and the ending of a frame is indicated
by the End Of Frame (EOF) delimiter ordered set. Fibre Channel
uses distinct SOF and EOF ordered sets to denote service class,
frame function, and possible error conditions. Table 5.21 lists the
different delimiters and their meaning.

5.4.6.2   Primitive Signals

Primitive signals are ordered sets with special meanings. Table 5.22
defines primitive signals and their meanings.

5.4.6.3   Primitive Sequences

Primitive sequences are transmitted to indicate conditions within
a port, or conditions detected by the receiver logic of a port.
Primitive sequences may be transmitted continuously. Table 5.23
defines primitive sequences and their meanings.

5.4.6.4   Running Disparity

Each 8 bits of data and each special character actually have two
possible encodings, referred to as Running Disparity Minus (RD−)
and Running Disparity Plus (RD+). At transmission time, the
transmitter will select one or the other encoding. Which encoding

Table 5.21 Fibre channel delimiters

Delimiter	Meaning
SOF Connect Class 1 (SOFc1)	Indicates start of class 1 dedicated connection – also indicates start of first sequence
SOF Initiate Class 1 (SOFi1)	Start of class 1 sequence other than first
SOF Normal Class 1 (SOFn1)	Start of class 1 frame other than first in sequence
SOF Initiate Class 2 (SOFi2)	Start of class 2 sequence
SOF Normal Class 2 (SOFn2)	Start of class 2 frame other than first in sequence
SOF Initiate Class 3 (SOFi3)	Start of class 3 sequence
SOF Normal Class 3 (SOFn3)	Start of class 3 frame other than first in sequence
SOF Fabric (SOFf)	Start of fabric frame used for intrafabric communication
SOF Circuit Activate Class 4 (SOFc4) - note 1	Activates Class 4 circuit
SOF Initiate Class 4 (SOFi4) - note 1	Start of Class 4 sequence
SOF Normal Class 4 (SOFn4) - note 1	Start of Class 4 frame other than first in sequence
EOF Terminate (EOFt)	Normal end of sequence
EOF Disconnect-Terminate (EOFdt)	Removes dedicated connection through a fabric – identifies last ACK of sequence
EOF Abort (EOFa)	Terminates partial frame due to link malfunction
EOF Normal (EOFn)	Normal end of frame without sequence termination, abort, disconnect, or invalid content indication
EOF Disconnect-Terminate-Invalid (EOFdti)	Invalid frame content – removes class 1 connection
EOF Normal-Invalid (EOFni)	Invalid frame content
EOF Remove Terminate (EOFrt) - note 1	Removes the Class 4 circuit
EOF Remove Terminate Invalid (EOFrti) - note 1	Invalid frame content

Note 1 - Class 4 delimiters added by Fibre Channel Framing and Signaling (FC-FS) Specification, Rev 1.90.

Table 5.22 Primitive signals and their meanings

Primitive signal	Meaning
Idle	Operational port ready for frame transmission/reception; transmitted when no frames are available for transmission
Receiver Ready (R_RDY)	Frame has been received and buffer is ready to accept next frame; does not pass through fabric

Table 5.23 Primitive sequences and their meanings

Primitive sequence	Meaning
Offline (OLS)	Transmitted to indicate that the port is (1) beginning link initialization, (2) receiving NOS, or (3) entering offline state
Not Operational (NOS)	Transmitted to indicate that the port has detected link failure or is offline
Link Reset (LR)	Transmitted to indicate entry of link reset protocol or to recover from link timeout
Link Reset Response (LRR)	Transmitted by port to indicate reception of LR

is chosen is based on the relative number of ones and zeroes in the transmission character. This is done in order to maintain the 'DC balance,' or ratio of ones to zeroes, in the bit stream.

5.4.7   FC0 Functions: Physical Layer

Fibre Channel supports coaxial cable and twisted pair electrical interfaces as well as optical fiber. The following sections define characteristics of the optical fiber interface; refer to the FC-PH specification for details of the supported copper wire interfaces.

5.4.7.1   Loss Budgets for Optical Interfaces

The Fibre Channel optical interface consists of an optical transmitter and receiver at each end of an Fibre Channel link. The Fibre Channel link consists of a pair of optical fibers, one for each direction of transmission. Table 5.24 gives link loss budgets and distance limitations for unrepeated Fibre Channel links at 1300 nm and 780 nm wavelength.

5.4.7.2   Multimode Interface Specifications

Table 5.25 defines output specifications and Table 5.26 defines input specifications for the Fibre Channel multimode optical signal. The parameters in this table are based on the requirement that the bit error rate not exceed 10^{-12}, including operation at the minimum interface power level.

5.4.7.3   Single Mode Interface Specifications

Table 5.27 gives specifications for the single mode output optical interface signal, and Table 5.28 gives specifications for the single mode input optical interface signal. The parameters in these tables are based on the requirement that the bit error rate not exceed 10^{-12}, including operation at the minimum interface power level.

5.4.8   Fibre Channel Summary

Fibre Channel is the dominant protocol used for storage networking today, with a large installed base. Its support of the SAN architecture, multiple service classes, flow control, and ability to

Table 5.24 Link loss budgets and distance limitations for Fibre Channel optical links

Bandwidth@ wavelength	Fiber type and size	Loss budget (dB)	Maximum distance	Notes
1062@780 nm	50 um MMF	6	500 m	Short wave laser; intermediate distance
531@780 nm	50 um MMF	8	1 km	Short wave laser; intermediate distance
266@780 nm	50 um MMF	12	2 km	Short wave laser; intermediate distance
266@1300 nm	62.5 um MMF	6	1.5 km	Long wavelength LED; intermediate distance
133@1300 nm	62.5 um MMF	6	1.5 km	Long wavelength LED; intermediate distance
1062@1300 nm	9 um SMF	14	10 km	Long wave laser; long distance
1062@1300 nm	9 um SMF	6	2 km	Long wave laser; intermediate distance
531@1300 nm	9 um SMF	14	10 km	Long wave laser; long distance
266@1300 nm	9 um SMF	14	10 km	Long wave laser; long distance
266@1300 nm	9 um SMF	6	2 km	Long wave laser; intermediate distance

support multiple operating systems has made it the protocol of choice for medium and large storage networks. The use of high transport rates, world wide names and the ability to extend the protocol over long distances make it well suited for use in distributed storage networks. The T11 Technical Committee has continued to develop Fibre Channel standards to meet evolving network requirements, including the specification of new service classes and 4 and 10 Gb/s interfaces.

Many believe that the primary competition for Fibre Channel will come from IP storage protocols as these technologies mature. However, it is unlikely that iSCSI or iFCP will ever completely

Table 5.25 Fibre Channel Multimode output optical interface signal

Parameter	Units	Short wave laser – intermediate distance			Long wave LED – intermediate distance	
Bit Rate	Mb/s	1062.5	531.25	265.625	265.625	132.812
Tolerance	ppm	+/−100	+/−100	+/−100	+/−100	+/−100
Operating Range	meters	500	1000	2000	1500	1500
Fiber Core Diameter	um	50	50	50	62.5	62.5
Transmitter Type		Laser	Laser	Laser	LED	LED
Spectral Center	nm (min)	770	770	770	1280	1270
Wavelength	nm (max)	850	850	850	1380	1380
Spectral Width	nm RMS (max)	4	4	4	NA	NA
	nm FWHM (max)	NA	NA	NA	(Note 1)	250
Launched Power Max	dBm (avg)	1.3	1.3	0	−14	−14
Launched Power Min	dBm (avg)	−7	−7	−5	−20	−22
Extinction Ratio	dB (min)	6	6	6	9	10
Max. Relative Intensity Noise (RIN_{12})	dB/Hz	−116	−114	−112	NA	NA
Eye Opening at 10^{-12} BER	% (min)	57	61	63	NA	NA
Deterministic Jitter	%(p-p)	20	20	20	16	24
Random Jitter	%(p-p)	NA	NA	NA	9	12
Optical Rise/Fall Time	ns. (max)	NA	NA	NA	2.0/2.2	4.0

Note 1 - See ANSI/INCITS X3.230-1994, Fibre Channel - Physical and Signaling Interface (FC-PH), Figure 26.

replace Fibre Channel as the predominant storage protocol. Rather, it is likely that each protocol will occupy a different market niche on the cost-versus-performance continuum, and will co-exist in many enterprise networks. In fact, IP storage can be seen as a compatible technology for extending Fibre Channel fabrics over the Internet in a cost-effective manner.

Table 5.26 Fibre Channel Multimode input optical interface signal

Parameter	Units	Short wave laser – intermediate distance			Long wave LED – intermediate distance	
Bit Rate	Mb/s	1062.5	531.25	265.625	265.625	132.812
Received Power (min)	dBm (avg)	−13	−15	−17	−26	−28
Received Power (max)	dBm (avg)	+1.3	+1.3	0	−14	−14
Optical Path Power Penalty	dB (max)	2	2	2	2	2
Return Loss of Receiver	dB (min)	12	12	12	NA	NA
Deterministic Jitter	%(p-p)	NA	NA	NA	19	24
Random Jitter	%(p-p)	NA	NA	NA	9	12
Optical Rise/Fall Time	ns. (max)	NA	NA	NA	2.5	4.3

Table 5.27 Fibre Channel Single mode output optical interface signal

Parameter	Units	Long wave laser – long distance			Long wave laser – intermediate distance	
Bit Rate	Mb/s	1062.5	531.25	265.625	1062.5	265.625
Tolerance	ppm.	+/−100	+/−100	+/−100	+/−100	+/−100
Operating Range	km.	10	10	10	2	2
Fiber Core Diameter	um.	9	9	9	9	9
Transmitter Type		Laser	Laser	Laser	Laser	Laser
Spectral Center Wavelength	nm. (min)	1285	1270	1270	1270	1270
	nm. (max)	1330	1355	1355	1355	1355
RMS Spectral Width	nm. (max)	3	3	6	6	30
Launched Power Max	dBm (avg)	−3	−3	−3	−3	−3
Launched Power Min	dBm (avg)	−9	−9	−9	−12	−12
Extinction Ratio	dB (min)	9	9	6	9	6
Max. Relative Intensity Noise (RIN_{12})	dB/Hz	−116	−114	−112	−116	−112
Eye Opening at 10^{-12} BER	% (min)	57	61	63	57	63
Deterministic Jitter	%(p-p)	20	20	20	20	20

Table 5.28 Fibre Channel Single mode input optical interface signal

Parameter	Units	Long wave laser – long distance			Long wave laser – intermediate distance	
Bit Rate	Mb/s	1062.5	531.25	265.625	1062.5	265.625
Received Power (min)	dBm (avg)	−25	−25	−25	−20	−20
Received Power (max)	dBm (avg)	−3	−3	−3	−3	−3
Optical Path Power Penalty	dB (max)	2	2	2	2	2
Return Loss of Receiver	dB (min)	12	12	12	12	12

5.5   GIGABIT ETHERNET (GigE) AND 10 GIGABIT ETHERNET (10 G ETHERNET)

Gigabit Ethernet is a member of the family of networking protocols standardized by the IEEE as part of the 802.3 group of standards. While ordinary Ethernet supports a data rate of 10 Mb/s, and Fast Ethernet runs at 100 Mb/s, Gigabit Ethernet runs at a rate of 1000 Mb/s over fiber optic cable. When operating in point-to-point switched mode, it is capable of transporting data for distances of up to 5 km. 10 gigabit Ethernet (10 G Ethernet) runs at a rate of approximately 10 Gb/s over fiber optical cable, and is capable of transporting data for distances of up to 30 km.

5.5.1   Applications

Gigabit Ethernet is used both to implement high-bandwidth Local Area Networks (LANs), and to provide point-to-point switched data transport. It is used both as a high-bandwidth backbone in existing networks, and to provide campus-wide network connectivity. Network Attached Storage (NAS) architectures typically use Gigabit Ethernet to support LAN-based file access; it is also being used increasingly as a storage protocol. 10G Ethernet is beginning to find application in these areas as well as bandwidth and performance requirements increase.

5.5.2   Standards

Ethernet and the Carrier Sense Multiple Access/Collision Detect (CSMA/CD) protocol are based on research done by Xerox Corporation, Intel Corporation, and Digital Equipment Corporation in the 1970s. The 10 Mb/s Ethernet standard was developed in the early 1980s by the Institute of Electrical and Electronics Engineers (IEEE) and released in 1985 as IEEE802.3.

Work on the Gigabit Ethernet standard began in 1996 with the formation of the IEEE 802.3z Gigabit Ethernet Task Force. The goal of the task force was to develop a standard for Gigabit-rate Ethernet with the following functional characteristics:

- Allow half- and full-duplex operation at a speed of 1000 Mb/s.
- Use the IEEE 802.3 Ethernet frame format.
- Use the CSMA/CD access method.
- Address backward compatibility with 10BASE-T and 100BASE-T technologies.

Work on the IEEE 802.3z standard was completed in 1998. IEEE 802.3z specifies a multimode fiber optic physical interface with a maximum distance of 550 meters, and a single mode fiber optic physical interface with a maximum distance of 5 kilometers. Work is ongoing to increase both the bandwidth and the maximum distance. The 10 Gigabit Ethernet specification, IEEE 802.3ae, was completed in 2002. The IEEE Ethernet in the First Mile (EFM) P802.3ah Task Force is currently developing a specification for Gigabit Ethernet with a maximum distance specification of 10 km.

5.5.3   Network Topology

Gigabit Ethernet supports both a LAN topology using CSMA/CD, and a switched point-to-point topology. Each is described below.

5.5.3.1   LAN Topology

Most Ethernet LANs today use a star or hub configuration, as shown in Figure 5.31. Each node is connected to a central hub or switch by means of twisted pair wiring or optical fibre.

Ethernet operation in a LAN environment uses the CSMA/CD protocol. CSMA/CD enables multiple stations to share a common transport medium without requiring a central arbitration function to determine which station is allowed to send at any time. *Carrier Sense* refers to the ability of each station to listen to the medium to determine if anyone else is sending, or if the medium is silent. *Multiple Access* means that multiple stations may attempt to transmit, if the medium is silent. *Collision Detect* means that if two stations begin transmitting simultaneously, they will interfere or collide with each other. Each station must be able to detect collisions and stop transmission if they occur. Each station will then wait an algorithmically-determined back-off time before trying to transmit again.

CSMA/CD operation allows half-duplex mode operation, in which a given station may receive or transmit at any time, but not both at the same time. Figure 5.32 shows operation of the CSMA/CD protocol for Ethernet.

5.5.3.2   Point-to-Point switched Topology

Full-duplex operation is an optional capability that allows simultaneous bidirectional communication over point-to-point links. Full duplex configurations are typically used for high-bandwidth

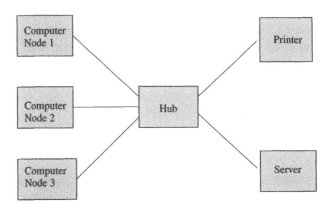

Figure 5.31   Conventional Ethernet LAN topology.

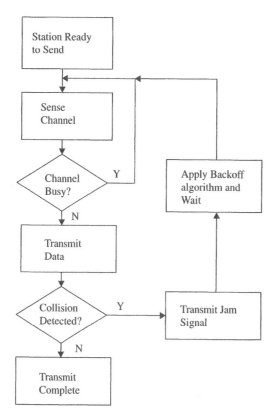

Figure 5.32   CSMA/CD protocol.

switch-to-switch links between networks. 10G Ethernet supports full-duplex operation only; it does not support half-duplex using CSMA/CD. Figure 5.33 shows a typical network configuration in which a point-to-point Gigabit Ethernet link is used to provide a high-bandwidth path for switched LAN-to-LAN traffic.

In full-duplex operation, each transmitter simply begins sending frames as soon as they are available. A 96-bit interframe gap (IFG) is placed between each frame. No carrier sense or collision detection is employed, and no frame extensions are required.

A flow control mechanism is employed to prevent receiver buffer overloading during congestion. If a receiving node becomes congested, it sends a *pause frame* to the transmitter to tell it to stop sending for a specified period of time. If the congestion is removed before the time period has elapsed, the receiver may send a second pause frame with a wait time of zero to enable the transmitter to begin sending again.

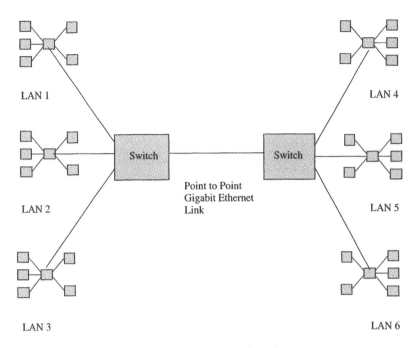

Figure 5.33 Point-to-point Gigabit Ethernet topology.

5.5.4   Protocol Architecture

The Gigabit Ethernet standards define the data link and physical layers only (layers 1 and 2 of the OSI model), and therefore do not address higher-level issues such as transport, routing, and Quality of Service (QoS). Figure 5.34 shows the relationship of the Ethernet standards to the common application and transport layers it typically supports. Normally, the TCP protocol is used to supply the layer 4 transport function, and IP is used to support the layer 3 networking function. NAS applications such as NFS and CIFS, and storage protocols such as iSCSI, often use TCP/IP on top of Ethernet. While a complete description of TCP/IP is beyond the scope of this book, a brief overview is given below.

5.5.4.1   TCP/IP

The Transmission Control Protocol, or TCP, is one of the fundamental protocols of the Internet and was defined by the Internet Engineering Task Force (IETF) in Request For Comments (RFC) 793 in 1981. TCP is a connection-oriented transport protocol designed

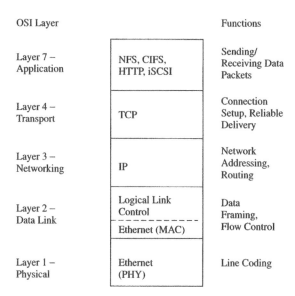

OSI Layer		Functions
Layer 7 – Application	NFS, CIFS, HTTP, iSCSI	Sending/ Receiving Data Packets
Layer 4 – Transport	TCP	Connection Setup, Reliable Delivery
Layer 3 – Networking	IP	Network Addressing, Routing
Layer 2 – Data Link	Logical Link Control - - - - - - - - - - Ethernet (MAC)	Data Framing, Flow Control
Layer 1 – Physical	Ethernet (PHY)	Line Coding

Figure 5.34   Relationship of Ethernet standards to OSI protocol stack.

to provide reliable communications between processors across a variety of reliable and unreliable networks. Figure 5.35 shows the state diagram for TCP connection establishment.

State definitions are as follows:

- *Listen* represents waiting for a connection request from any remote TCP and port.
- *SYN Sent* represents waiting for a matching connection request after having sent a connection request.
- *SYN Received* represents waiting for a confirming connection request acknowledgment after having both received and sent a connection request.
- *Established* represents an open connection, data received can be delivered to the user. The normal state for the data transfer phase of the connection.
- *FIN Wait* represents waiting for a connection termination request from the remote TCP, or an acknowledgment of the connection termination request previously sent.
- *FIN Wait2* represents waiting for a connection termination request from the remote TCP.
- *Close Wait* represents waiting for a connection termination request from the local user.

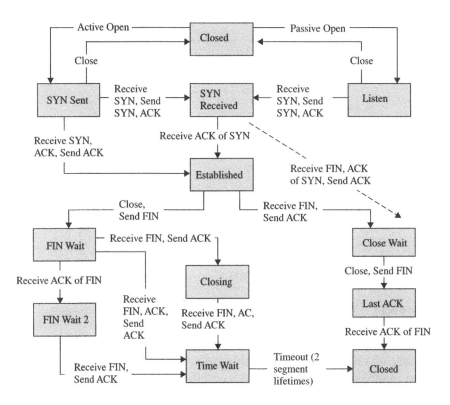

Figure 5.35 TCP connection state diagram.

- *Closing* represents waiting for a connection termination request acknowledgment from the remote TCP.
- *Last ACK* represents waiting for an acknowledgment of the connection termination request previously sent to the remote TCP (which includes an acknowledgment of its connection termination request).
- *Time Wait* represents waiting for enough time to pass to be sure the remote TCP received the acknowledgment of its connection termination request.
- *Closed* represents no connection state at all.

TCP uses a three-way handshake to establish a connection. Figure 5.36 shows simple state and message sequences for normal connection establishment and closing. In this figure, TCP A initiates connection setup by sending a SYN message to TCP B, and entering the *SYN Sent* state. TCP B responds by acknowledging TCP A's

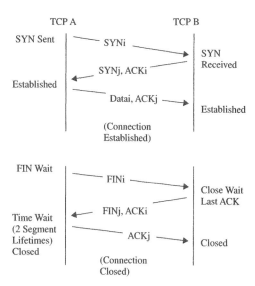

Figure 5.36   TCP connection establishment sequence.

SYN, sending its own SYN to TCP A, and entering the *SYN Received* state. When TCP A receives the SYN and acknowledgment from B, it enters the *Established* state, sends an ACK for TCP B's SYN, and begins transmitting numbered data segments. Upon receipt of the ACK from TCP A, TCP B also enters the *Established* state and begins receiving data segments.

To close the connection upon receipt of a CLOSE message from the user, TCP A sends a FIN message, indicating no more data to transmit, to TCP B and enters the FIN Wait state. After this point, TCP A will accept no more SENDs from its user. TCP B acknowledges TCP A's FIN, and enters the Close Wait state. After TCP B receives a CLOSE from its user, it sends its own FIN to TCP A, and enters the Last ACK state. When TCP A receives TCP B's FIN, it returns an ACK to TCP B and enters the Time Wait state. When TCP B receives the ACK, it enters the Closed state. TCP A waits for two segment lifetimes after sending the ACK, and enters the Closed state, closing the connection.

TCP uses window-based flow control. The receiving TCP notifies the sending TCP of the number of bytes it is prepared to receive, starting with the acknowledgement number.

5.5.4.2   IP

The Internet Protocol (IP) is the most commonly used internet-working protocol in the world today. IP normally comprises the networking layer of the TCP/IP protocol suite. It interfaces with the TCP transport layer by means of two service primitives: *Send*, which is used by the transport layer to request delivery of a data unit; and *Deliver*, which is used to notify the transport layer of the arrival of a data unit.

The IP datagram format for the 32-bit address version of IP, referred to as IP Version 4 (IPv4) is shown in Figure 5.37. (The bit values shown indicate the start of each field, except for bit 31, which is the last bit in each word.) The individual fields are defined below:

- *Version* – a 4-bit field which indicates the protocol version number.
- *Internet Header Length* – a 4-bit field indicating the length of the header in 32-bit words; minimum length = 5.
- *Type of Service* – an 8-bit field specifying reliability, precedence, delay, and throughput parameters.
- *Total Length* – 16-bit field indicating total length of datagram.
- *Identifier* – 16-bit field sequence number used to identify datagram.
- *Flags* – 3-bit field; *More* bit is used for segmentation/reassembly; *Don't Fragment* bit prohibits fragmentation when set. Third bit currently unused.

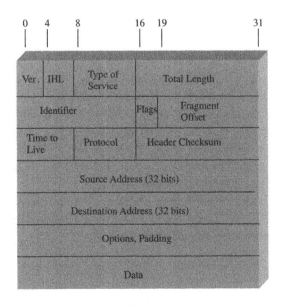

Figure 5.37 IP datagram format (IPv4).

- *Fragment Offset* – 13-bit field indicating where this fragment belongs in the original datagram this fragment is part of. Measured in 64-bit units.

- *Time to Live* – an 8-bit field specifying datagram lifetime, measured in router hops.

- *Protocol* – an 8-bit field specifying the next higher level protocol to receive the data at the destination.

- *Header Checksum* – a 16-bit error-detecting code applied to the header only. Because some header fields change during transit, this must be recomputed at each router.

- *Source Address* – 32-bit address (ipv4) specifying source network and end system.

- *Destination Address* – 32-bit address (ipv4) specifying destination network and end system.

- *Options* – variable-length field encoding options specified by user.

- *Padding* – variable-length field used to ensure that header length is a multiple of 32 bits.

- *Data* – variable length field containing user data. Length must be an integer multiple of 8 bits and less than 65,535 octets.

IP datagrams are routed through a network on an individual basis, using destination address. Networks use interior routing protocols, such as Open Shortest Path First (OSPF) to route datagrams among end systems. For exchange of network-to-network traffic, exterior routing protocols, such as Border Gateway Protocol (BGP) are used to exchange routing information among networks.

Originally, IP supported only one class of service, referred to as *best effort*. In this class of service, the network will attempt to deliver each packet to its destination, but no guarantees about performance are made, and no resources are dedicated for delivery of the packet. Services which demand higher levels of service, such as realtime voice, video, and storage data, have created requirements for guaranteed quality of service. The Integrated Services Architecture (IntServ) was developed by the IETF in 1994 and standardized as RFC1633. It defines a *flow* as a stream of packets with a common source address, destination address, and port number, and creates a requirement to maintain a state for each flow in the network. IntServ uses *admission control* to check to see if the processor or router is able to support each service request, a *packet classifier* to determine which class each packet belongs to, and a *packet scheduler* to schedule each packet for transmission on the outbound link. IntServ provides two classes of service in addition to best effort: *guaranteed service*, which supports real-time traffic with bounds on delay and is defined in RFC2212; and *controlled load*, which provides an approximation of best-effort service over an uncongested network, and is defined in RFC2211.

IntServ uses a reservation protocol called the *Resource Reservation Protocol*, or RSVP, to create a path and reserve resources for a flow. RSVP is defined by RFC2205. The data source sends a Path message to the destination. The Path message is used to mark a route and to collect information about the QOS characteristics of each router along the route. When the destination receives the Path message, it returns a RSVP reservation (RESV) message to the source. If sufficient resources are available through the entire path, those resources are reserved specifically for that flow.

One limitation of RSVP is that it is not scaleable. State must be maintained for each flow in the network, and each flow state must be periodically updated as conditions change. Another approach to QOS is provided by *Differentiated Services (DiffServ)*, defined in RFC 2474. Instead of maintaining a separate state for each flow, DiffServ classifies service requests at the edge of the network and aggregates individual flows into a few service classes for transport through the network. Packets with similar QoS requirements are aggregated into *Behavior Aggregates* (BA), and each BA receives a specified *Per-Hop-Behavior* (PHB) as it moves from router to router, specified in terms of queuing and delay. The IETF Working Group has defined two broad service categories: *Expedited Forwarding* (EF), RFC2598, and *Assured Forwarding* (AF), RFC2597. EF supports low packet loss, low delay, and low jitter. AF is divided into four relative classes of service, each subdivided into three levels of packet drop precedence. When congestion is encountered, packets with lower drop precedence are dropped before packets with higher drop precedence.

While IP has proven itself as a vital component of the Internet, it has significant limitations which are becoming more apparent as the global use of the Internet increases. One of these is address space. The 32-bit addresses defined by ipv4 provide only 4 billion distinct addresses, which is less than the total population of the earth. Address availability is further limited by the inefficiencies imposed by a two-level addressing scheme in which each address is broken down into variable-length host and network addresses. In response to this, the IETF has developed a next-generation addressing scheme, known as *IPv6*. IPv6 provides a 128-bit address, and incorporates some additional functionality, such as integrated multicasting and IPsec security. Initial adoption of IPv6 has been slow, due to the large installed base of IPv4 networks, but is expected to gain momentum as global demand for Internet connectivity increases.

The IPv6 header uses a simplified 40-byte fixed-length header defined in RFC2460, consisting of a 16-byte source address, a 16-byte destination address, and an 8-byte field for general header information. Options may be specified using extension headers, which are located after the fixed-length header. Five fields which were part of the IPv4 header have been removed: Header Length; Identification; Flags; Fragment Offset; and Header Checksum. Three fields have been renamed and modified: Traffic Class (formerly Type of Service); Next Header (formerly Protocol Type); and Hop Limit (formerly Time to Live). A new field, Flow Label, has been added. Figure 5.38 shows the fields of the IPv6 header. (Bit values, except for bit 31, indicate starting bit of each field.)

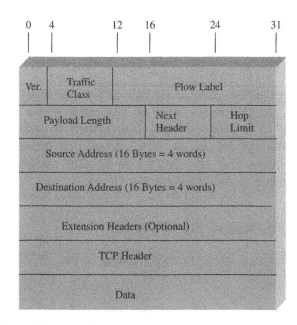

Figure 5.38   Ipv6 header format.

The IPv6 header may be followed by zero or more extension headers. The presence of an extension header is indicated by the value in the Next Header field of the standard IPv6 header. If there is no extension header, this field will indicate a TCP header as the next header. If there is an extension header, it will be identified by the value in the Next Header field, and its Next Header field will specify either the TCP header, if it is the only extension header, or the type of the next extension header. Currently specified extension headers include a hop-by-hop options header, a routing header, a fragment header, a destination options header, an authentication header, and an encrypted security payload header. The first four are defined in RFC2460; the authentication header is defined in RFC2402 and the encrypted security payload header is defined in RFC2406.

5.5.5   Ethernet Data Framing

The data link layer specified in the OSI standards is implemented as two sublayers in the IEEE 802 specifications: a Media Access Control (MAC) client layer and a MAC layer. If the node implementing the Ethernet layer is an end station or Data Terminal Equipment (DTE), then the MAC client level is a Logical Link Control (LLC) layer as defined by IEEE 802.2. If the node implementing the Ethernet layer is an intermediate station or Data Communications Equipment (DCE), then the MAC client layer is a bridge entity as defined by IEEE 802.1.

As the application data is passed down the protocol stack, a TCP header, an IP header, and an LLC header are added. This becomes the LLC protocol data unit which is encapsulated in the basic Ethernet frame, or MAC frame, as described below. Figure 5.39 shows the different levels of data encapsulation and their relationship to the MAC frame.

5.5.5.1   Basic Ethernet Frame Format

The basic Ethernet frame format defined in IEEE802.3 consists of seven fields:

- *Preamble (PRE)* – consists of 7 bytes. An alternating pattern of 1s and 0s that tells receiving stations that a frame is coming. It

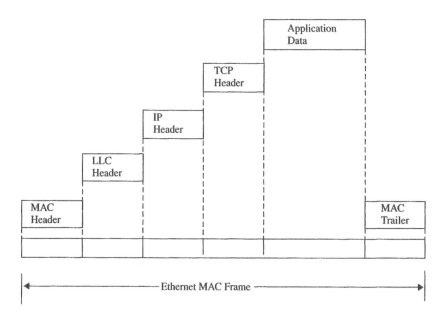

Figure 5.39   MAC frame data encapsulation and protocol layers.

also enables synchronization of the incoming bit stream with the receiving physical layer.

- *Start Of Frame delimiter (SOF)* – consists of 1 byte. The SOF is an alternating pattern of 1s and 0s, ending with 2 consecutive 1 bits, indicating that the next bit is the leftmost bit in the leftmost byte of the destination address.

- *Destination Address (DA)* – consists of 6 bytes. Indicates which station(s) should receive the frame. The leftmost bit in the DA field indicates whether the DA is an individual address (0) or a group address (1). The second bit from the left indicates whether the DA is globally administered (0) or locally administered (1). The remaining 46 bits are a uniquely assigned value that identifies a single station, a defined group of stations, or all stations on the network.

- *Source Address (SA)* – consists of 6 bytes. The SA field identifies the sending station. The SA is always an individual address and the left-most bit in the SA field is always 0.

- *Length/Type* – consists of 4 bytes. This field indicates either the number of MAC client data bytes that are contained in the data field of the frame, or the frame type ID if the frame is assembled using an optional format. If the Length/Type field value is less than or equal to 1500, the number of LLC bytes in the data field is equal to the Length/Type field value. If the Length/Type field value is greater than 1536, the frame is an optional frame, and the Length/Type field value identifies the type of frame being sent or received.

- *Data* – a sequence of n bytes of any value, where n is less than or equal to 1500. If the length of the data field is less than 46, the data field must be extended by adding a filler sufficient to bring the data field length to 46 bytes.
- *Frame Check Sequence (FCS)* – consists of 4 bytes. This sequence contains a 32-bit cyclic redundancy check (CRC) value, which is created by the sending MAC and is recalculated by the receiving MAC to check for damaged frames. The FCS is generated over the DA, SA, Length/Type, and Data fields.

For proper operation of the CSMA/CD protocol at gigabit speeds, the minimum size of the frame must be expanded for Gigabit Ethernet by adding an extender field if the basic frame is less than 416 bytes for 1000BaseX or 520 bytes for 1000BaseT. Note that the FCS does not include the extender field. (The extender field is not required for full-duplex Gigabit Ethernet operation.) Figure 5.40 shows the format of an Ethernet Frame.

Individual addresses are referred to as *unicast* addresses. They refer to a single MAC and are assigned by the NIC manufacturer from a block assigned by the IEEE. Group addresses, or *multicast* addresses, identify the end stations in a work group and are assigned by the network manager. A special group address of all 1s is referred to as the *broadcast* address and indicates all stations on the network.

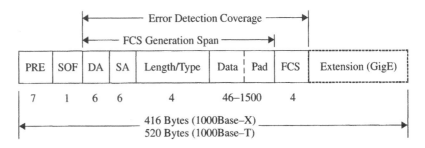

Figure 5.40 Ethernet frame format. PRE: Preamble; SOF: Start of Frame; DA: Destination Address; SA: Source Address; FCS: Frame Check Sequence.

5.5.5.2 Virtual LANs and Quality of Service

A virtual LAN (VLAN) is a logical subset of a LAN that is based on geographical location, user type, work group, or similar criteria. VLANs are defined in IEEE 802.1q. Each VLAN consists of a broadcast domain for its users; a broadcast on a specific VLAN will only propagate to the users on that VLAN. From a NAS perspective, VLANs may be used in a manner similar to zones in Fibre Channel. Groups of users with similar access requirements can be given access to specific files, and work groups can be extended across geographical areas. VLANs can be used for security purposes as well.

IEEE 802.1D provides Quality of Service (QoS) for Ethernet packets by enabling user priority values to be encoded in packets that represent different traffic classes. The user priority value is located in the frame header using the extended frame format defined in IEEE 802.1q. RSVP sessions can be mapped to the user priority values specified in IEEE 802.1D.

5.5.6 Physical Layer – Gigabit Ethernet

Gigabit Ethernet uses 8B/10B line coding, in which each 8 bits of data to be transmitted is encoded into a 10-bit transmission character, which is sent serially over the fiber link. At the receiving end, each transmission character is decoded into the original 8 bits of data. In addition to the transmission characters, which may be decoded into the 256 possible 8-bit combinations, there are additional transmission characters, referred to as *special characters*, which are used for purposes which require them to be distinct from frame contents. Groups of special characters, called *ordered sets*, are used as frame delimiters, primitive signals, and primitive sequences.

Several different physical interfaces are supported. A short-wave interface, 1000BASE-SX, is targeted at low-cost horizontal and shorter backbone applications using MMF. A long-wave interface, 1000BASE-LX, is intended for longer building backbones using MMF and campus backbones using SMF. A copper-based interface, 1000BASE-CX, may be used for equipment interconnect.

5.5.6.1 Loss Budgets for Gigabit Ethernet Interfaces

Table 5.29 gives link loss budgets for Gigabit Ethernet physical interfaces.

Table 5.29 Link loss budgets and distance limitations for Gigabit Ethernet optical links

Bandwidth@ wavelength	Fiber type and size	Loss budget (dB)	Maximum distance	Modal bandwidth (MMF)
1000@850 nm 1000Base-SX[1]	50 um MMF	3.6	500 m	400 MHz-km; using mode conditioning patch cable
1000@850 nm 1000Base-SX[1]	50 um MMF	3.6	550 m	500 MHz-km; using mode conditioning patch cable
1000@1310 nm 1000Base-LX[1]	50 um MMF	2.4	550 m	400 MHz-km; using mode conditioning patch cable
1000@1310 nm 1000Base-LX[1]	50 um MMF	2.4	550 m	500 MHz-km; using mode conditioning patch cable
1000@850 nm 1000Base-SX	62.5 um MMF	2.6	275 m	200 MHz-km
1000@1310 nm 1000Base-LX[1]	62.5 um MMF	2.4	550 m	500 MHz-km; using mode conditioning patch cable
1062@1310 nm 1000Base-LX[1]	9–10 um SMF	4.6	5 km	

1. Actual transmitted bitrate is 1.25 Gb/s due to 8B/10B encoding

5.5.6.2   Gigabit Ethernet Optical Interface Specifications

Tables 5.30 through 5.33 give optical interface specifications for 1000BASE-SX and 1000BASE-LX interfaces. Table 5.31 lists specifications for the multimode input optical interface signal. Table 5.32 gives specifications for the 1000BASE-LX MMF/SMF output optical interface signal. Table 5.33 lists specifications for the single mode input optical interface signal.

5.5.7   Physical Layer – 10 G Ethernet

IEEE 802.3ae defines two separate physical interfaces for 10 gigabit Ethernet. The 10GBASE-R interface uses 64B/66B block coding to support 850 nm short range (10GBASE-SR), 1310 nm long range (10GBASE-LR), and 1550 nm extra long range (10GBASE-ER) links. Alternatively, the WAN Interface Sublayer (WIS) may be used to encapsulate 10GBASE-R data into frames that are compatible with the 10 G SONET STS-192c and SDH VC-4-64c standards (see Section 7.2 for details). The WIS supports 850 nm short range

Table 5.30   1000BASE-SX (MMF) output optical interface signal

Parameter	62.5/50 um MMF	Unit
Transmitter Type	Shortwave laser	
Signaling Speed	1.25 +/− 100 ppm	Gb/s
Wavelength	770 to 860	nm
RMS Spectral Width (max)	0.85	nm
Rise Time (T_r) 20–80%	0.26	ns
Fall Time (T_f) 80–20%	0.21	ns
Average Launch Power (max)	(note 1)	dBm
Average Launch Power (min)	−9.5	dBm
Average Launch Power of OFF transmitter (max)[2]	−30	dBm
Extinction Ratio (min)	9	dB
RIN (max)	−117	dB/Hz
Coupled Power Ratio (min)[3]	9	dB
Total Jitter at TP3[4,5]	0.510/408	UI/ps
Deterministic Jitter at TP3[4,5]	0.250/200	UI/ps

1. Average launch power is the lesser of the class 1 safety limit defined by IEC 60825-1 or the average receive power (max) defined in Table 5.31.
2. Examples of an OFF transmitter are: no power supplied to the PMD, laser shutdown for safety condition, activation of a transmit disable, or other optional laser shutdown conditions.
3. CPR is defined in 802.3-2002, Part 3, Section 38.6.10. Radial overfilled launches as defined in IEC 60793-1-4 [B24], while they meet CPR ranges, should be avoided.
4. Test Point 3 (TP3) is defined in 802.3-2002, Part 3, Section 38.2.1, Figure 38.1.
5. Total jitter is composed of both deterministic and random components. The allowed random jitter equals the total jitter minus the deterministic jitter at that point.

Table 5.31   1000BASE-SX (MMF) input optical interface signal

Parameter	62.5 um	50 um	Unit
Signaling Speed	1.25 +/− 100 ppm		Gb/s
Wavelength	770 to 860		nm
Average Receive Power (max)	0		dBm
Receive Sensitivity	−17		dBm
Return Loss (min)	12		dB
Stressed Receive Sensitivity[1,2]	−12.5	−13.5	dBm
Vertical Eye Closure Penalty[3]	2.60	2.20	dB
Receive Electrical 3 dB Upper Cutoff Frequency (max)	1500		MHz

1. Measured with conformance test signal at TP3 as defined in 802.3-2002, Part 3, Section 38.6.11, for BER = 10^{-12} at the eye center.
2. Measured with a transmit signal having a 9 dB extinction ratio. If another extinction ratio is used, the stressed receive sensitivity should be corrected for the extinction ratio penalty.
3. Vertical eye-closure penalty is a test condition for measuring stressed receive sensitivity. It is not a required characteristic of the receiver.

Table 5.32   1000BASE-LX (single mode) output optical interface signal

Parameter	62.5 um MMF	50 um MMF	9–10 um SMF	Unit
Transmitter Type		Longwave Laser		
Signaling Speed (range)		1.25 +/− 100 ppm		Gb/s
Wavelength (range)		1270–1355		nm.
T_{rise}/T_{fall} (max, 20–80% response time)		0.26		ns
RMS Spectral Width (max)		4		nm
Average Launch Power (max)		−3		dBm
Average Launch Power (min)	−11.5	−11.5	−11.0	dBm
Average Launch Power of OFF Transmitter (max)		−30		dBm
Extinction Ratio (min)		9		dB
Relative Intensity Noise (max)		−120		dB/Hz
Coupled Power Ratio (CPR)[1]	28<CPR<40	12<CPR<20	N/A	dB
Total Jitter at TP3[2,3]		0.510/408		UI/ps
Deterministic Jitter at TP3[2,3]		0.250/200		UI/ps

1. CPR is defined in 802.3-2002, Part 3, Section 38.6.10. Due to the dual media (MMF/SMF) support of the LX transmitter, fulfillment of this specification requires a single-mode fiber offset launch mode conditioning patch cord as described in 802.3-2002, Part 3, Section 38.11.4, for MMF operation.
2. Test Point 3 (TP3) is defined in 802.3-2002, Part 3, Section 38.2.1, Figure 38.1.
3. Total jitter is composed of both deterministic and random components. The allowed random jitter equals the total jitter minus the deterministic jitter at that point.

(10GBASE-SW), 1310 nm long range (10GBASE-LW), and 1550 nm extended range (10GBASE-EW) links. The frames also contain path, line, and section overheads similar to those defined in Section 7.2 for SONET. However, the electrical and optical characteristics of the WIS differ from the SONET specifications.

The 10 G Ethernet physical coding sublayer uses 64B/66B line coding, in which each 8 octets of data to be transmitted are encoded into a 66-bit block of data, which is sent serially over the fiber link. At the receiving end, each block is decoded into the original 8 octets

Table 5.33   1000BASE-LX (single mode) input optical interface signal

Parameter	Value	Unit
Signaling Speed (range)	1.25 +/− 100 ppm	Gb/s
Wavelength (range)	1270 to 1355	nm
Average Receiver Power (max)	−3	dBm
Receiver Sensitivity	−19	dBm
Return Loss (min)	12	dB
Stressed Receive Sensitivity[1,2]	−14.4	dBm
Vertical Eye-close Penalty[3]	2.60	dB
Receive Electrical 3 dB Upper Cutoff Frequency (max)	1500	MHz

1. Measured with conformance test signal at TP3 as defined in 802.3-2002, Part 3, Section 38.6.11, for BER $= 10^{-12}$ at the eye center.
2. Measured with a transmit signal having a 9 dB extinction ratio. If another extinction ratio is used, the stressed receive sensitivity should be corrected for the extinction ratio penalty.
3. Vertical eye-closure penalty is a test condition for measuring stressed receive sensitivity. It is not a required characteristic of the receiver.

of data. In addition to the transmission characters, which may be decoded into the original octets, there are additional transmission characters, referred to as *control characters*, which are used for purposes which require them to be distinct from frame contents. Groups of control characters and data characters, called *ordered sets*, are used as frame delimiters, primitive signals, and primitive sequences. One control character, the idle character, is also used for rate adaptation between the 10GBASE-R rate of 10.3125 Gb/s and the STS-192c/VC-4-64c rate of 9.95328 Gb/s. (Note that it is also necessary for the WIS to reverse the byte order, since Ethernet sends the least significant bit first, while SONET/SDH sends the most significant bit first.)

5.5.7.1   Loss Budgets for 10 G Ethernet Interfaces

Table 5.34 gives link loss budgets for 10 G Ethernet physical interfaces.

5.5.7.2   10 G Ethernet Optical Interface Specifications

Tables 5.35 through 5.40 give optical interface specifications for 10 G Ethernet interfaces. Table 5.36 lists specifications for the multimode input optical interface signal. Table 5.37 gives specifications for the 10GBASE-LR and 10GBASE-LW SMF output optical interface

Table 5.34 Link loss budgets and distance limitations for 10 G Ethernet optical links

Bandwidth@ wavelength	Fiber type and size	Loss budget (dB)	Maximum distance	Modal bandwidth (MMF)
10G@850 nm	50 um MMF	7.3	66 m	400 MHz-km
10G@850 nm	50 um MMF	7.3	82 m	500 MHz-km
10G@850 nm	50 um MMF	7.3	300 m	2000 MHz-km
10G@850 nm	62.5 um MMF	7.3	26 m	160 MHz-km.
10G@850 nm	62.5 um MMF	7.3	33 m	200 MHz-km
10G@1310 nm	9–10 um SMF	9.4	10 km	
10G@1550 nm	9–10 um SMF	15.0	30 km (40 km)[1]	

1. Links > 30 km. for the same power budget are considered to be engineered links.

Table 5.35 10GBASE-SR/SW (MMF) output optical interface signal

Parameter	10GBASE-SR	10GBASE-SW	Unit
Signaling Speed	10.3125	9.95328	Gb/s
Signaling Speed Variation	+/−100	+/−20	ppm
Center Wavelength Range	840 to 860		nm.
RMS Spectral Width[1]	2		
Average Launch Power (max)	3		dBm
Average Launch Power (min)[4]	−7.3		dBm
Average Launch Power of OFF transmitter (max)[5]	−30		dBm
Extinction Ratio (min)	3		dB
RIN$_{12}$ OMA (max)	−128		dB/Hz
Optical Return Loss Tolerance (min)	12		dB
Transmitter Eye Mask	6		
Total Jitter	7		
Deterministic Jitter	7		

1. Average Spectral Width is the standard deviation of the spectrum.
2. Trade-offs are possible among spectral width, center wavelength, and optical modulation amplitude (OMA). See IEEE802.3ae, Section 52, for details.
3. 10GBASE-S average launch power shall be the lesser of the class 1 safety limit specified in IEEE802.3ae, 52.10.2, or the average receive power (max) specified in Table 5-36.
4. Average launch power (min) is informative and does not ensure compliance.
5. Examples of an OFF transmitter are: no power supplied to the PMD, laser shutdown for safety condition, activation of a transmit disable, or other optional laser shutdown conditions.
6. See IEEE802.3ae, Figure 52.8.
7. Acceptable transmitted jitter is achieved by compliance with IEEE802.3ae, 52.9.7, Transmitter Optical Waveform, and 52.9.10, Transmitter and Dispersion Penalty.

signal. Table 5.38 lists specifications for the 10GBASE-LR and 10GBASE-LW single mode input optical interface signal. Table 5.39 gives specifications for the 10GBASE-ER and 10GBASE-EW SMF output optical interface signal. Table 5.40 lists specifications for

Table 5.36   10GBASE-SR/SW (MMF) input optical interface signal

Parameter	10GBASE-SR	10GBASE-SW	Unit
Signaling Speed	10.3125	9.95328	Gb/s
Signaling Speed Variation from Nominal (max)	100		ppm
Center Wavelength (range)	840 to 860		nm
Average Receive Power (max)[1]	−1.0		dBm
Average Receive Power (min)[2]	−9.9		dBm
Receiver Sensitivity (max) in OMA[3]	0.077 (−11.1)		mW(dBm)
Receiver Reflectance (max)	−12		dB
Stressed Receiver Sensitivity in OMA[4,5]	0.18 (−7.5)		mW(dBm)
Vertical Eye Closure Penalty[6]	3.5		dB
Stressed Eye Jitter (min)[7]	0.3		UI pk to pk
Receive Electrical 3 dB Upper Cutoff Frequency (max)	12.3		GHz

1. The receiver shall be able to tolerate continuous exposure to an optical input signal having a power level equal to the Average Receive Power (max) plus 1 dB without damage.
2. Average receive power (min) is informative and does not ensure compliance.
3. Receiver sensitivity is informative.
4. Measured with conformance test signal at TP3 as defined in 802.3ae, 52.9.9.2, for BER = 10^{-12}.
5. The stressed sensitivity values in the table are for system level BER measurement which include the effects of Clock and Data Recovery (CDR) circuits. It is recommended that at least 0.4 dB additional margin be allocated if component level measurements are made without the effect of CDR circuits.
6. Vertical eye-closure penalty is a test condition for measuring stressed receive sensitivity. It is not a required characteristic of the receiver.
7. Stressed eye jitter is a test condition for measuring stressed receiver sensitivity. It is not a required characteristic of the receiver.

the 10GBASE-ER and 10GBASE-EW single mode input optical interface signal.

5.5.8   Gigabit Ethernet Summary

Ethernet continues to be the commonest and most cost-effective networking technology being deployed. According to an industry survey, 87% of all installed network connections used Ethernet in 2000. Use of Gigabit Ethernet continues to grow as network applications demand more and more bandwidth, and the price of GigE hardware continues to fall; it is expected that over 50% of all installed Ethernet will be Gigabit Ethernet in 2003. GigE is seeing increasing use as a point-to-point transport media, especially in the MAN,

Table 5.37 10GBASE-LR/LW (single mode) output optical interface signal

Parameter	10GBASE-LR	10GBASE-LW	Unit
Signaling Speed	10.3125	9.95328	Gb/s
Signaling Speed Variation	+/− 100	+/− 20	ppm
Center Wavelength Range	1260 to 1355		nm.
Side Mode Suppression Ratio (min)	30		dB
Average Launch Power (max)	0.5		dBm
Average Launch Power (min)[1]	−8.2		dBm
Launch power (min) in OMA minus Transmitter and Dispersion Penalty (TDP)	−6.2		dBm
Optical Modulation Amplitude (min)[2]	−5.2		dBm
Transmitter and Dispersion Penalty (max)	3.2		dB
Average Launch Power of OFF transmitter (max)[3]	−30		dBm
Extinction Ratio (min)	3.5		dB
RIN_{12} OMA (max)	−128		dB/Hz
Optical Return Loss Tolerance (min)	12		dB
Transmitter Reflectance (max)[4]	−12		dB
Transmitter Eye Mask	[5]		
Total Jitter	[6]		
Deterministic Jitter	[6]		

1. Average launch power (min) is informative and does not ensure compliance.
2. Even if TDP < 1 dB, OMA (min) must exceed this value.
3. Examples of an OFF transmitter are: no power supplied to the PMD, laser shutdown for safety condition, activation of a transmit disable, or other optional laser shutdown conditions.
4. Transmitter Reflectance is defined looking into the transmitter.
5. See IEEE802.3ae, Figure 52-8.
6. Acceptable transmitted jitter is achieved by compliance with IEEE802.3ae, 52.9.7, Transmitter Optical Waveform, and 52.9.10, Transmitter and Dispersion Penalty.

and carriers are increasing their marketing of metropolitan Gigabit Ethernet service at both gigabit and 10 G levels. While native-mode Gigabit Ethernet is limited to 5 km distance, it is easily transported over MAN distances using WDM, and the IEEE EFM Task Force is developing a specification for GigE with a range of 10 km. Gigabit Ethernet is widely used for NAS, both as a high-bandwidth LAN technology and for switched point-to-point transport.

One performance limitation associated with Gigabit Ethernet has nothing to do with the GigE protocol itself, but rather with TCP/IP performance. TCP/IP is generally implemented in software in

Table 5.38   10GBASE-LR/LW single mode input optical interface signal

Parameter	10GBASE-LR	10GBASE-LW	Unit
Signaling Speed	10.3125	9.95328	Gb/s
Signaling Speed Variation from Nominal (max)	100		ppm
Center Wavelength (range)	1260 to 1355		nm
Average Receive Power (max)[1]	0.5		dBm
Average Receive Power (min)[2]	−14.4		dBm
Receiver Sensitivity (max) in OMA[3]	0.055 (−12.6)		mW(dBm)
Receiver Reflectance (max)	−12		dB
Stressed Receiver Sensitivity in OMA[4,5]	0.093 (−10.3)		mW(dBm)
Vertical Eye Closure Penalty[6]	2.2		dB
Stressed Eye Jitter (min)[7]	0.3		UI pk to pk
Receive Electrical 3 dB Upper Cutoff Frequency (max)	12.3		GHz

1. The receiver shall be able to tolerate continuous exposure to an optical input signal having a power level equal to the Average Receive Power (max) plus 1 dB without damage.
2. Average receive power (min) is informative and does not ensure compliance.
3. Receiver sensitivity is informative.
4. Measured with conformance test signal at TP3 as defined in 802.3ae, 52.9.9.2, for BER = 10^{-12}.
5. The stressed sensitivity values in the table are for system level BER measurement which include the effects of CDR circuits. It is recommended that at least 0.4 dB additional margin be allocated if component level measurements are made without the effect of CDR circuits.
6. Vertical eye-closure penalty is a test condition for measuring stressed receive sensitivity. It is not a required characteristic of the receiver.
7. Stressed eye jitter is a test condition for measuring stressed receiver sensitivity. It is not a required characteristic of the receiver.

most operating systems, and uses up many processor cycles in buffering and ordering packets. As much as 90% of processor time in NAS applications may be consumed by TCP/IP processing. This processing overhead may be minimized by using a custom processor that does TCP/IP processing in hardware, called an *accelerator adapter* or *TCP/IP Offload Engine* (TOE).

Another TCP/IP-related issue is packet loss under congested conditions. Gigabit Ethernet typically reaches maximum utilization at about 70% of total bandwidth, when packet loss begins to occur. This requires the sender to re-transmit packets, reducing performance and introducing delay. One way to reduce the likelihood of packet loss is to upgrade the network to 10 G Ethernet, which is unlikely to experience enough congestion to cause packet loss.

Table 5.39 10GBASE-ER/EW (single mode) output optical interface signal

Parameter	10GBASE-ER	10GBASE-EW	Unit
Signaling Speed	10.3125	9.95328	Gb/s
Signaling Speed Variation	$+/-100$	$+/-20$	ppm
Center Wavelength Range	1530 to 1565		nm.
Side Mode Suppression Ratio (min)	30		dB
Average Launch Power (max)	4.0		dBm
Average Launch Power (min)[1]	-4.7		dBm
Launch power (min) in OMA minus Transmitter and Dispersion Penalty (TDP)	-2.1		dBm
Optical Modulation Amplitude (min)[2]	-1.7		dBm
Transmitter and Dispersion Penalty (max)	3.0		dB
Average Launch Power of OFF transmitter (max)[3]	-30		dBm
Extinction Ratio (min)	3.0		dB
RIN_{21} OMA (max)[4]	-128		dB/Hz
Optical Return Loss Tolerance (min)	21		dB
Transmitter Eye Mask	[5]		
Total Jitter	[6]		
Deterministic Jitter	[6]		

1. Average launch power (min) is informative and does not ensure compliance.
2. Even if TDP < 0.4 dB, OMA (min) must exceed this value.
3. Examples of an OFF transmitter are: no power supplied to the PMD, laser shutdown for safety condition, activation of a transmit disable, or other optional laser shutdown conditions.
4. RIN measurement is made with a return loss at 21 dB.
5. See IEEE802.3ae, Figure 52-8.
6. Acceptable transmitted jitter is achieved by compliance with IEEE802.3ae, 52.9.7, Transmitter Optical Waveform, and 52.9.10, Transmitter and Dispersion Penalty.

5.6 PROTOCOL SUMMARY

Storage protocols have evolved in response to a variety of user requirements, technological innovations, and improvements in equipment and network technology. By looking at this evolution, it is possible to see some trends that have guided the development of storage protocols. The need for increased bandwidth and greater distance range drove the evolution from parallel copper-based protocols, such as SCSI and bus/tag, to high-speed serial protocols over optical fiber. ESCON/SBCON was the first storage protocol to provide high bandwidth over an extended range; FICON improves upon ESCON by providing higher transport bandwidth and better

Table 5.40   10GBASE-ER/EW single mode input optical interface signal

Parameter	10GBASE-ER	10GBASE-EW	Unit
Signaling Speed	10.3125	9.95328	Gb/s
Signaling Speed Variation from Nominal (max)	100		PPm
Center Wavelength (range)	1530 to 1565		nm
Average Receive Power (max)	−1.0		dBm
Average Receive Power (min)[1]	−15.8		dBm
Maximum Receive Power (Damage threshold)	4.0		dBm
Receiver sensitivity (max) in OMA[2]	0.039 (−14.1)		mW(dBm)
Receiver Reflectance (max)	−26		dB
Stressed Receiver Sensitivity in OMA[3,4]	0.074 (−11.3)		mW(dBm)
Vertical Eye Closure Penalty[5]	2.7		dB
Stressed Eye Jitter (min)[6]	0.3		UI pk to pk
Receive Electrical 3 dB Upper Cutoff Frequency(max)	12.3		GHZ

1. Average receive power (min) is informative and does not ensure compliance.
2. Receiver sensitivity is informative.
3. Measured with conformance test signal at TP3 as defined in 802.3ae, 52.9.9.2, for BER $= 10^{-12}$.
4. The stressed sensitivity values in the table are for system level BER measurement which include the effects of CDR circuits. It is recommended that atleast 0.4 dB additional margin be allocated if component level measurements are made without the effect of CDR circuits.
5. Vertical eye-closure penalty is a test condition for measuring stressed receive sensitivity. It is not a required characteristic of the receiver.
6. Stressed eye jitter is a test condition for measuring stressed receiver sensitivity. It is not a required characteristic of the receiver.

I/O performance over large distances. Fibre Channel adds refinements including flow control, classes of service, and a global naming service. Gigabit Ethernet provides high bandwidth data transport using familiar LAN topology and low-cost hardware.

6

InfiniBand

6.1 APPLICATIONS

InfiniBand™ is a network architecture for connecting multiple host processor nodes, I/O platforms, and I/O devices together to form a system area network. As such, it defines not only a storage network architecture, but also a processor architecture that is based on switched I/O access, rather than the shared-bus I/O typical of many previous CPU architectures.

6.2 STANDARDS

The InfiniBand Architecture (IBA) is defined in two specification volumes which were released by the InfiniBand Trade Association in 2000, and updated in 2002 (Infiniband, 2002). Volume 1 covers network and processor architecture and concepts. Volume 2 covers the storage link physical interfaces.

6.3 NETWORK TOPOLOGY

IBA defines a scaleable architecture that can range from a single processor and a few storage devices to a massively parallel configuration consisting of hundreds of processors and thousands of

Distributed Storage Networks   Thomas C. Jepsen
© 2003 John Wiley & Sons, Ltd   ISBN: 0-470-85020-5

storage units. High bandwidth, low latency, and enhanced reliability are provided by allowing multiple paths through the storage fabric; each node may support multiple concurrent high-bandwidth transfers using multiple ports.

Figure 6.1 shows a single-processor configuration. The processor node consists of one or more CPUs, system memory, and a memory controller. Switched access to I/O devices is provided by a Host Channel Adapter (HCA), which is a separate hardware unit, (Although the HCA is architecturally separate from the processors, it is generally included in the processor physical configuration.) Use of a separate processor for managing storage I/O operations is reminiscent of the channel architecture used by mainframe computers.

Target storage devices have a Target Channel Adapter (TCA), which provides an interface to the InfiniBand fabric. Target devices may be a single storage device, or multiple devices, such as a RAID array. TCAs may provide interworking between InfiniBand and other storage protocols (e.g. SCSI, Fibre Channel, Gigabit Ethernet) to support storage devices using these protocols and interfaces to existing storage networks. Switched storage connectivity is provided by a fabric switch. Multiple fabric switches may be cascaded in large configurations. Routers may optionally be included in the configuration to provide WAN connectivity. InfiniBand storage ports use IPv6-compatible addressing which enables IP-based networking.

Multiple processors may be clustered to provide high-performance parallel processing. Fabric switches may be configured

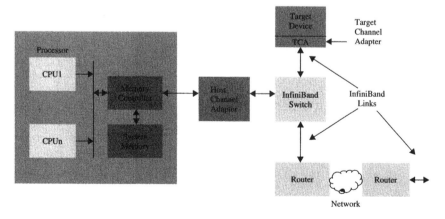

Figure 6.1   InfiniBand architecture – single processor configuration.

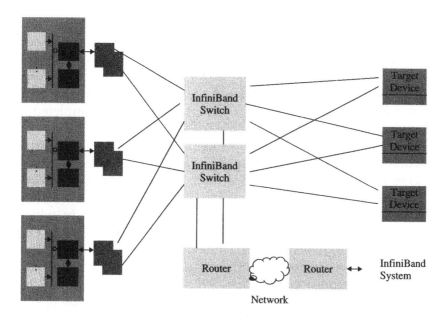

Figure 6.2 Multi-processor InfiniBand configuration.

redundantly to provide additional availability and reliability. Figure 6.2 shows an InfiniBand configuration supporting multiple processors, switches, and I/O devices.

Each channel adapter (HCA or TCA) constitutes a fabric node. Each processor or target device may support multiple channel adapters, and therefore appear to consist of multiple fabric nodes. Each channel adapter supports one or more ports. Each port has multiple pairs of dedicated transmit and receive buffers, so it can transmit and receive data concurrently. Each pair of buffers is managed as a *Virtual Lane* (VL), which has its own flow control characteristics. Each port has multiple VLs associated with it; one VL is reserved for management messages.

IBA provides direct memory access for memory *consumers*, including both I/O controllers and host software processes. Thus, applications requesting data can communicate directly with I/O functions, with no additional data copying required.

IBA enables consumers to queue up a set of instructions for the hardware to process in *work queues*. Work queues are created in pairs; a send work queue and a receive work queue together are called a *Queue Pair* (QP). The send work queue holds instructions that cause data to be transferred between a consumer's memory and another consumer's memory; the receive work queue hold instructions that tell where to place data received from another consumer.

A consumer creates a work request, which causes a Work Queue Element (WQE) to be placed in the appropriate work queue. The channel adapter executes WQEs in the order in which they were placed in the work queue. When WQE execution is completed, a Completion Queue Element (CQE) is placed on a completion queue.

Each consumer has its own work queues; each pair of work queues operates independently of the others. Because some work queues require acknowledgment from the remote node and some WQEs use multiple packets, a given work queue may have several WQEs in progress at the same time. Thus the order in which CQEs are placed in the completion queue is not necessarily related to the order in which WQEs were placed in the work queue. Figure 6.3 shows operation of the work and completion queues for the channel adapter.

Three different operations are defined for a send queue operation. A SEND operation specifies a block of data in the consumer's memory space to be sent to a destination; a receive WQE in the destination's work queue specifies where to put the data in the destination's memory. A Remote Memory Access (RDMA) operation specifies a block of data to be sent to or received from a destination, and also specifies the data location in the destination's memory.

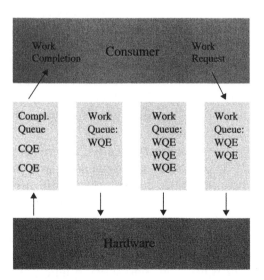

Figure 6.3 InfiniBand work and completion queues.

A Memory Binding operation allows a consumer to specify which portions of its memory it will allow other nodes to access, and to specify read/'write access permissions.

Only one operation is defined for a receive queue operation. A Receive WQE specifies where the hardware is to place data received from another consumer that executed a SEND operation.

6.4   ADDRESSING

IBA supports both datagram and connection-oriented transport. For connection-oriented service, each queue pair is associated with only one remote consumer. The local QP maintains information about the remote consumer's QP consisting of a port identifier and a QP identifier. The port identifier consists of a Local ID (LID) assigned by a *subnet manager*. A subnet manager is an entity attached to a subnet that is responsible for configuring and managing switches, routers, and channel adapters. Ports are also globally identified by a globally unique ID (GUID) assigned by the hardware vendor, similar to an Ethernet MAC address. This information is exchanged during communication establishment. For datagram transport, there is no fixed relationship between the local QP and the destination. Instead, information in the WQE identifies the destination.

Figure 6.4 shows the relationship of the IBA to the OSI protocol model. As shown in the figure, consumers communicate requests

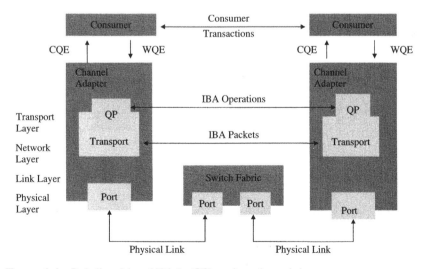

Figure 6.4   Relationship of IBA to OSI protocol model.

to the channel adapters using WQEs. For send queue operations, the channel adapter interprets the WQE, creates a request message, segments the message into multiple packets if necessary, adds the appropriate routing headers, and sends the packet out the appropriate port. The port logic transmits the packet over the link where switches and routers relay the packet through the fabric to the destination.

When the destination receives a packet, the port logic validates the integrity of the packet. The channel adapter associates the packet with a particular QP and uses the context of that QP to process the packet and execute the operation. If necessary, the channel adapter creates an acknowledgment and sends it back to the originator.

Reception of certain request messages causes the channel adapter to consume a WQE from the work queue. When it does, the CQE corresponding to the WQE is returned to the consumer.

Fabric switches are used for transferring packets within a subnetwork. Packets within the subnetwork are routed by LID. Each switch maintains a forwarding table based on the LID of each node. The subnet manager loads the forwarding tables for the switches after creating the LIDs for the individual subnetwork ports. Multiple paths may be provided through the fabric for redundancy or load sharing.

Routers are used to route packets among subnetworks. Packets are routed among subnetworks based on LID and a *global identifier* (GID). The GID consists of the vendor-specified GUID and a subnet identifier. The subnet manager configures routers with subnet information, including LID and VL information.

6.5 DATA FRAMING

The following sections describe service classes and packet formats for Infiniband packets.

6.5.1 Service Classes

When QPs are created, they are configured to provide one of the following service classes:

- *Reliable Connection* (acknowledged; connection oriented)
- *Reliable Datagram* (acknowledged, multiplexed)

- *Unreliable Connection* (unacknowledged; connection oriented)
- *Unreliable Datagram* (unacknowledged; connectionless)
- *Raw Datagram* (unacknowledged; connectionless).

A Reliable Connection associates a local QP with one and only one remote QP. A connected service requires a consumer to create a QP for each consumer it wishes to communicate with. Reliable connections are considered reliable because the channel adapter maintains sequence numbers and acknowledges all messages, and therefore is able to request retransmission of errored packets.

Unreliable Connections also associate a local QP with a single remote QP. A SEND buffer request placed on one QP causes data to be written into the receive buffer of the associated QP. Unreliable connections are unreliable because they do not acknowledge packets and do not have the ability to request retransmission.

Unreliable Datagram service allows the consumer of the QP to communicate with any unreliable datagram QP on any node. A receive operation allows incoming messages from any unreliable datagram QP on any node. Although the unreliable datagram service provides a lower level of service than the reliable services, it provides increased scaleability and reduces the need for state management. All unreliable datagrams are limited to one packet in size.

The Reliable Datagram service multiplexes packets over connections between nodes called End-to-End Contexts (EEC). EECs allow each reliable datagram QP to communicate with any other reliable datagram QP in any node. Multiple QPs can use the same EEC, and one QP may use multiple EECs.

The Raw Datagram service is a data link service that allows QPs to send and receive raw datagrams. Two types of raw datagram service are supported: IPv6 and EtherType. IPv6 datagram service enables standard protocols, such as TCP and UDP, to be layered on top of IPv6 packets, and allows delivery of native IPv6 packets to IBA ports. Ethertype enables similar support of standard protocols layered on top of Ethernet (see Section 5.5 for details).

6.5.2 IBA Packet Format

An IBA packet is bounded by start and end delimiters. The transport, network, and link level protocols add additional header and

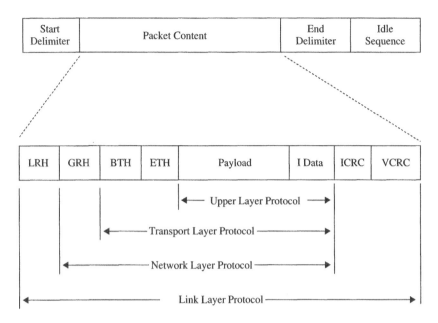

Figure 6.5 IBA packet framing.

trailer information to the upper layer protocol data. Format of an IBA packet is shown in Figure 6.5.

The *Local Route Header* (LRH) is always present and identifies the local source and destination ports used for switch routing. For local routing, the LRH contains the LID of the destination channel adapter. For internetwork routing, the LRH contains the LID of the destination router. The LRH also identifies the service level and VL used. The VL value may change as the packet traverses the network.

Each packet contains two CRC fields. The *Invariant CRC* (ICRC) contains a CRC checksum for the fields that do not change as the packet traverses the fabric or network. The *Variant CRC* (VCRC) covers all the fields of the packet. Use of two CRCs allows the network to modify data fields during routing and still maintain data integrity.

Link level flow control uses a credit-based system where each receiver sends credits to the transmitter indicating how may packets it may send without overloading the receive buffer. Credits are issued on a per-VL basis.

The *Global Route Header* (GRH) is present in packets that traverse multiple subnetworks. The GRH identifies source and destination ports using a GID in the form of an IPv6 address. As the packet traverses different subnetworks, routers may modify the content of the GRH and replace the LRH; however, use of ICRC and VCRC guarantees data integrity.

The *Base Transport Header* (BTH) is present in all packets except for raw datagrams. It specifies the destination QP, the operation code, the packet sequence number, and the partition. The *operation code* identifies the packet as the first, last, intermediate, or only packet of a message, and specifies the operation (SEND or RDMA). The packet sequence number is initialized as part of the communications establishment process, and is incremented each time the QP creates a new packet. The receiving QP tracks the sequence number to detect missing packets. For reliable service, the receiver sends ACK or NAK messages back to the sender to inform it that a packet was or was not received.

The *Extended Transport Header* (ETH) is used for a variety of functions. For reliable datagram service, the ETH indicates the EEC used by the QP. For RDMA functions, the ETH contains the virtual address of the data buffer to read or write.

6.6   PHYSICAL LAYER

Physical transport media may consist of 1, 4, or 12 *lanes*, each representing a separate physical interface. Each lane has a transport speed of 2.5 Gb/s; therefore, the 1-, 4-, and 12-lane interfaces represent signal speeds of 2.5, 10, and 30 Gb/s, respectively.

The link physical layer provides the interface between the packet byte stream of the link layer and the serial bit stream on the physical transport medium. The packet byte stream is byte striped across all available physical lanes (i.e. a single byte is written to each lane in order). The byte stream on each lane is encoded using 8B/10B encoding, similar to Fibre Channel, FICON, and Gigabit Ethernet.

6.6.1   8B/10B Transmission Coding

InfiniBand fiber optic physical interfaces use 8B/10B line coding, in which each 8 bits of data to be transmitted is encoded into a 10-bit transmission character, which is sent serially over the fiber link. Use of 8B/10B encoding results in 25% overhead; thus a 2.5 Gb/s transport lane consists of 2 Gb/s of 8B/10B encoded user data. At the receiving end, each transmission character is decoded into the original 8 bits of data. In addition to the transmission characters which may be decoded into the 256 possible 8-bit combinations, there are additional transmission characters, referred to as *special characters*, which are used for purposes which require them to be distinct from frame contents. InfiniBand uses special characters as frame delimiters and link control symbols. The following link control symbols are defined:

- *COM* – character boundary alignment symbol. The COM symbol is used by the physical lane receiver to identify symbol boundaries. It is also used as the start of ordered set delimiter.
- *SDP* – start of data packet delimiter. The SDP is used to identify the start of a data packet.
- *SLP* – start of link packet delimiter. The SLP is used to identify the start of a link control packet.
- *EGP* – end of good packet delimiter. The EGP is used to identify the end of each packet as it is transmitted by the originating port.
- *EBP* – end of bad packet delimiter. The EBP is used to identify the end of a bad packet as it is transmitted by a switch or router. When an error is detected (e.g. decode error, CRC error), the EGP delimiter is replaced by the EBP delimiter.
- *PAD* – packet padding symbol. The PAD symbol is used for physical lane alignment.
- *SKP* – skip symbol. The SKP symbol is used for clock tolerance compensation.

Other special characters are reserved for future use and vendor-specific operations.

Combinations of special characters are called *ordered sets*. Infiniband uses ordered sets to perform certain control functions. A *SKIP* ordered set consists of a COM and three SKP symbols. *Link Training Sequence 1* (TS1) and *Link Training Sequence 2* (TS2) ordered sets consist of a COM and a series of lane identifiers, and are used for lane control functions.

6.6.2 InfiniBand Optical Loss Budgets and Operating Distances

InfiniBand defines a number of optical link interfaces with different optical characteristics and loss budgets. Optical link interfaces may

Table 6.1   Link loss budgets and distance limitations for InfiniBand optical links

Bandwidth@ wavelength	Fiber pairs	Fiber type and size	Loss budget (dB)	Maximum distance	Modal bandwidth (MMF)
2.5 G/850 nm (1B-1X-SX)	1	62.5/125 um MMF	6	125 m	200 MHz-km
2.5 G/850 nm (1B-1X-SX)	1	50/125 um MMF	6	250 m	500 MHz-km
2.5 G/850 nm (1B-1X-SX)	1	50/125 um MMF	6	500 m	2000 MHz-km
2.5 G/1300 nm (1B-1X-LX)	1	9–10 um SMF	9	10 km	
10 G/850 nm (1B-4X-SX)	4	62.5/125 um MMF	4.8	75 m	200 MHz-km
10 G/850 nm (1B-4X-SX)	4	50/125 um MMF	4.8	125 m	500 MHz-km
10 G/850 nm (1B-4X-SX)	4	50/125 um MMF	4.8	200 m	2000 MHz-km
10 G/1300 nm (1B-4X-LX)	1	9–10 um SMF	9.4	10 km	
30 G/850 nm (1B-12X-SX)	12	62.5/125 um MMF	4.8	75 m	200 MHz-km
30 G/850 nm (1B-12X-SX)	12	50/125 um MMF	4.8	125 m	500 MHz-km
30 G/850 nm (1B-12X-SX)	12	50/125 um MMF	4.8	200 m	2000 MHz-km

be short reach (SX) using multimode fiber, or long reach (LX) using single mode fiber. Each link interface consists of a number of pairs of fibers for receiving and transmitting. Thus a 1X-SX interface is a single pair of short-range fibers, and a 12X-SX interface consists of 12 pairs of short-range fibers. The optical bit rate is 2.5 Gb/s for each transmit/receive fiber pair except the 4X-LX, which uses a single pair of fibers running at 10 Gb/s. Table 6.1 lists supported optical interfaces.

6.6.3   InfiniBand MultiMode 1X-SX Optical Output Specifications

Table 6.2 gives optical output specifications for the InfiniBand multimode fiber interface.

Table 6.2 InfiniBand multimode IX-SX optical output specifications

Parameter	Minimum	Maximum	Units
Transmitter Type	Laser		
Center Wavelength	830	860	nm.
RMS Spectral Width		0.85	nm.
Average Launched Power[1]		−4.0	dBm
Optical Modulation Amplitude (OMA)[2]	0.196		mW
RMS mean of 20–80% Rise/Fall Time[3]		150	ps
RIN_{12} (OMA)		−117	DB/Hz

1. Average launched power (max) is the lesser of the eye safety limit or average receiver power (max).
2. Optical modulation amplitude values are peak-to-peak.
3. Optical rise and fall time specifications are based on unfiltered waveforms.

Table 6.3 InfiniBand multimode 1X-SX optical input specifications

Parameter	Minimum	Maximum	Units
Average Received Power		−1.5	dBm
Optical Modulation Amplitude (OMA)[1]	0.050		mW
Return Loss of Receiver	12		dB
Stressed Receiver Sensitivity (OMA)[1]	0.102		mW
Stressed Receiver ISI Test	2.0		dB
Stressed Receiver DCD Component of deterministic jitter (at Tx)	40		ps
Receiver electrical 3 dB upper cutoff frequency		2.8	GHz
Receiver electrical 10 dB upper cutoff frequency		6.0	GHz

1. Optical Modulation Amplitude values are peak-to-peak.

6.6.4   InfiniBand Multimode 1X-SX Optical Input Specifications

Table 6.3 gives optical input specifications for the InfiniBand multimode fiber interface.

6.6.5   Infiniband Single Mode 1X-LX Optical Output Specifications

Table 6.4 gives optical output specifications for the InfiniBand 1X-LX single mode fiber interface.

Table 6.4   InfiniBand single mode IX-LX optical output specifications

Parameter	Minimum	Maximum	Units
Transmitter Type	Laser		
Center Wavelength	1270	1360	nm.
RMS Spectral Width[1]		5.4	nm.
Average Launched Power[2]		−3.0	dBm
Optical Modulation Amplitude (OMA)[3]	0.186		mW
RMS mean of 20–80% Rise/Fall Time[4]		150	ps
RIN$_{12}$ (OMA)		−120	DB/Hz

1. Maximum value at 1312 nm; see specification for details.
2. Average launched power (max) is the lesser of the eye safety limit or average receiver power (max).
3. Optical modulation amplitude values are peak-to-peak.
4. Optical rise and fall time specifications are based on unfiltered waveforms.

Table 6.5   InfiniBand single mode 1X-LX optical input specifications

Parameter	Minimum	Maximum	Units
Average Received Power		−1.5	dBm
Optical Modulation Amplitude (OMA)[1]	0.0234		mW
Return Loss of Receiver	20		dB
Stressed Receiver Sensitivity (OMA)[1]	0.0365		mW
Stressed Receiver ISI Test	0.58		dB
Stressed Receiver DCD Component of DJ (at Tx)	40		ps
Receiver electrical 3 dB upper cutoff frequency		2.8	GHz
Receiver electrical 10 dB upper cutoff frequency		6.0	GHz

1. Optical Modulation Amplitude values are peak-to-peak.

6.6.6   InfiniBand Single Mode 1X-LX Optical Input Specifications

Table 6.5 gives optical input specifications for the InfiniBand 1X-LX single mode fiber interface.

6.6.7   InfiniBand MultiMode 4X-SX Optical Output Specifications

Table 6.6 gives optical output specifications for the InfiniBand 4X-SX multimode fiber interface.

Table 6.6 InfiniBand multimode 4X-SX optical output specifications

Parameter	Minimum	Maximum	Units
Transmitter Type	Laser		
Center Wavelength	830	860	nm.
RMS Spectral Width		0.85	nm.
Average Launched Power[1]		−2.5	dBm
Optical Modulation Amplitude (OMA)[2]	0.150		mW
RMS mean of 20–80% Rise/Fall Time[3]		150	ps
RIN_{12} (OMA)		−117	DB/Hz

1. Average launched power per fiber (max) is the lesser of the eye safety limit or average receiver power (max).
2. Optical modulation amplitude values are peak-to-peak.
3. Optical rise and fall time specifications are based on unfiltered waveforms.

Table 6.7 InfiniBand MultiMode 4X-SX optical input specifications

Parameter	Minimum	Maximum	Units
Average Received Power		−1.5	dBm
Optical Modulation Amplitude (OMA)[1]	0.050		mW
Return Loss of Receiver	12		dB
Stressed Receiver Sensitivity (OMA)[1]	0.085		mW
Stressed Receiver ISI Test	0.90		dB
Stressed Receiver DCD Component of deterministic jitter (at Tx)	60		ps
Receiver electrical 3 dB upper cutoff frequency		2.8	GHz
Receiver electrical 10 dB upper cutoff frequency		6.0	GHz

1. Optical Modulation Amplitude values are peak-to-peak.

6.6.8 InfiniBand Multimode 4X-SX Optical Input Specifications

Table 6.7 gives optical input specifications for the InfiniBand multimode 4X-SX fiber interface.

6.6.9 Infiniband Single Mode 4X-LX Optical Output Specifications

The InfiniBand single mode 4X-LX optical output specifications are the same as the specifications for the 10GBASE-LR interface given in Section 5.5.7 (Table 5.37), except that the signaling speed is 10.0 Gb/s instead of 10.3125 Gb/s.

6.6.10 InfiniBand Single Mode 4X-LX Optical Input Specifications

The InfiniBand single mode 4X-LX optical input specifications are the same as the specifications for the 10GBASE-LR interface given in Section 5.5.7 (Table 5.38), except that the signaling speed is 10.0 Gb/s instead of 10.3125 Gb/s.

6.6.11 InfiniBand MultiMode 12X-SX Optical Output Specifications

Table 6.8 gives optical output specifications for the InfiniBand 12X-SX multimode fiber interface.

6.6.12 InfiniBand Multimode 12X-SX Optical Input Specifications

Table 6.9 gives optical input specifications for the InfiniBand multimode 12X-SX fiber interface.

Table 6.8 InfiniBand multimode 12X-SX optical output specifications

Parameter	Minimum	Maximum	Units
Transmitter Type	Laser		
Center Wavelength	830	860	nm.
RMS Spectral Width		0.85	nm.
Average Launched Power[1]		−4.0	dBm
Optical Modulation Amplitude (OMA)[2]	0.150		mW
RMS mean of 20–80% Rise/Fall Time[3]		150	ps
RIN$_{12}$ (OMA)		−117	DB/Hz

1. Average launched power per fiber (max) is the lesser of the eye safety limit or average receiver power (max).
2. Optical modulation amplitude values are peak-to-peak.
3. Optical rise and fall time specifications are based on unfiltered waveforms.

Table 6.9 InfiniBand multimode 12X-SX optical input specifications

Parameter	Minimum	Maximum	Units
Average Received Power		−1.5	dBm
Optical Modulation Amplitude (OMA)[1]	0.050		mW
Return Loss of Receiver	12		dB
Stressed Receiver Sensitivity (OMA)[1]	0.085		mW
Stressed Receiver ISI Test	0.90		dB
Stressed Receiver DCD Component of deterministic jitter (at Tx)	60		ps
Receiver electrical 3 dB upper cutoff frequency		2.8	GHz
Receiver electrical 10 dB upper cutoff frequency		6.0	GHz

1. Optical Modulation Amplitude values are peak-to-peak.

6.7 SUMMARY

InfiniBand is more than just a storage protocol; it is a revolutionary storage-centric architecture that integrates storage networking into the core architecture and implements many innovations and improvements from previous storage protocols. Infiniband incorporates IP networking, and specifically IPv6 addressing, into its core architecture. Like most innovations that are revolutionary rather than evolutionary, Infiniband has limited acceptance at present, and so far has been confined to the development of special-purpose high-performance computing systems that can make effective use of its switched I/O and tightly coupled memory to do synchronous network processing.

One promising offshoot of the InfiniBand architecture is Remote Direct Memory Access (RDMA) over TCP. This effort, currently being developed by the RDMA Consortium (http://www.rdmaconsortium.com), uses the RDMA zero-copy capability of Infini-Band for low-latency remote memory access, but uses 10 G Ethernet as the physical layer transport, rather than the InfiniBand protocol described above. When used with a TCP/IP Offload Engine (TOE), 10 G Ethernet provides nearly the same access latency performance as InfiniBand, at a lower implementation cost.

7

MAN/WAN Protocols for Distributed Storage Networking

When storage protocols must be transported for extended distances across a Metropolitan Area Network (MAN) or Wide Area Network (WAN), long-haul transport protocols must be employed. This section discusses four common protocols for the MAN and WAN: Wavelength Division Multiplexing (WDM), Synchronous Optical Network (SONET), Asynchronous Transfer Mode (ATM), and Generic Framing Procedure.

7.1 WAVELENGTH DIVISION MULTIPLEXING (WDM)

Wavelength Division Multiplexing (WDM) is a way to take advantage of the high bandwidth capability of optical fiber without requiring high modulation rates at the transmitter. WDM has been widely used in telecommunications, and is now being increasingly used in enterprise networking applications as well.

WDM, like many other optical networking technologies, is based on techniques that have a long history in wire-based analog telecommunications networks. WDM is the optical equivalent of frequency division multiplexing, which has been used in the public switched telephone network for almost 100 years to carry multiple telephone

Distributed Storage Networks   Thomas C. Jepsen
© 2003 John Wiley & Sons, Ltd   ISBN: 0-470-85020-5

conversations on the same wire.[1] In frequency division multiplexing, each phone conversation is used to modulate a different carrier frequency. All the carrier frequencies are transmitted to the far end over the same wire, separated out at the far end using filters, and then demodulated.

Using a separate optical fiber for each SONET, ATM, ESCON, Fibre Channel, or Gigabit Ethernet channel would be an inefficient use of the fiber's bandwidth. This is because a fiber optic link is capable of transmitting many terabits of data per second, and these protocols transmit at most only a few gigabits per second. Using WDM, each of these individual channels can be used to modulate a laser operating at wavelengths spaced approximately 1 nanometer (nm) apart in the 1550 nm region. These separate wavelengths are then combined using a diffraction grating, and coupled into a single mode fiber for transmission. At the receive end, the individual wavelengths are again separated out, using a similar diffraction grating, and demodulated separately. Figure 7.1 shows the operating principle for WDM.

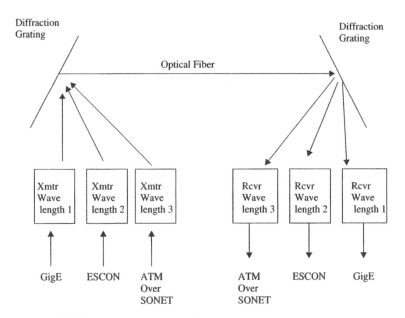

Figure 7.1   WDM principle of operation.

---

[1] Actually you can go back even further than that, and argue that WDM is the optical descendant of the harmonic telegraph, invented in 1875 by Elisha Gray to transmit multiple telegraph messages simultaneously on the same wire by using a different carrier frequency for each individual message.

The theoretical maximum number of channels that could be transmitted over a single fiber using WDM is in the range of several thousand, and is constrained in the real world by the techniques used to etch the diffraction gratings. Most commercially available systems used for enterprise networks in the MAN support 8, 16 or 32 wavelengths ('coarse division wavelength multiplexing'). WDM systems used by carriers for long distance telecommunications transport support higher wavelength densities ("dense wavelength division multiplexing," or DWDM), and can support as many as 170 wavelengths on a single fiber. DWDM systems also use a higher bandwidth per wavelength, typically 10 Gb/s.

Operation in the 1550 nm region provides minimum attenuation for light waves traveling in optical fiber, and therefore WDM systems can provide transport for storage protocols for distances in excess of 50 km without the use of repeaters. For greater distances, however, amplification is required. One such technique is the use of *Erbium Doped Fiber Amplifiers* (EDFAs). An EFDA is a length of optical fiber that has had traces of the element erbium added. A shorter-wavelength laser is used to inject energy into the doped fiber and raise the energy state of the erbium. The excited erbium atoms in turn add energy to the incoming signal, which increases its amplitude. Thus, EFDAs enable amplification to be performed optically, without the need to regenerate the electrical signals.

WDM topologies in the MAN are usually point-to-point, mesh, or ring. Point-to-point connectivity is often used for enterprise private networking, as it is typically the least expensive option. Figure 4.4 shows a point-to-point WDM configuration for the MAN. Mesh networks provide multiple paths between endpoints, and therefore provide additional reliability at the cost of additional fiber spans; Figure 4.5 shows a WDM mesh configuration.

Ring configurations provide additional redundancy and reliability, and enable multi-site and/drop capability. Ring configurations may be used by enterprise networks, and by public carriers providing managed service offerings. Figure 4.6 shows a WDM ring configuration used in the MAN.

One drawback to the use of WDM technology is the lack of standards for network management and error correction. WDM equipment from multiple vendors may use different methods for configuration, provisioning, and fault detection, and may not be interoperable. Also, since the modulation technique used is amplitude modulation, there is no simple way to provide error detection and correction in the transport path. A number of optical standards groups are currently working to address these issues.

7.2   TIME DIVISION MULTIPLEXING AND SONET

The Synchronous Optical Network (SONET) is an optical transmission interface originally developed by BellCore (now Telcordia) for use by the Bell operating companies for digital transport of voice telephony. The SONET standards define a synchronous hierarchical digital transport network, which forms the basis of the North American telecommunications network. A similar set of standards, called the Synchronous Digital Hierarchy (SDH), was standardized by the ITU-T, and is in wide use in Europe. One of the strengths of SONET is its extensive set of operations, administration, and maintenance (OAM) features which provide enhanced reliability and maintainability.

7.2.1   SONET/SDH Standards

The SONET standards were developed in the mid-1980s by BellCore and released as a specification, *GR-253-CORE: Synchronous Optical Network (SONET) Transport Systems: Common Generic Criteria*.[2] SDH specifications were developed by the ITU-T and issued as G.707, G.708, and G.709.

7.2.2   SONET Network Architecture

A SONET network may use a point-to-point or ring configuration. Figure 7.2 shows an example of a point-to-point configuration, and indicates path, line, and section terminations. SONET paths are terminated by *Path Terminating Elements* (PTEs), which provide service mapping and concentration of lower-level (e.g. DS-1, DS-3) signals. Sections are terminated by *regenerators*, which are used to regenerate the SONET signal when it is extended over long

---

[2] The current version is GR-253-CORE, Synchronous Optical Network (SONET) Transport Systems: Common Generic Criteria, Issue 3; Telcordia Technologies, September 2000. SONET formats are also documented in ANSI T1.105-1995, Telecommunications – Synchronous Optical Network (SONET) – Basic Description including Multiplex Structures, Rates and Formats.

distances. Lines are terminated by PTEs, *Add/Drop Multiplexers* (ADMs), or *Digital Cross-Connects* (DCSs). An ADM adds or drops lower-level tributary signals. A DCS is used to cross-connect SONET tributaries and change payload data from one SONET payload envelope to another.

High-capacity SONET networks used by telecommunications carriers for long-distance transport often use a ring configuration for redundancy and reliability. The use of protection switching bits in the line overhead enables a fault to be quickly detected and traffic to be switched to an alternate path or link in less than 50 milliseconds. There are several ring configurations in common use. The Unidirectional Path Switched Ring (UPSR) shown in Figure 7.3 performs path switching in the event of a fiber fault. Each traffic originating ring node creates duplicate outgoing paths in each direction, and transmits the same data on each path. The terminating ring node listens to both incoming signals, and selects the best one as the working path. If an error occurs in the working path (or if the fiber carrying the working path is cut), the receiver simply begins listening to the duplicate (protection) path from the opposite direction.

The two-fiber Bidirectional Link Switched Ring (BLSR) config-uration shown in Figure 7.4 uses a single fiber in each direction. Each fiber has half its bandwidth reserved for working traffic and half reserved for protection. If a fiber is cut, its working traf-fic is moved to the protection side of the other fiber. Unlike the UPSR configuration, where protection bandwidth must be dupli-cated end-to-end for each path, the BLSR configuration allows node-to-node switching to take place.

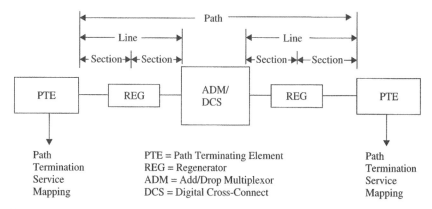

Figure 7.2 SONET point-to-point architecture.

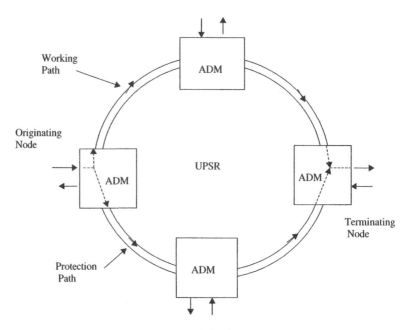

Figure 7.3   SONET Unidirectional Path Switched Ring (UPSR) configuration.

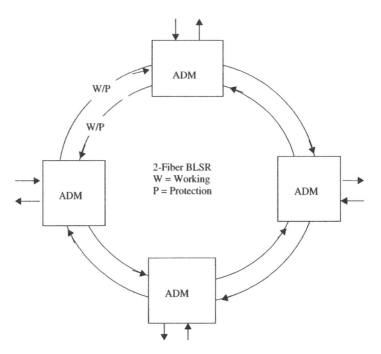

Figure 7.4   SONET two-fiber Bidirectional Link Switched Ring (BLSR) configuration.

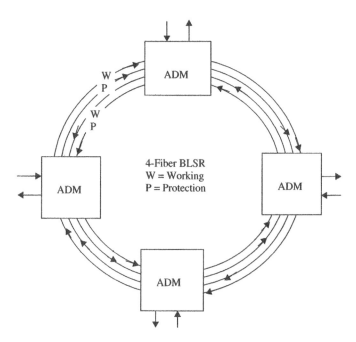

Figure 7.5   SONET four-fiber Bidirectional Link Switched Ring (BLSR) configuration.

The four-fiber BLSR configuration shown in Figure 7.5 uses two working fibers and two protection fibers in each direction. If a working fiber is cut, its traffic is shifted to the protection fiber running in the same direction. The four-fiber BLSR provides faster protection switchover than the two-fiber configuration.

7.2.3   Time Division Multiplexing and the Digital Hierarchy

Time Division Multiplexing (TDM) was originally intended for transport of voice telephony. Pulse Code Modulation (PCM) techniques for digitizing voice make use of Nyquist's theorem, which requires that an analog signal be sampled at a rate equal to twice its bandwidth. Thus to digitize a human voice signal with a bandwidth of 4 KHz, the sample rate must be 8 KHz. If each sample consists of 1 byte, then the resulting digital signal is 64 Kb/s. This is the encoding technique specified by the original PCM standard, ITU-T G.711; however, most voice encoding is done today with more efficient adaptive and predictive techniques that result in a lower bit rate.

Multiple PCM streams may be transported on a single high-bandwidth medium using TDM. In this scheme, each PCM stream is assigned a time slot or channel on the transport medium, and is allowed to send one byte of data during its assigned interval. The North American DS-1 standard defines a frame of 24 time slots plus 1 framing bit, for a total of $8 \times 24 + 1$ bits, or 193 bits per frame. If the frames are sampled at an 8 KHz rate, then the total transmitted bandwidth for 24 channels is 193×8000, or 1.544 Mb/s. The equivalent ITU-T E1 standard allows 32 channels to be sampled at an 8 kHz rate, creating a total transmitted bandwidth of $8 \times 32 \times 8000$, or 2.048 Mb/s.

While originally intended for digital transport of voice telephony, the DS-1 and E1 TDM encoding schemes are also well suited for transmission of digital data. Interleaving schemes are used to provide TDM transport at higher rates; the North American standards specify TDM rates of 6.312 Mb/s (DS-2), 44.736 Mb/s (DS-3), and 274.176 Mb/s (DS-4). The ITU-T standards also specify higher transport rates, including 34.368 Mb/s (E3), and 139.264 Mb/s (E4).

7.2.4 SONET and the Optical Hierarchy

The TDM standards are intended for use over relatively short distances using copper transport media. Also, the transmitted signals are nonsynchronous, and may require bit rate adjustment at network-to-network interfaces. With the introduction of optical fiber into the public switched telephone network in the 1970s and 1980s, a need arose to extend the digital hierarchy to support higher transport bandwidths and synchronous operation, and to include Operations, Administration and Maintenance (OAM) functionality in the encoded data stream.

The basic concept in SONET is the Synchronous Transport Signal, Level 1 (STS-1) frame. As with the basic TDM scheme, the sample rate is 8 kHz; however, the sampled data can be visualized as a frame consisting of 9 rows of 90 bytes each, for a total of 810 bytes. Thus, the transport bit rate for an STS-1 signal is $810 \times 8 \times 8000$, or 51.84 Mb/s. The digitized voice or data to be transported consists of nine rows of 87 bytes, and is referred to as the Synchronous Payload Envelope (SPE). A single STS-1 SPE supports a user bandwidth capability of 50.112 Mb/s, and thus has the capacity to transport 28 DS-1s, 1 DS-3, or 21 E1s. In addition to the SPE, the STS-1 frame contains nine rows of three bytes each of *overhead* information, which is used for OAM, error detection, and data communications between network elements. Generally speaking, the section overhead (SOH) is used for communication between regenerators. The line overhead (LOH) is used for communications between PTEs and ADMs or DCSs. Within the SPE, the path overhead (POH) is used for PTE-to-PTE communication; the H1 and H2 pointers within the LOH indicate the position of the POH within the SPE. The pointer bytes (H1, H2, H3) are also used to indicate the start of payload, and to compensate for small differences in clock timing (frequency justification). Figure 7.6 shows the format for the SONET STS-1 frame.

Lower-speed nonsynchronous data may be transported over SONET by means of *Virtual Tributaries* (VTs). Each 1.728 Mb/s VT1.5 tributary is capable of transporting a single 1.544 Mb/s DS-1 TDM stream. SDH supports a similar sub-STS rate referred to as a *Tributary Unit* (TU).

In a synchronous network, all digital transitions occur at the same time. This is accomplished by the use of a clock signal that is distributed throughout the network and traceable back to a primary reference clock. Depending on its position in the network, a SONET element may obtain its timing information from the received SONET signal, or from a Building Integrated Timing Supply (BITS) clock signal traceable back to the primary reference.

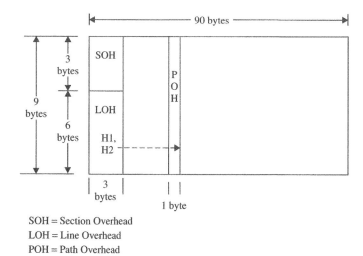

SOH = Section Overhead
LOH = Line Overhead
POH = Path Overhead

Figure 7.6 SONET STS-1 frame format.

Table 7.1 SONET STS-1 overhead bytes

Transport Overhead Type	Byte 1 (Column 1)	Byte 2 (Column 2)	Byte 3 (Column 3)	Path Overhead (Pointed to by H1, H2)
SOH:				
Byte 1	A1	A2	C1	J1
(SOH Row 1)	Framing	Framing	STS-ID	Trace
Byte 2	B1	E1	F1	B3
(SOH Row 2)	BIP-8	Orderwire	User	BIP-8
Byte 3	D1	D2	D3	C2
(SOH Row 3)	Data Com	Data Com	Data Com	Signal Label
LOH:				
Byte 4	H1	H2	H3	G1
(LOH Row 1)	Pointer	Pointer	Pointer Action	Path Status
Byte 5	B2	K1	K2	F2
(LOH Row 2)	BIP-8	APS	APS	User
Byte 6	D4	D5	D6	H4
(LOH Row 3)	Data Com	Data Com	Data Com	Multiframe
Byte 7	D7	D8	D9	Z3
(LOH Row 4)	Data Com	Data Com	Data Com	Growth
Byte 8	D10	D11	D12	Z4
(LOH Row 5)	Data Com	Data Com	Data Com	Growth
Byte 9	Z1	Z2	E2	Z5
(LOH Row 6)	Growth	Growth	Order Wire	Growth

Table 7.1 shows the locations of the overhead bytes in the SOH, LOH, and POH. Table 7.2 explains the meaning and use of each.

The STS-1 frame defines the format for the electrical signal; the equivalent optical format is the Optical Carrier (OC-1) format. Higher-rate SONET interfaces may be *concatenated* or *unconcatenated*. For concatenated SONET interfaces, the entire bandwidth is available for a single packet or cell flow, while an unconcatenated SONET interface is channelized into multiple lower-rate flows. Unconcatenated SONET rates are created by simply combining multiple STS-1 frames to form a higher rate. Concatenated rates are created by byte interleaving the transport overheads of multiple STS-1 frames, and then interleaving the SPEs. Concatenated rates are designated by adding a small 'c' to the rate designation (e.g. STS-3c, OC3c). A common SONET transport bandwidth is the 155.52 Mb/s OC-3 format, which is created by combining 3 OC-1

Table 7.2 Overhead bytes and their meaning

Overhead byte	Meaning
Section Overhead	
A1, A2	Framing bytes used to synchronize the beginning of the frame
B1	Bit interleaved parity byte providing even parity over previous STS frame
C1	Identifies the STS-1 number of each STS frame within an STS-N format
D1–D3	192 Kb/s data communications channel for OAM
E1	Section-level 64 Kb/s PCM order wire
F1	64 Kb/s user channel
Line Overhead	
B2	Bit interleaved parity for line level error monitoring
D4–D12	576 Kb/s data communications channel for line OAM
E2	64 Kb/s line order wire
H1–H3	Pointer bytes; used for frame alignment and frequency adjustment of payload
K1,K2	Automatic protection switching signaling
Z1, Z2	(Reserved)
Path Overhead	
B3	Bit interleaved parity – path level
C2	STS path signal label to designate equipped versus unequipped STS signals.
F2	64 Kb/s Path user channel
G1	Status byte sent from path terminating equipment back to path originating equipment
H4	Multiframe indicator for payloads longer than a single STS frame
J1	64 Kb/s channel used to send path integrity pattern
Z3–Z5	(Reserved)

frames ($51.84 \times 3 = 155.52$ Mb/s.). Higher-transport rate SONET formats include OC-12 (622.08 Mb/s) and OC-48 (2488.32 Mb/s.).

7.2.5   Use of TDM/SONET for Storage Networking

7.2.5.1   Fibre Channel over SONET

Transport of Fibre Channel packets over SONET is defined in ANSI INCITS 342-2001, Fibre Channel Backbone (FC-BB). This document specifies a Fibre Channel Backbone WAN (FC-BBW_SONET)

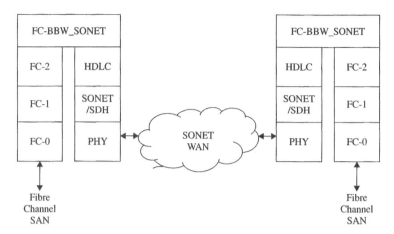

Figure 7.7 Protocol layering for SONET/SDH transport of Fibre Channel packets.

interface which supports both SONET and SDH transport of Fibre Channel packets over the wide area network. High-Level Data Link Control (HDLC) framing is used to synchronously transport Fibre Channel packets over the SONET network. Figure 7.7 shows the protocol layering involved in SONET/SDH transport of Fibre Channel frames.

FC-BBW_SONET mapping supports service classes 2, 3, and 4, as well as F (intra-fabric frames). Service class 1 is not supported. Standard HDLC information (I), supervisory (S) and unnumbered (U) messages are used to initiate connections, transfer packets, and acknowledge receipt of packets. All Fibre Channel frames and FC-BBW_SONET messages have a Logical Link Control/Sub Network Access Protocol (LLC/SNAP) header to designate protocol type, and a BBW_header to indicate optional flow control type. The FC-BB specification defines two types of flow control: Selective Recovery (SR), a sliding-window protocol which supports both flow control and error recovery; and Simple Flow Control (SFC), which uses a PAUSE byte in the BBW_header to request permission to transmit for a specified interval. Figure 7.8 shows the layering of the encapsulations used to transport Fibre Channel frames using HDLC.

For WAN transport of Fibre Channel frames, special attention must be paid to the timeout values E_D_TOV and R_A_TOV (see Section 5.4.5.6). For switched topology, R_A_TOV is equal to the E_D_TOV plus two times the maximum time that a frame may be delayed within the fabric and still be delivered. Both E_D_TOV and R_A_TOV must take network propagation time into account.

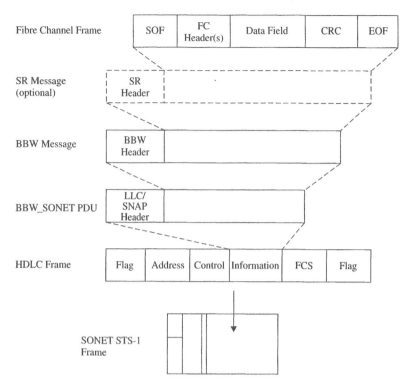

Figure 7.8 Encapsulation of Fibre Channel frames using HDLC.

The SOF and EOF frame delimiters used by the Fibre Channel protocol are 10-bit ordered sets and have no 8-bit equivalents (see Section 5.4.6.1). The FC frame encapsulation values for SOF and EOF used by FC-BBW_SONET and FC-BBW_ATM are given in Table 7.3. The byte value is mapped into a 32-bit word as the first eight bits

FC service class 1 is not supported for frame encapsulation, and therefore SOFc1, SOFi1, and SOFn1 do not have byte encodings.

Other frame-based storage protocols, such as ESCON/SBCON or Gigabit Ethernet, may be transported over SONET using HDLC framing in a similar fashion.

7.2.5.2 SONET Summary

Since it was originally developed for voice telephony applications, SONET is well-suited for applications requiring low latency and a low bit error rate, including storage networking. However, there are some limitations to the use of SONET as a transport protocol. Bandwidth must be provisioned, and cannot be allocated on an

Table 7.3 FC frame encapsulation byte values for SOF and EOF

FC frame delimiter	Byte encoded value	FC service class
SOFf	0 × 28	(intra-fabric communication)
SOFi2	0 × 2D	2
SOFn2	0 × 35	2
SOFi3	0 × 2E	3
SOFn3	0 × 36	3
EOFn	0 × 41	2,3,4,F
EOFt	0 × 42	2,3,4,F
EOFni	0 × 49	2,3,4,F
EOFa	0 × 50	2,3,4,F

'on-demand' basis. Thus the bandwidth will be wasted during idle periods. Also, bandwidth must be allocated in fixed VT1.5 or STS-1 increments and cannot be allocated in smaller increments. For these reasons, Asynchronous Transfer Mode (ATM) over SONET is often employed to allow on-demand allocation of variable amounts of bandwidth.

7.3 ASYNCHRONOUS TRANSFER MODE (ATM)

Asynchronous Transfer Mode (ATM) is a circuit-based, connection-oriented technology that was developed in the early 1990s to provide a single packet-based format for transport of digital voice and data across telecommunications networks. Some of the important characteristics of ATM include the following:

- *ATM uses a standard cell size of 53 bytes*[3]. An ATM cell consists of a 5-byte header and a 48-byte user data field. Use of a standard cell size enables ATM switching to be done in hardware for high speed and performance.
- *ATM defines service categories.* ATM supports continuous bit rate, real-time variable bit rate, non-real-time variable bit rate, and unspecified classes of service.

---

[3] The nonintuitive cell size of 53 bytes came about as a compromise between two user groups. One favored a 32-byte payload optimized for voice traffic, and another wanted a 64-byte payload for data traffic. As a compromise, a 48-byte payload was selected, which together with the 5-byte header, makes a 53 byte packet.

- *ATM is circuit-based.* ATM addressing is based on virtual circuits, which may be permanent (PVC) or switched (SVC).
- *ATM is connection-oriented.* Connections may be virtual path connections (VPC) or virtual channel connections (VCC).
- *ATM permits user-specified quality of service.* Quality of Service (QoS) parameters such as peak cell rate, sustained cell rate, cell loss priority, and cell delay variation are specified as part of connection setup. Use of resource reservation enables support of absolute rather than relative QoS.

7.3.1   Standards

ATM standards were developed by the ATM Forum, an industry standards group, and by the International Telecommunications Union (ITU) in the early 1990s. The primary difference between the two sets of standards is in document organization; the ATM Forum standards tend to aggregate the ATM specifications into a few volumes, while the ITU standards are more granular in terms of scope and function. While there are minor technical differences between the ATM Forum standards and the ITU standards, they are largely identical in terms of function. Table 7.4 lists the primary ATM Forum and ITU-T specifications.

7.3.2   ATM Protocol Architecture

ATM protocol architecture is shown in Figure 7.9. ATM can be considered to be primarily a layer 2 data link protocol from

Table 7.4   ATM standards from the ATM Forum and ITU-T

Subject	ATM Forum Standard (Date)	ITU-T Standard (Date)
ATM Layer	ATM UNI 3.1 (1994) B-ICI 2.0 (1995)	I.361 (1999)
AAL5		I.363.5 (1996)
SSCOP		Q.2110 (1994)
SSCF		Q.2130 (1994)
Signaling	UNI SIG 4.1 (2002)	Q.2931 (1995)
Traffic Management	TM 4.1 (1999)	I.371 (2000)

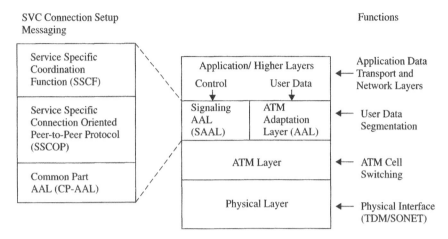

Figure 7.9   ATM protocol architecture.

the standpoint of the OSI model. Transport and networking are assumed to be higher-level functions. ATM consists of a control plane, which is responsible for connection setup, and a user data plane, which provides ATM adaptation for application PDUs.

7.3.2.1   Cell Format

Figure 7.10 shows ATM cell format. Each ATM cell is divided into two parts – a 5-byte header and a 48-byte user data field. The header is slightly different for *User-Network Interface* (UNI) ATM cells which pass between a user terminal and the network, and *Network-Network Interface* (NNI) ATM cells which pass between switches in the network. For ATM UNI cells, the header consists of a 4-bit *Generic Flow Control* (GFC) field, an 8-bit *Virtual Path Identifier* (VPI) field, a 12-bit *Virtual Channel Identifier* (VCI) field, a 3-bit *Payload Type* (PT) field, a *Cell-Loss Priority* (CLP) bit, and an 8-bit *Header Error Control* (HEC) field.

The GFC field is used for local flow control at the UNI; its coding is application-specific. The VPI field is used to specify a virtual path for the cell traffic. The VCI field specifies a virtual channel within the VPI. The PT bits are used to indicate if the cell is used for user data, Operations, Administration and Maintenance (OAM) data, or resource management. PT bits are also used to indicate beginning and end of ATM Adaption Layer (AAL) frame boundaries. The CLP bit is used to indicate discard priority of the cell in the event of

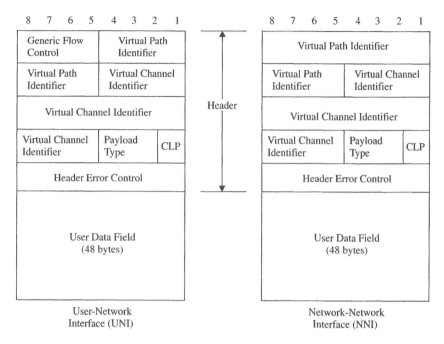

Figure 7.10 ATM cell format.

network congestion. The HEC field is used for header error detection and correction; the generator polynomial is $X^8 + X^2 + X + 1$.

The NNI header is identical to the UNI header, with the exception of the GFC field, which is not used, and the VPI field, which is expanded to 12 bits to allow for more virtual paths among switches in the network.

7.3.2.2 ATM Adaptation Layers

The ATM Adaptation Layers (AAL) are provided to support adaptation of non-ATM protocols, such as pulse code modulation (PCM) voice and Frame Relay Link Access Procedure for Frame-Mode Bearer Services (LAPF). ITU-T I.362 and I.363.2 define 4 specific AAL types for different service classes. AAL1 is a connection-oriented constant bit rate (CBR) service, intended primarily for PCM-encoded voice telephony. AAL2 is similar to AAL1, but provides higher bandwidth efficiency for multiple voice channels through the use of compression and silence suppression. AAL3/4 is a connectionless variable bit rate data service, primarily used to support Switched Multi-Megabit Data Service (SMDS). AAL5 is a connection-oriented variable bit rate (VBR) service intended for data packet service, including Frame Relay, IP, and storage protocols.

Each AAL consists of two sublayers: a common part convergence sublayer (CPCS) and a Segmentation And Reassembly (SAR) sublayer. The AAL5 CPCS provides the interface with the higher layer; it adds user-to-user information, a length indicator, and a CRC checksum to the application data, and padding, when required, to create a CPCS PDU that is an even multiple of the ATM payload size of 48 bytes. The SAR layer segments the CPCS PDU into 48-byte segments in the outgoing direction, and reassembles ATM cell payloads into a CPCS PDU in the incoming direction. AAL5 is defined in ITU-T I.363. Figure 7.11 shows the functions of the CPCS and SAR sublayers for AAL5.

ATM guarantees in-order delivery of cells, so no sequence number is needed. The CRC field in the CPCS can be used to check for missing data. The ATM user to ATM user (AAU) bit of the PT header field is used to indicate CPCS boundaries. All SAR PDUs in a CPCS PDU except the last will have AAU set to 0; the last SAR PDU will have AAU set to 1.

7.3.3   Virtual Paths and Virtual Channels

ATM makes use of logical channels referred to as *virtual paths* and *virtual channels* to control the flow of user data through the

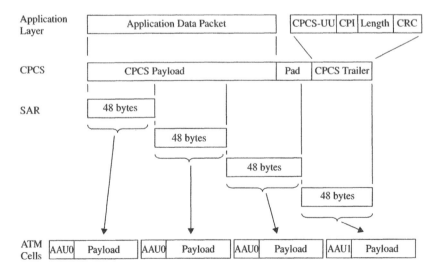

Figure 7.11   CPCS and SAR sublayer for AAL5.

network. Each cell belongs to the virtual path and virtual channel specified by the VPI and VCI fields of the cell header. Network switches use the VPI/VCI fields to route ATM cells through the network. VPIs and VCI enable a hierarchical routing scheme to be employed. All VCIs for a specific destination or service level can be grouped together into a single VPI for management purposes. The UNI cell header allocates 8 bits for the VPI value, meaning that a maximum of 256 virtual paths can be specified for a single user-network interface. The UNI cell header allocates 16 bits for the VCI value, allowing a maximum of 65,536 virtual channels to be specified. The NNI cell header allocates 12 bits for the VPI value, allowing a maximum of 4096 network-to-network virtual paths.

VCIs can be concatenated across the network to form a user-to-user Virtual Channel Connection (VCC). Each VCC has its own traffic contract and quality of service parameters. Similarly, VPIs can be concatenated across the network to form a user-to-user Virtual Path Connection (VPC). In this case, traffic for all the individual VCIs will be managed according to the traffic contract and QoS parameters established for the VPC.

Figure 7.12 shows the relationship of VCIs to VPIs, and illustrates example VCC and VPC connections.

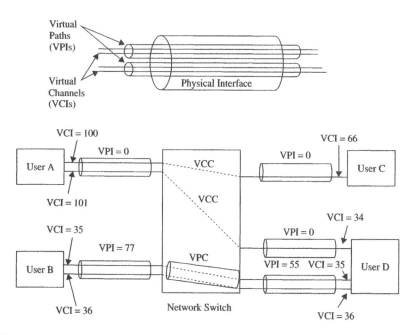

Figure 7.12   ATM VCIs, VPIs, and connections.

7.3.3.1   Permanent Virtual Connections

ATM connections may be set up on a permanent basis, or set up for short-term use using signaling. Permanent connections are referred to as *Permanent Virtual Connections* (PVCs) and are set up administratively by network management functions. The network administrator sets parameters such as traffic class and QOS, and manually selects a route across the network. Parameters which may be specified for a connection include *Peak Cell Rate* (PCR), *Cell Delay Variation* (CDV), *Sustainable Cell Rate* (SCR), and *Cell Loss Priority* (CLP). Connections are bidirectional, and these parameters must be set for both the forward and backward directions. (A unidirectional connection simply has the cell rate parameters set to zero in one direction.) Once configured, a PVC is always available with no connection setup latency required. However, if there is no traffic to send, the allocated bandwidth and network resources are wasted.

7.3.3.2   Switched Virtual Connections

ATM connections set up for short-term use on an on-demand basis using signaling are referred to as *Switched Virtual Connections* (SVCs). SVC setup involves using signaling messages as defined in ITU-T Q.2931. The Signaling ATM Adaptation Layer (SAAL) provides the protocol stack for connection setup and response messages. The SAAL is further subdivided into a Service Specific Coordination Function (SSCF), a Service Specific Connection Oriented Peer-to-peer Protocol (SSCOP) sublayer, and a Common Part AAL (CP-AAL). SSCF maps the SSCOP to the needs of the SSCF user and is defined in ITU-T Q2130. SSCOP is used to transfer variable-length service data units (SDUs) between SSCOP users and is defined in ITU-T Q.2110. CP-AAL provides information transfer using AAL5. A signaling channel (VPI = 0, VCI = 5) is set up between each user node and network switch, and between network switches, to convey signaling messages and responses. Figure 7.13 shows SVC connection setup across the network.

7.3.4   Service Categories

The ATM traffic management specifications define five basic service categories for ATM traffic: Constant Bit Rate (CBR), real time Variable Bit Rate (rt-VBR), non-real time Variable Bit Rate (nrt-VBR), Available Bit Rate (ABR), and Unspecified Bit Rate (UBR).

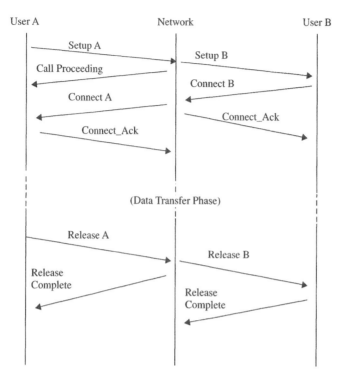

Figure 7.13 SVC connection setup.

The CBR service category is intended for real-time applications requiring tightly controlled delay variation, such as voice, video, or circuit emulation. Rt-VBR is also intended for real-time applications with controlled delay, but a bursty data source is assumed. Nrt-VBR is intended for non-real-time applications with bursty data characteristics; low cell loss is assumed. ABR enables the service parameters to change based on network conditions; a user specifies maximum and minimum bandwidth requirements at connection establishment, and a flow control feedback mechanism is used to change allocated bandwidth, based on relative priority and network conditions. UBR is a 'best effort' service in which minimum cell loss and cell delay are not guaranteed.

7.3.5   Traffic and QoS Parameters

Each of the service categories has certain traffic and Quality of Service (QoS) parameters associated with it. These parameters must have values specified at connection establishment in order to guarantee the requested QoS. Traffic and QoS parameters defined by the ATM standards include the following:

- *Peak Cell Rate (PCR)* – the maximum cell rate supported by the connection. For CBR service, this is the same as sustained cell rate (SCR).
- *Sustained Cell Rate (SCR)* – the average cell rate over the life of the connection.
- *Maximum Burst Size (MBS)* – the maximum number of cells which may be delivered at PCR for a VBR connection.
- *Cell Delay Variation Tolerance (CDVT)* – the amount of cell arrival time variation allowed for this connection.
- *Minimum Cell Rate (MCR)* – the minimum usable cell rate allowed for this connection.
- *Peak-to-peak CDV* – cumulative cell delay variation across the network.
- *Cell Transfer Delay (CTD)* – total end-to-end cell transit delay across the network.
- *Cell Loss Priority (CLP)* – specifies cell discard priority during congestion.

Table 7.5 lists the Traffic and QoS parameters required for each service category.

7.3.5.1   Traffic Control Functions

Specification of traffic and QoS parameters at connection setup time creates a *traffic contract* for the connection which ensures a guaranteed level of service to the user. ATM uses the following traffic control functions to enforce the traffic contract for each connection:

- *Connection Admission Control (CAC)* is defined as the set of actions taken by the network during the call setup phase to determine if the connection request QoS specifications can be supported, or if the connection request should be rejected.
- *Feedback controls* are defined as the set of actions taken by the network and end systems to regulate the traffic submitted on ATM connections to maintain QoS requirements.
- *Usage Parameter Control (UPC)* is defined as the set of actions taken by the network to monitor and control traffic, and to detect and react to violations of the traffic contract, at the end system access.

Table 7.5 QoS parameters specified for each service category

Attribute	ATM Layer Service Category				
	CBR	Rt-VBR	Nrt-VBR	UBR	ABR
Traffic Parameters					
PCR and CDVT[4,5]	Specified			Specified[2]	Specified[3]
SCR, MBS, and CDVT[4,5]	n/a	Specified		n/a	
MCR[4]	n/a			n/a	Specified
QoS Parameters					
Peak-to-peak CDV	Specified		Unspecified		
maxCTD	Specified		Unspecified		
CLR[4]	Specified			Unspecified [1]	
Other Attributes					
Feedback	Unspecified				Specified

1. CLR is low for sources that adjust cell flow in response to control information. Whether a quantitative value for CLR is specified is network specific.
2. May not be subject to CAC and UPC procedures.
3. Represents the maximum rate at which the ABR source may send. The actual rate is subject to control information.
4. These parameters are either explicitly or implicitly specified for SVCs and PVCs.
5. CDVT refers to the cell delay variation tolerance. CDVT is not signaled. In general, CDVT need not have a unique value for a connection. Different values may apply at each interface along the path of a connection.

- *Cell Loss Priority (CLP) Control* defines actions taken to protect the QoS of existing connections by selectively discarding low-priority cells.
- *Traffic shaping* may be used to achieve a desired modification of the traffic characteristics.
- *Network Resource Management (NRM)* allows logical separation of connections by service characteristics, for example by using multiple virtual paths.
- *Frame Discard* may be employed by networks to deal with congestion.
- *ABR Flow Control* may be used to adaptively share the available bandwidth among participating users.

7.3.6 Physical Layer

ATM may be transported as SONET or TDM payloads. The ATM specifications define physical layers for the DS-1 (1.544 Mb/s) and

DS-3 (44.736 Mb/s) TDM rates, and for the OC3c (155.52 Mb/s), OC12c (622.08 Mb/s) and OC48 (2488.32 Mb/s) SONET rates.

7.3.6.1   SONET Physical Layers

The physical layer for the STS-3c (OC3c) consists of two sublayers: a Transmission Convergence (TC) layer and a Physical Media Dependent (PMD) sublayer. OC3c concatenation provides an SPE capacity of 149.760 Mb/s. Since the SPE capacity is not an even number of ATM cells, cells may overlap SPEs. Figure 7.14 shows the functions of the TC and PMD sublayers.

HEC generation/verification consists of generating (transmit direction) or validating (receive direction) the checksum for the header contents using the generator polynomial specified above in Section 7.3.2.1. The HEC checksum covers the entire header, including the HEC field itself. The checksum enables multiple bit errors to be detected, and a single errored bit to be corrected.

Cell scrambling/descrambling randomizes the payload content to avoid continuous non-variable bit patterns and improve cell delineation.

Cell delineation determines cell boundaries using the HEC.

Path signal identification is performed using the C2 overhead byte. For ATM, the C2 byte is a fixed value of 00010011.

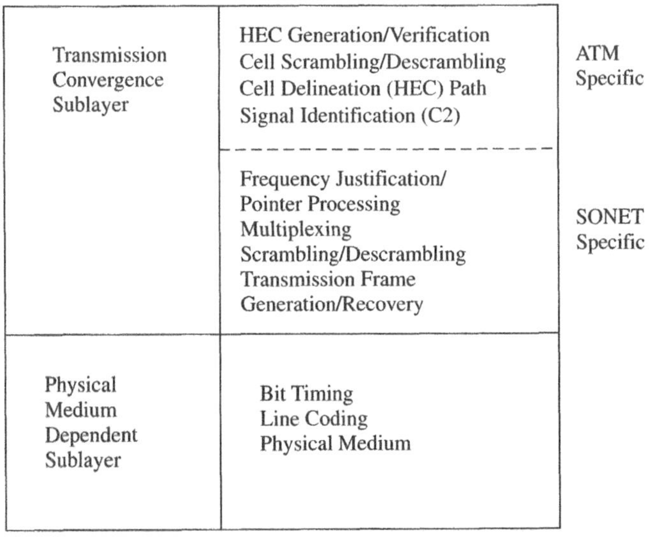

Transmission Convergence Sublayer	HEC Generation/Verification Cell Scrambling/Descrambling Cell Delineation (HEC) Path Signal Identification (C2)	ATM Specific
	Frequency Justification/ Pointer Processing Multiplexing Scrambling/Descrambling Transmission Frame Generation/Recovery	SONET Specific
Physical Medium Dependent Sublayer	Bit Timing Line Coding Physical Medium	

Figure 7.14   TC and PMD layer functions.

The remaining TC functions (frequency justification, pointer processing, multiplexing, scrambling/descrambling, transmission frame generation/recovery) are identical to SONET operation. Pointers are used to compensate for timing differences and to identify actual start of payload.

The PMD functions (bit timing, line coding) are also identical to SONET operation.

7.3.7   Interworking with Storage Protocols

7.3.7.1   Fibre Channel over ATM

Transport of Fibre Channel packets over ATM is defined in ANSI INCITS 342-2001, Fibre Channel Backbone (FC-BB). This document specifies a Fibre Channel Backbone WAN (FC-BBW_ATM) interface which supports ATM transport of Fibre Channel packets over the wide area network. Figure 7.15 shows the protocol layering involved in ATM transport of Fibre Channel frames.

FC-BBW_ATM mapping supports service classes 2, 3, and 4, as well as F (intra-fabric frames). Service class 1 is not supported. FC-BBW_ATM makes use of the AAL5 adaptation layer and the nrt-VBR service category. Fibre Channel frames are mapped into the CPCS-PDU. FC-BBW_ATM messages are transported transparently across the ATM network using AAL5 encapsulation. Each FC-BBW_ATM message has a Logical Link Control/Sub Network

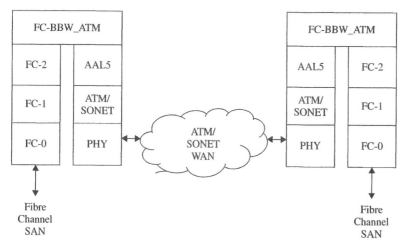

Figure 7.15   Protocol layering for ATM transport of Fibre Channel packets.

Access Protocol (LLC/SNAP) header to designate protocol type, and a BBW_header to indicate optional flow control type; both are mapped into the CPCS-PDU. The FC-BB specification defines two types of flow control: Selective Recovery (SR), a sliding-window protocol which supports both flow control and error recovery; and Simple Flow Control (SFC), which uses a PAUSE byte in the BBW_header to request permission to transmit for a specified interval. Figure 7.16 shows the layering of the encapsulations used to transport Fibre Channel frames using ATM AAL5.

FC-BBW_ATM may use either provisioned PVCs or use Q.2931 signaling to initiate an SVC. QoS and traffic parameters must be specified for the connection. The FC-BBW_ATM layer contains a routing table that maps Fibre Channel Destination Identifiers (D_IDs) to ATM addresses.

For WAN transport of Fibre Channel frames, special attention must be paid to the timeout values E_D_TOV and R_A_TOV (see Section 5.4.5.6). For switched topology, R_A_TOV is equal to the E_D_TOV plus two times the maximum time that a frame may be delayed within the fabric and still be delivered. Both

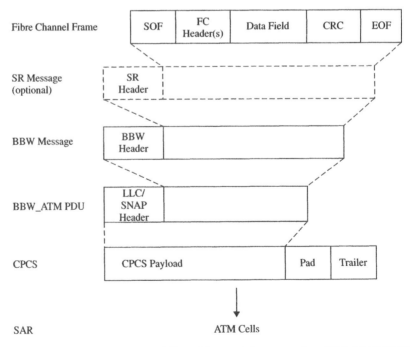

Figure 7.16 Encapsulation of Fibre Channel frames using ATM AAL5 CPCS-PDU.

E_D_TOV and R_A_TOV must take network propagation time into account.

The SOF and EOF frame delimiters used by the Fibre Channel protocol are 10-bit ordered sets and have no 8-bit equivalents (see Section 5.4.6.1). The FC frame encapsulation values for SOF and EOF used by FC-BBW_ATM are given in Table 7.3.

Other frame-based protocols, such as ESCON/SBCON and Gigabit Ethernet, may be transported over ATM using AAL5 in a similar fashion.

7.3.7.2   ATM Summary

Storage protocols can be transported over ATM by using the proper AAL (generally AAL5), and setting up a connection with the proper traffic and QOS parameters. Advantages of ATM include the ability to specify an arbitrary amount of bandwidth on a per-VC basis, low latency and cell loss, and the ability to set absolute bounds on QoS parameters such as cell delay variation, cell loss ratio, and peak cell rate. All of these factors make ATM a good choice for applications requiring real-time performance and low data loss, such as synchronous mirroring.

7.4   GENERIC FRAMING PROCEDURE (GFP)

Generic Framing Procedure (GFP) is a standard for mapping a wide variety of data formats, including storage protocols, over SONET/SDH or directly over WDM. Work on GFP was begun by ANSI in 1999; it was standardized by the ITU-T as G.7041 in 2001. GFP provides two types of payload mappings: frame-mapped GFP, which may be used for variable-length packet data such as PPP or Ethernet; and transparent-mapped GFP, which is intended for block-encoded data such as ESCON, FICON, and Fibre Channel. (Note that Gigabit Ethernet could be transported either as variable-length Ethernet frames, or as block-encoded 8B/10B data.)

7.4.1   GFP Framing

A GFP frame consists of a payload area and a core header, as shown in Figure 7.17. The core header is used for GFP specific link management functions. The core header contains a 2-byte Payload Length Indicator (PLI) field which indicates the size of the payload area, and a 2-byte core header error control (cHEC) field which is

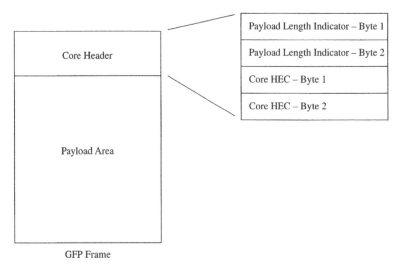

GFP Frame

Figure 7.17 GFP frame.

used to ensure the integrity of the core header. The cHEC uses a CRC-16 sequence which provides multiple-bit error detection and single-bit error correction capabilities.

7.4.2 GFP Payload Area

The GFP payload area supports two different formats for frame-mapped GFP (GFP-F) and transparent-mapped GFP (GFP-T), as shown in Figure 7.18. Both payload formats begin with a payload header and are optionally terminated with a frame check sequence (FCS) trailer. The payload header is a variable-length sequence from 4–64 bytes in length. It consists of a two-byte type field and associated two-byte type HEC (tHEC) field, and optional extension headers. The payload type field indicates whether the GFP frame is a user data frame or management frame, whether or not the FCS trailer is present, whether or not any extension headers are present, and the type of payload. The tHEC field is a CRC-16 sequence which is used to ensure the integrity of the type field.

For GFP-F frames, the payload information field contains the framed PDU (PPP/IP or Ethernet MAC). For GFP-T frames, the block encoded data is first decoded from its original 8B/10B encoding into either an 8-bit data value or a control character. The control characters are mapped into 8-bit GFP control characters. The data bytes and control characters are then block encoded again using a 64B/65B block code. The extra bit is a flag bit which indicates

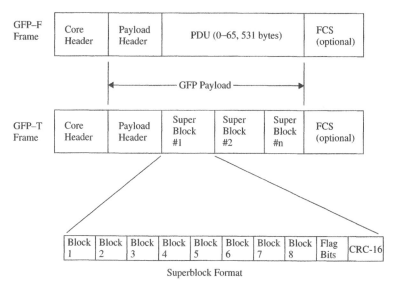

Figure 7.18   GFP-F and GFP-T payload format.

whether or not control characters are included in the block. Control characters are placed at the beginning of the block. Each 8-bit GFP control character contains a Last Control Character (LCC) bit which indicates if it is the last control character in the block, a 3-bit Control Code Locator (CCL), which indicates the original location of the control character in the sequence of data values in the block, and a 4-bit Control Code Indicator (CCI) representing the original 8B/10B control character.

Finally, 8 64B/65B blocks are grouped into a 520 byte 'superblock'. The flag bits are removed from each 64B/65B block and grouped into a single byte at the end of the superblock. A CRC-16 checksum is computed and appended to the superblock. A variable number of superblocks may be present in a single GFP-T frame, depending on the SONET/SDH transport rate. The GFP core and GFP-T payload headers are then added to the superblocks to form a complete GFP frame.

Both GFP-F frames and GFP-T frames may be optionally terminated with a 4-byte FCS. The FCS consists of a CRC-32 sequence that protects the contents of the payload information field.

7.4.3   Physical Layer Interface

GFP uses a HEC-based frame delineation procedure, similar to ATM. Frames are placed on the physical link according to the byte boundary requirements of the medium in use (SONET/SDH or WDM). Both the core header and the payload information area contents are scrambled when transmitted and de-scrambled when received. If no GFP frames are available for transmission, idle frames are inserted into the transmission byte stream.

7.4.4 GFP Summary

The use of 64B/65B block encoding provides a block encoding for storage protocols that is much more efficient in terms of bandwidth usage than conventional 8B/10B encoding, and provides the low latency required for critical storage applications. The use of superframes enables GFP frames to be sized appropriately for the SONET/SDH transport rate employed, and enables efficient use of the fixed-rate bandwidth allocation provided by SONET/SDH. While GFP is relatively new, it is likely to be widely deployed for transport of storage protocols over SONET/SDH and WDM.

7.5 *SUMMARY – WAN/MAN PROTOCOLS*

WDM, SONET, and ATM are all widely used for storage transport over MAN and WAN distances, and each offers a different set of advantages. WDM offers low cost and high bandwidth capabilities, but lacks advanced OAM features. SONET is the most mature technology and offers advanced OAM and reliability features; it may be used for direct transport of storage protocols, IP over SONET, or ATM over SONET. However, bandwidth is assigned in fixed units, and will be wasted if not consumed. Also, use of HDLC framing for transport of data packets over SONET makes it necessary to encode escape sequences for flag and control characters found in user data, and increases the possibility of loss of data synchronization due to single-bit errors. ATM provides the ability to assign bandwidth in user-specifiable units, and provides a robust set of QOS guarantees. However, ATM is a relatively expensive option compared to the others, and makes somewhat inefficient use of bandwidth due to the 5-byte header overhead present in each cell. GFP is a new protocol which promises to make efficient use of SONET bandwidth while preserving the low latency and low error rate required for transport of critical storage data. Network developers should choose which protocol to use based on their unique requirements for cost-effectiveness, performance, and scaleability.

8

Storage Over IP

8.1 OVERVIEW

Transport of block storage data using the Internet and the TCP/IP protocol suite is a desirable goal, due to the ubiquity and availability of these technologies. Storage solutions making use of TCP/IP would provide the cost/performance advantages of Internet technology, and extend the distance over which the protocol would operate. Doing so requires the mapping of storage protocols, such as SCSI or Fibre Channel, to the standard TCP/IP protocol stack.

Applications making use of storage over IP technology would enable consolidation, pooling, and clustering of local storage, and would provide network client access to remote storage. Data mirroring could be supported as well as local and remote backup and recovery.

8.1.1 Standards

Work on IP storage was begun by the IETF IP Storage Working Group. This group has produced an RFC defining the requirements for SCSI over the Internet, RFC 3347, *Small Computer Systems Interface protocol over the Internet (iSCSI) Requirements and Design Considerations*. Drafts are currently in progress for the standards for Internet SCSI (iSCSI) (Satran *et al.*, 2003), Fibre Channel over

Distributed Storage Networks   Thomas C. Jepsen
© 2003 John Wiley & Sons, Ltd   ISBN: 0-470-85020-5

IP (FCIP) (Rajagopal *et al.*, 2002), and Fibre Channel over Internet, (iFCP) (iFCP, 2002). A draft is also in progress for the proposed iSCSI naming service, or iSNS (Tserg *et al.*, 2003).

Since the above-mentioned IETF documents are still at draft status as this book goes to press, the technical information in this section is subject to change and should be used for informational purposes only.

8.2 INTERNET SCSI (iSCSI)

The iSCSI protocol maps the SCSI remote procedure invocation model over the TCP protocol. (See Section 5.1 for a description of the SCSI protocol, and Section 5.5 for a description of TCP operation.) SCSI commands and responses are transported via iSCSI requests and iSCSI responses. An iSCSI request for which a response is expected is referred to as an iSCSI *task*. From the SCSI protocol viewpoint, communication between the initiator and the target is carried out by means of messages instead of by setting values on the control and data buses; the arbitration and selection phases of SCSI SPI are replaced by request/response messages. Instead of following the strict command/data/status/message subphases used in SCSI, iSCSI allows these phases to be combined for greater efficiency. For example, a command and its associated data may be combined into a single message. from the initiator to the target, and data and status may be returned from a target to an initiator in a single message. Figure 8.1 shows conceptual architecture for iSCSI.

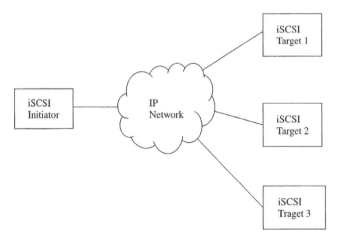

Figure 8.1 ISCSI conceptual architecture.

8.2.1   iSCSI Protocol Architecture

The iSCSI architecture uses a layered approach in which Command Descriptor Blocks (CDBs) are passed from the SCSI layer to the iSCSI layer. The iSCSI layer then builds iSCSI PDUs and passes them to the TCP layer, which provides initiator-target communication using one or more TCP connections. The set of TCP connections connecting an initiator to a target is referred to as a *session*. Across the session, the initiator sees a single target image on all connections, and the target sees a single initiator image on all TCP connections. Figure 8.2 shows the layering concept used in iSCSI.

8.2.2   Command, Response, and Data Sequence Numbering

Commands are numbered to ensure ordered delivery of commands over multiple connections during a session. iSCSI status responses

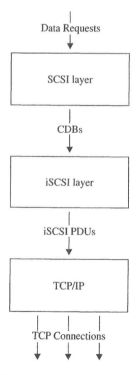

Figure 8.2   iSCSI protocol layering concept.

are also numbered for in-order delivery on a per-connection basis, to enable detection and recovery of missing status. Data sequences are numbered on a per-command basis to enable detection and recovery of missing data. Sequence numbers for commands, responses, and data sequences are contained in the iSCSI PDUs. Commands may be marked for immediate delivery.

8.2.3 iSCSI Login

iSCSI uses a login process to add a TCP connection to a session, authenticate the participating parties, and negotiate session parameters. Initiators connect to TCP ports to initiate login; targets listen on well-known port numbers for incoming connections. Once authentication has occurred and parameters have been set, the session transitions to the Full Feature phase and iSCSI commands and data may be sent by the initiator to the LUNs associated with the target. Figure 8.3 shows the state transitions for an iSCSI session for normal data transfer.

8.2.4 Command Allegiance

Once a session is established, *command allegiance* must be observed. This means that for any iSCSI request sent over a connection, the

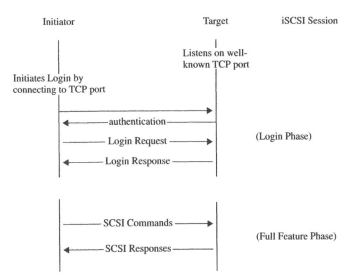

Figure 8.3   iSCSI session state transitions – normal data transfer.

corresponding data sequences and/or responses must be returned over the same connection.

8.2.5 Data Transfer

Data transfer from the initiator to the target may be solicited or unsolicited. Solicited data is sent in response to a ready-to-transfer (r2t) PDU sent by the target. Unsolicited data is immediate data sent as part of a request PDU, or in separate data PDUs. The maximum amount of unsolicited data that may be sent must be negotiated at login.

8.2.6 Connection Termination

Normal termination of a TCP connection is accomplished by the use of the FIN message (see Section 5.5.4.1, TCP/IP). For normal operation, the TCP connection is not terminated until after the session has left the Full Feature Phase.

8.2.7 iSCSI PDU Format

iSCSI PDUs consist of a basic header segment, optional additional header segments, an optional data segment, and an optional data digest segment. Figure 8.4 shows the format of the iSCSI PDU.

8.2.7.1 Basic Header Segment

The basic header is a fixed-length 48-byte segment. Figure 8.5 shows the format of the iSCSI PDU base header. All base headers must contain an opcode and a data segment length.

The I bit (byte 0, bit 1) indicates that the PDU is marked for immediate delivery. Opcodes (byte 0, bits 2-7) indicate the function of the PDU. Initiators and targets have separate opcode sets. Request PDUs use initiator opcodes. Response PDUs use target opcodes. Tables 8.1 and 8.2 list initiator and target opcodes, respectively.

The F (final) bit (byte 1, bit 0) indicates that this is the final (or only) PDU of a sequence. Meanings of the opcode-specific fields are dependent on the individual opcodes. The TotalAHSLength

Byte 0	Byte 1	Byte 2	Byte 3

Basic Header Segment (48 bytes)
Additional Header Segment 1 (optional)
Additional Header Segment 2 (optional)
Additional Header Segment n (optional)
Header Digest (optional)
Data Segment (optional)
Data Digest (optional)

Figure 8.4   iSCSI PDU format.

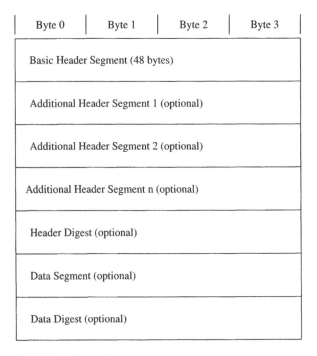

Figure 8.5   iSCSI PDU basic header segment format.

Table 8.1 Request PDU initiator opcodes

OpCode value	Name	Meaning
0×00	NOP – Out	Used by initiator to verify that a connection/session is still active
0×01	SCSI Command	PDU Encapsulates SCSI Command Descriptor Block
0×02	SCSI Task Management Function Request	Enables initiator to explicitly control execution of one or more tasks
0×03	Login Request	Used by initiator to initiate login to target
0×04	Text Request	Used to exchange information
0×05	SCSI Data Out	For Write operations
0×06	Logout Request	Used to perform a controlled closing of a connection
0×10	SNACK Request	Used by initiator to request retransmission of numbered responses, data, or R2T PDUs
0×1C–0×1E	Vendor-Specific Codes	

(byte 4) field gives the total length of the additional header segments in 4-byte segments, including padding. The DataSegmentLength (bytes 5-8) is the total length of the data segment payload, excluding padding. The LUN field (bytes 8-15) indicates the logical unit that the opcode operates on. The Initiator Task Tag (bytes 16-19) uniquely identifies a task within a session.

8.2.7.2 Additional Header Segments

Additional Header Segments are integer multiples of 4 bytes. Currently defined Additional Header Segments include Extended CDBs and Expected Bidirectional Read Data Length.

8.2.7.3 Header Digests and Data Digests

Header Digests and Data Digests are used to protect the integrity of the header and data segments. The Header Digest is located after the header segments and the data digest is located after the payload data of the PDU.

8.2.7.4 Data Segment

The data segment contains the PDU payload data. It is padded if necessary to an integer multiple of 4 bytes.

Table 8.2 Response PDU target opcodes

OpCode Value	Name	Meaning
0×20	NOP – In	Used by initiator to verify that a connection/session is still active
0×21	SCSI Response	Contains SCSI status and possibly sense information or other response information
0×22	SCSI Task Management Function Response	Response returned by target after performing requested task
0×23	Login Response	Indicates the progress and/or end of login phase
0×24	Text Response	Contains the target's response to the initiator's text request
0×25	SCSI Data In	For Read operations
0×26	Logout Response	Used by target to indicate if cleanup operation for the connection has completed
0×31	Ready to Transfer (R2T)	Sent by target when it is ready to receive data
0×32	Asynchronous Message	Sent by target to indicate special conditions
0×3C–0×3E	Vendor Specific Codes	
0×3F	Reject	Used to indicate an iSCSI error condition

8.2.8 iSCSI Names

Both targets and initiators use names for identification. An iSCSI node name is the SCSI device name of the iSCSI device. Note that the name is associated with the node, rather than with the HBA or interface card, to enable HBAs to be moved in the network without loss of state information. Since the range of operation over TCP/IP is world-wide, iSCSI names must be globally unique. An initiator may discover the names of targets to which it has access by using a discovery function.

iSCSI nodes also have iSCSI addresses. An iSCSI address consists of the iSCSI name plus an optional TCP transport (port) address. The iSCSI name may have one of three formats:

- An IPv4 address.
- An IPv6 address.
- A host name (e.g. mystorage.example.com).

For initiators, no port is specified. For targets, if no port is specified, the default IANA-assigned port of 3260 is used. iSCSI addresses may be assigned dynamically, and may change over time.

8.2.9 iSCSI Security

The use of a storage protocol over an IP network requires that security features be implemented. For iSCSI, this means that target and initiator logins must be validated to ensure that each request originates from a known legitimate node, and data packets must be protected against unauthorized 'eavesdropping.'

Two separate mechanisms are used to provide security for iSCSI implementations. In-band authentication is used to validate initiators and targets at the connection level, and IPSec, as specified in RFC2401, is used to provide packet protection at the IP level.

Targets must authenticate the initiator during login and initiators may optionally authenticate targets. Authentication is performed on every new iSCSI connection by an exchange of Login PDUs. Several different authentication implementations are possible; options are discussed in the iSCSI RFC.

The IPSec implementation must provide cryptographic integrity, data authentication, and confidentiality. Cryptographic integrity and data authentication are provided by means of a cryptographic keyed message authentication code sent in every packet. Confidentiality is provided by encrypting the data in every packet. The IPSec implementation for iSCSI must support Encapsulating Security Payload (ESP) for tunnel mode, and may support ESP for transport mode (see Section 10 for an overview of IPSec and ESP modes). For details, refer to the iSCSI RFC and the IPSec RFCs.

8.2.10 iSCSI Naming and Discovery

The iSCSI discovery mechanism enables each initiator to find the targets to which it has access, and to find the address of each target. There are several ways for iSCSI discovery to be performed. The simplest is to use static configuration to create a list of targets for each initiator. A more complex approach is to use a discovery mechanism to dynamically create a list of all available targets in the network, or all available targets at a specific network element.

Dynamic discovery may involve the use of a Storage Name Server (SNS), which can be queried by the initiator in a fashion similar to the use of DNS for the conventional Internet. There are several general-purpose discovery mechanisms which may be used by iSCSI. One that has been developed specifically for iSCSI by the IP Storage Working Group is Internet Storage Name Service (iSNS), which currently has the status of a working draft.

iSNS is intended to provide naming service and discovery capability similar to that provided by the Fibre Channel nameserver capability; it may be used not only by iSCSI networks, but also by iFCP networks which integrate Fibre Channel and IP. iSNS is intended to allow an IP storage network to be managed from a single point by employing an iSNS server to perform discovery for all iSNS clients.

iSNS clients initiate communication with an iSNS server using the iSNS Protocol (iSNSP). The iSNS server maintains a database of attribute information about all clients that have registered with the server. Functions of the iSNS server include the following:

- *Name Registration Service* – the name registration service enables storage network entities to register with and query the database. For iSCSI, both targets and initiators may register and query the database for information about other nodes.
- *Discovery Domain and Login Control* – the discovery domain allows storage nodes to be grouped into manageable domains, and to limit login attempts to those nodes in specific domains. Login control allows access control to be delegated to the iSNS server, so that only authorized initiators are allowed to login to specific targets.
- *State Change Notification* – state change notification allows the iSNS server to issue notifications about the operational state of storage nodes. Clients register to receive information about operational state changes.
- *Open Mapping between Fibre Channel and iSCSI Services* – the iSNS database stores information about both iSCSI and Fibre Channel devices, and is capable of storing mappings between both Fibre Channel devices and iSCSI proxy images, and between iSCSI devices and proxy Fibre Channel World Wide Names.

Figure 8.6 shows iSNS client registration and query operation.

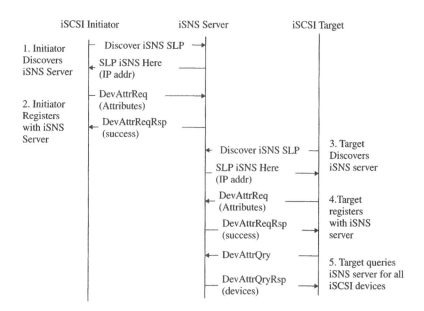

Figure 8.6 iSNS registration and query operation.

iSNS clients use the Service Location Protocol (SLP) to discover the IP address (or fully qualified domain name) of the iSNS server. Each client multicasts an SLP discovery message to obtain the iSNS server address. Once the client has the address of the iSNS server, it can send a Device Attribute Registration Request (DevAttrReg) message to the server containing operating attributes. If the request is successful, a Device Attribute Registration Request Response (DevAttrRegRsp) is returned with a 'success' parameter.

A registered client may query the iSNS server for the operating attributes of all storage nodes within its Discovery Domain by using a Device Attribute Query (DevAttrQry) message. The iSNS server will return a Device Attribute Query Response (DevAttrQryRsp) containing operating attributes for all storage devices specified in the message key of the DevAttrQry message.

8.3 FIBRE CHANNEL AND IP NETWORKS

The IETF IP Storage Working Group is currently developing two standards for providing transport of Fibre Channel frames over IP networks. Fibre Channel over TCP/IP (FCIP) is a tunneling mechanism which allows Fibre Channel SANs to be interconnected over

LAN, MAN, or WAN distances using IP networking. The Internet Fibre Channel Protocol (iFCP) standard specifies an implementation of Fibre Channel fabric functionality for an IP network. iFCP replaces the Fibre Channel switching and routing infrastructure described in Section 5.4 with IP components.

Both FCIP and iFCP make use of a generic Fibre Channel frame encapsulation format which enables transport of Fibre Channel frames over IP networks.

8.3.1 Fibre Channel Frame Encapsulation Format

The IETF IP Storage Working Group has defined an encapsulation format for Fibre Channel Frames which enables them to be transported as the payload of an IP packet (see Section 5.5.4.2 for IPv4 and IPv6 packet formats). The encapsulation format defines a 7-byte standard header for Fibre Channel frames, and provides an encoding for the Start Of Frame (SOF) and End Of Frame (EOF) frame delimiters. Figure 8.7 shows the encapsulation format used for transport of Fibre Channel frames over IP.

8.3.1.1 Header Field Definitions

The *Protocol#* field in word 0 contains an IANA-assigned value indicating which encapsulation protocol is in use. The *Version* field in word 0 indicates which version of the FC encapsulation is in use

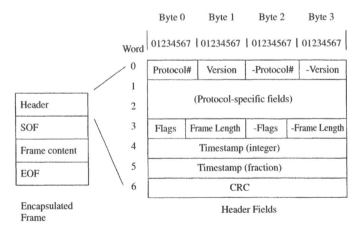

Figure 8.7 Fibre channel frame encapsulation format.

(currently 0×01). The *-Protocol#* and *-Version* fields contain the ones' complement of *Protocol#* and Version, respectively, and may be compared with those fields to validate a received encapsulated frame. Words 1 and 2 are reserved for use by the specific encapsulation protocol (e.g. FCIP or iFCP). All the bits of the *Flags* field (word 3, bits 0–5) are reserved for future use except bit 5, CRC Valid (CRCV). This bit is set to one when the CRC is valid; otherwise it is set to zero. The *Frame Length* (word 3, bits 6–15) contains an integer count of the total length of the encapsulated FC frame, including header, SOF, and EOF fields, in 32-bit words. *-Flags* and *-Frame Length* are the ones' complement of the Flags and Frame Length fields, respectively.

The *Timestamp (integer)* value in word 4 contains either (1) the number of elapsed seconds since midnight, January 1, 1900, at the time the encapsulated frame is placed in an output stream, or (2) the value zero, indicating an invalid time stamp. The *Timestamp (fraction)* field in word 5 contains a value indicating a fractional value of a whole second (e.g. a value of $0\times80000000 = 0.5$ second). The integer and fractional timestamp values are used to compute network transit time and to specify the lifetime of the encapsulated FC frame. The CRC field in word 6 contains either zero, if CRCV is zero, or a valid CRC for header words 0–5 if CRCV is equal to one.

Two mechanisms are defined for validating the header contents. The header may be validated by either comparing individual fields and their respective ones' complements, or by CRC validation.

8.3.1.2   SOF and EOF Fields

The SOF and EOF frame delimiters used by the Fibre Channel protocol are 10-bit ordered sets and have no 8-bit equivalents (see Section 5.4.6.1). Since TCP/IP is byte-ordered, equivalent values must be defined to enable transport of FC frame delimiters. The FC frame encapsulation values for SOF and EOF are given in Table 8.3.

FC service class 1 is not supported for frame encapsulation, and therefore SOFc1, SOFi1, and SOFn1 do not have byte encodings. The SOF and EOF encapsulation fields permit use of ones' complement fields for validation, similar to the header.

8.3.2   Fibre Channel over TCP/IP (FCIP)

Fibre Channel over IP (FCIP) enables Fibre Channel SANs to be interconnected using TCP/IP and the IP network. The FCIP

Table 8.3 FC frame encapsulation byte values for SOF and EOF

FC frame delimiter	Byte encoded value	FC service class
SOFf	0×28	(intrafabric communication)
SOFi2	0×2D	2
SOFn2	0×35	2
SOFi3	0×2E	3
SOFn3	0×36	3
SOFi4	0×29	4
SOFn4	0×31	4
SOFc4	0×39	4
EOFn	0×41	2,3,4,F
EOFt	0×42	2,3,4,F
EOFni	0×49	2,3,4,F
EOFa	0×50	2,3,4,F
EOFdt	0×46	4
EOFdti	0×4E	4
EOFrt	0×44	4
EOFrti	0×4F	4

standard defines an architecture for interworking between Fibre Channel and IP networks, the use and setup of TCP connections for control and data transport, and an encapsulation format.

8.3.2.1   FCIP Architecture

From a protocol layering standpoint, FCIP provides a mapping between the Fibre Channel FC0-FC2 layers (see Figure 5.22) and the TCP/IP protocol stack for network connectivity (see Figure 5.33). Figure 8.8 shows FCIP protocol layering.

Figure 8.9 shows a conceptual view of FCIP. In the FCIP architecture, an *FCIP entity* communicates with a peer FCIP entity across the IP network, and also with an *FC entity*, which provides an interface to a Fibre Channel fabric, as defined in Section 5.4. The connectivity across the IP network is referred to as an *FCIP Link*.

8.3.2.2   FCIP Classes of Service

FCIP supports Fibre Channel service classes 2, 3, and 4. Classes 1 and 6 are not supported.

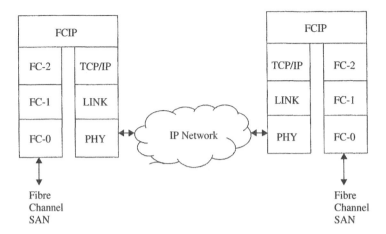

Figure 8.8   FCIP protocol layering.

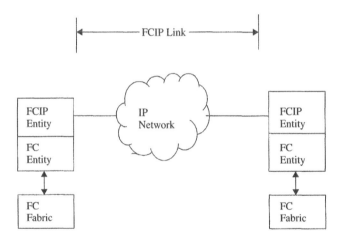

Figure 8.9   FCIP conceptual architecture.

8.3.2.3   FCIP Entity

An FCIP entity is a functional component which enables FCIP protocol exchanges across the IP network. It consists of two sub-components: (1) a *control and services module*; and (2) one or more *FCIP link endpoints*. Figure 8.10 shows FCIP entity architecture.

The Control & Services module provides control functions such as link initialization, and an interface to TCP/IP functions such as TCP connection establishment and discovery. It also implements security functions.

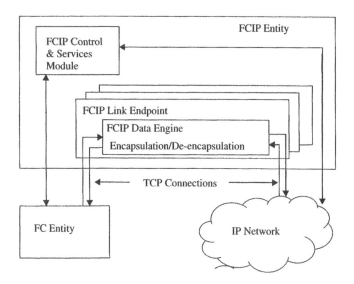

Figure 8.10 FCIP entity architecture.

TCP connections are established for each link endpoint that wishes to transfer storage data. When an FCIP entity determines that a new connection is needed, it finds the IP address, worldwide name, QoS information, and security information relating to the peer FCIP entity and sends a connection request to it on the well-known port number for FCIP (3225). Multiple connections may exist simultaneously between two FCIP entities.

Each FCIP link endpoint contains an *FCIP data engine*, which performs encapsulation of FC frames in the FC-to-IP direction, and de-encapsulation of FCIP frames in the IP-to-FC direction.

8.3.2.4 FCIP Frame Encapsulation

Figure 8.11 shows the encapsulation format for FCIP. Table 8.4 lists FCIP encapsulation fields and their meanings.

8.3.2.5 FCIP Special Frame (FSF)

An FCIP Special Frame (FSF) is the first frame sent on a newly created TCP connection. Only one FSF is sent in each direction. Figure 8.12 shows the format of an FSF. The *Source FC/FCIP Entity Identifier* in words 10–11 is a unique identifier assigned by the FC fabric entity whose world wide name is given in words 8–9.

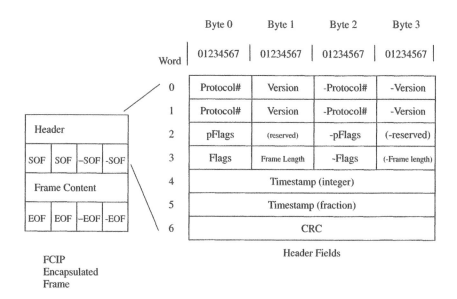

Figure 8.11   FCIP encapsulation format.

Table 8.4   FCIP encapsulation fields and their meanings

Field	Meaning
Protocol#	IANA-assigned protocol number (iFCP = 1)
Version	Encapsulation version
-Protocol#	Ones' complement of protocol#
-Version	Ones' complement of version
pFlags	Protocol specific flags. SF (bit 7): Special Frame bit. Indicate FC encapsulated frame (SF = 0) or FCIP special frame (FSF) (SF = 1). Ch (bit 0): Changed bit. Indicates FSF unchanged (Ch = 0); FSF changed (Ch = 1).
(reserved)	Reserved (all 0s)
-pFlags	Ones' complement of pFlags
(-reserved)	Ones' complement of reserved (255)
Flags	Encapsulation flags. For FCIP, CRCV must be 0.
Frame Length	Length of entire encapsulated FC frame in 32-bit words, including header, SOF word, and EOF word
-Flags	Ones' complement of Flags field
-Frame Length	Ones' complement of Frame Length field
Time Stamp (integer)	Integer component of time stamp
Time Stamp (fraction)	Fractional component of time stamp
Header CRC	Set to all 0s

Byte 0   Byte 1   Byte 2   Byte 3

Word | 01234567 | 01234567 | 01234567 | 01234567 |

Word	
0–6	Header
7	(reserved)
8–9	Source FC Fabric Entity World Wide Name
10–11	Source FC/FCIP Entity Identifier
12–13	Connection Nonce
14	Connection Usage Flags | (reserved) | Connection Usage Code
15–16	Destination FC Fabric Entity World Wide Name
17	Keep Alive Timeout Value (KA_TOV)
18	(reserved)

Figure 8.12 FCIP Special Frame (FSF) format.

The *Connection Nonce* in words 12–13 is a 64-bit random number assigned to uniquely identify a TCP connection request.[1] Bits 0–3 of the *Connection Usage Flags* indicate if frames for intrafabric communication, service class 2, class 3 or class 4, respectively, will be transported via the TCP connection. The *Connection Usage Code* field contains information on how the connection will be used as specified in FC-BB-2.[2] The Connection Usage Flags and the Connection Usage Codes together define the QOS requirements for the connection. The *Keep Alive Timeout Value (KA_TOV)* specifies the FC keep alive timeout value to be applied to the new TCP connection.

If all the contents of the FSF are correct and acceptable to the receiving FCIP entity, it simply echoes the FSF back to the sender with no changes. If the receiver wishes to makes changes to FSF fields (e.g. change the destination FC fabric entity world wide name), the FSF is returned back with the necessary changes and the changed flag in the header set to 1 (Ch = 1).

8.3.2.6 FCIP Security

FCIP uses IPSec for authentication and confidentiality, and uses Internet Key Exchange (IKE) for the key management protocol. Both are discussed in Chapter 10.

---

[1] According to *Webster's Dictionary*, a 'nonce' is a word coined for a single occasion.
[2] *Fibre Channel Backbone–2 (FC-BB-2)*, T111 Project 1466-D, http://www.t11.org/t11/docreg.nsf/1d1/fc-bb-2.

8.3.3   Internet Fibre Channel Protocol (iFCP)

8.3.3.1   iFCP Architecture

Figure 8.13 shows an example iFCP fabric implementation. In this model, Fibre Channel devices accessing the iFCP fabric are assigned to gateway regions, each with an iFCP gateway. Similar to the standard Fibre Channel architecture, Fibre Channel devices perform N-Port-to-N_Port communication through F-Ports on the iFCP fabric gateway. The iFCP gateway appears to be a fabric switch to the connected Fibre Channel devices. Each iFCP gateway has an iFCP portal which provides an interface to the IP network. An iFCP layer is implemented to provide the following functions:

- Frame addressing and mapping.
- Encapsulation/De-encapsulation of Fibre Channel frames.
- Establishment of an iFCP session in response to a PLOGI.

8.3.3.2   iFCP Classes of Service

iFCP supports Fibre Channel service classes 2 and 3. Classes 1, 4, and 6 are not supported.

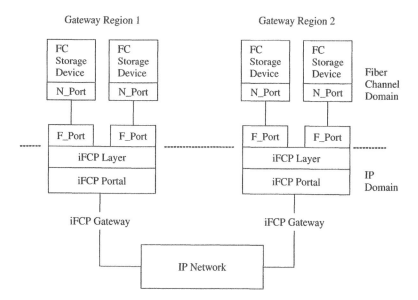

Figure 8.13   Example iFCP fabric implementation.

8.3.3.3   iFCP Discovery and Management Functions

iFCP uses iSNS for discovery and configuration management purposes. iSNS must support the following functions for iFCP:

- Fibre Channel nameserver functions, including notification of configuration changes;
- Support of zoning through the use of device discovery domains;
- Storage and distribution of security policies;
- Support of the Fibre Channel broadcast mechanism.

8.3.3.4   iFCP Bounded and Unbounded Fabrics

iFCP gateways may be part of a bounded fabric, or an unbounded fabric. In a bounded fabric, each N_Port address has fabric-wide scope. The Domain ID part of the N_Port address (see Section 5.4.5.4) is assigned to each iFCP gateway by the iSNS server. In bounded fabrics, a transparent addressing scheme is used in which the destination N_Port address is used directly for N_Port-to-N_Port communication. However, the scaleability of bounded networks is limited by the range of Domain IDs which may be assigned by the iSNS server (1–239).

To address this issue, unbounded fabrics may be used. In an unbounded fabric, N_Port addresses have local scope only. A principal switch element within a gateway region assigns Domain IDs to individual iFCP gateways. An address translation scheme is used to permit communication with remote N_Ports residing in different gateway regions. In this scheme, each iFCP gateway assigns local-scope addresses to each of its local N_Ports. It may also assign an address referring to an N_Port on a remote gateway. To communicate with that remote N_Port, the local gateway establishes an N_Port alias for the remote N_Port during device discovery. The local gateway then creates a descriptor consisting of the World Wide Name of the remote port and its N_Port alias. When the remote gateway receives incoming frames with the destination alias address in the header, it replaces the destination alias address with the local-scope address of the N_Port, replaces the source address with its alias address for the source, and recomputes the CRC checksum for the frame.

All iFCP gateways must support unbounded fabrics and address translation. Support of bounded fabrics and transparent addressing is optional.

8.3.3.5 iFCP Sessions

An iFCP session consists of a pair of N_Ports connected by a single TCP/IP connection. Only a single session may exist at any time between two N_Ports. An N_Port participating in an iFCP session is uniquely identified by its N_Port ID and an iFCP portal address, consisting of an IP address and TCP port.

iFCP may create pools of TCP connections for use in session creation, in order to reduce connection setup time. A TCP connection currently participating in a session is referred to as a *bound* connection, and a connection not currently participating in a session is referred to as an *unbound* connection. When the iFCP layer creates a new session, it may select an existing unbound connection, or establish a new connection.

8.3.3.6 iFCP Frame Encapsulation

iFCP encapsulates Fibre Channel frames by adding a 7-byte header to the frame and providing encodings for the SOF and EOF ordered sets. Figure 8.14 shows encapsulation for Fibre Channel frames. Table 8.5 lists the header, SOF, and EOF fields and their meanings.

Note that the SOF and EOF encodings appear in the header as well as at the beginning and end of the frame content. The SOF byte appears twice in the SOF word preceding the frame content,

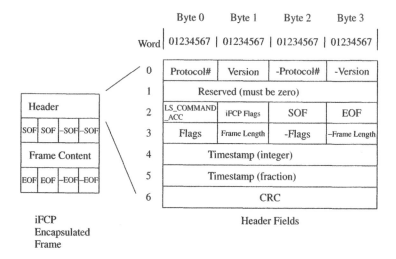

Figure 8.14 iFCP Fibre Channel frame encapsulation.

Table 8.5 iFCP Fibre Channel frame encapsulation fields and their meanings

Field	Meaning
Protocol#	IANA-assigned protocol number (iFCP = 2)
Version	Encapsulation version
-Protocol#	Ones' complement of protocol#
-Version	Ones' complement of version
LS_COMMAND_ACC	Used for special link service ACC response
iFCP Flags	Flags specifying special control frame (TRP and SPC = 0), address transparent mode enabled (TRP = 1), address translation mode enabled (TRP = 0, or frame is part of link service message requiring special processing (SPC = 1)
SOF	Start of Frame encoding.
EOF	End of Frame encoding.
Flags	Encapsulation flags. For iFCP, CRCV must be 1.
Frame Length	Length of entire encapsulated FC frame in 32-bit words, including header, SOF word, and EOF word
-Flags	Ones' complement of Flags field
-Frame Length	Ones' complement of Frame Length field
Time Stamp (integer)	Integer component of time stamp
Time Stamp (fraction)	Fractional component of time stamp
Header CRC	Header CRC

in bytes 0 and 1; its ones' complement appears in bytes 3 and 4. The EOF word following the frame content is formatted identically.

8.3.3.7 R_A_TOV and Use of Time Stamp

In the Fibre Channel protocol, the R_A_TOV timer is used to determine the maximum amount of time that a frame from a failed exchange may remain in the fabric (see Section 5.4.5.6). For iFCP, R_A_TOV is used to enforce a maximum 'time to live' value for encapsulated iFCP packets by using the time stamp values in the header. For iFCP, R_A_TOV should include both the propagation delays through the gateways and the propagation delay through the IP network. The propagation delay through the IP network is referred to as IP_TOV, and should be stored in the iSNS server. R_A_TOV should be set to twice the value of IP_TOV.

8.3.3.8   iFCP Security

iFCP uses IPSec for authentication and confidentiality, and uses Internet Key Exchange (IKE) for the key management protocol. Both are discussed in Chapter 10.

8.4   SUMMARY

While IP-based storage has been widely discussed in the media, actual adoption has been slow, due in part to a lack of standards. The IETF is currently in the process of finalizing the specifications for iSCSI, FCIP, and iFCP, and it is envisioned that the completion of these standards will lead to widespread adoption of IP storage technologies. IP storage uses well known and inexpensive technologies, and can operate over virtually unlimited distances. However, there are some practical limitations to storage transport over IP that must be considered. First of all, delay is not bounded in the public Internet, and is difficult to control even in private networks. High-performance, low latency applications using traditional storage protocols such as ESCON or Fibre Channel normally assume constant delay for proper operation; operations may time out if unanticipated delay occurs. Secondly, high rates of packet loss are the norm in IP networks. Typically, between 0.3% and 1% of all packets in the Internet are lost and must be re-transmitted. Applications which require low latency and cannot tolerate packet loss, such as real-time synchronous database mirroring, are not well suited for IP storage protocols. Storage applications tend to retransmit lost data at the block level, which is more performance-affecting than recovery at the byte or packet level.

Another issue is the use of TCP as the transport protocol for IP storage. The use of TCP has caused much controversy during the development of the IP storage specifications. TCP is byte-oriented, rather than block-oriented; software implementations are inefficient and use up much processing time. TCP's sliding window flow control is incompatible with the credit-based flow control used by storage protocols such as Fibre Channel. TCP also discards packets when congestion occurs. Some have argued that TCP should be replaced with a block-oriented protocol specifically intended for storage transport. However, others argued for the advantages of using a widely used and well understood protocol, and as a result, TCP was retained as the transport layer for IP storage.

One solution to the TCP performance problem has been to use TCP/IP Offload Engines (TOEs), which implement a TCP/IP protocol stack in hardware, rather than in software as part of the operating system, as is normally done. However, this approach may cause conflicts with other applications over protocol specifics such as load balancing and routing paths.

Nevertheless, distributed storage applications that are not delay-sensitive, such as remote backup, electronic vaulting, or non-realtime asynchronous mirroring, may well benefit from the cost-effective use of IP storage. Also, iSCSI will likely see much use as an inexpensive alternative to Fibre Channel for extending the range of SCSI buses locally, in the building or across the campus.

9

Storage Management Requirements

Storage networks are typically heterogeneous networks embedding products from multiple vendors and using multiple protocols. Most vendors provide management tools intended to facilitate the installation, operation, and maintenance of their products. While these tools are useful for performing vendor-specific functions, their use of vendor- and product-specific schemas for equipment codes, location codes, and error conditions make it difficult to provide the system user with a single unified view of the network. The use of multiple protocols and geographically distributed locations adds to the complexity of storage management. This chapter discusses techniques for integrating storage management, and standardization work being undertaken by the Storage Networking Industry Association (SNIA).

9.1 OVERVIEW

Clearly, development of a vendor- and protocol-neutral storage management architecture is a desirable goal. Such an architecture would address the following requirements:

- *Ubiquitous management* – the ability to monitor and control all network resources from any location at any time.

Distributed Storage Networks   Thomas C. Jepsen
© 2003 John Wiley & Sons, Ltd   ISBN: 0-470-85020-5

- *Outage impact assessment* – the ability to show the impact of component outages on applications and users.
- *User friendliness* – the ability to provide a consistent, intuitive, and secure user interface.
- *Security* – the ability to manage user access and administrative domains
- *Common information model* – the use of a common information model enables information sharing.
- *High availability* – a high-availability architecture supports non-stop processing.
- *Scaleability* – scaleable from standalone solutions to enterprise frameworks.
- *Compatibility* – the ability to support existing instrumentation and management protocols.
- *Coordination* – the ability to synchronize management operations with applications.

Integrated storage management also leads to a lower total cost of ownership for managed storage networks. For networks with nonintegrated management, the cost of performing management functions is significant, and may exceed the cost of hardware. Use of an integrated management solution leads to significantly reduced management costs over time.

9.2 STANDARDS

Standardization of storage management is a major focus of the Storage Networking Industry Association (SNIA), an international computer industry forum consisting of over 100 storage vendors. The SNIA has a number of working groups focused on storage management issues, including:

- A shared storage model, providing a generic model for storage system architecture, including distributed storage systems.
- Implementation of the Common Information Model (CIM) developed by the Distributed Management Task Force (DMTF), for representing storage network components and functions in an object-oriented fashion.

- Implementation of the Web-Based Enterprise Management (WBEM) model, developed by the DMTF for web-based management of storage systems.

The SNIA is working with other industry organizations and standards groups to produce these standards, including the DMTF, the ANSI T10 and T11 Technical Committees, the IEEE, the IETF, and the Fibre Channel Industry Association (FCIA).[1]

9.3 THE SNIA SHARED STORAGE MODEL

So far, we have dealt with the architecture of various distributed storage networks by simply describing them in an ad hoc fashion, with no attempt to define underlying concepts or create a unified architectural model. However, to create management applications for distributed storage networks that may use equipment from multiple vendors or multiple protocols, a generic model is needed.

9.3.1 Shared Storage Model Architecture Overview

One of the primary requirements for management of a storage network is a generic layered architectural model which enables management to be performed transparently in a vendor- and protocol-neutral manner. The SNIA shared storage model, as illustrated in Figure 9.1, provides such a framework.

As shown in Figure 9.1, the SNIA model divides the storage domain into a *file/record layer*, a *block layer*, and a *services subsystem*. The file/record layer allows application clients to directly access database records, perform file-based database access, and perform file system access of file-structured documents. The block layer includes both low-level storage devices and block-based aggregation. It provides three levels of abstraction for block-structured data: *host blocking*, the block structure used by the host computer; *network blocking*, the blocking used by the storage network protocol; and *device blocking*, the block structure used by the actual storage device. The services subsystem provides the functions to manage the storage components.

---

[1] As this books goes to press, the SNIA has just released a preliminary version of its Storage Management Initiative Specification (SMI-S), which provides a common object and management model to support multi-vendor storage interoperability.

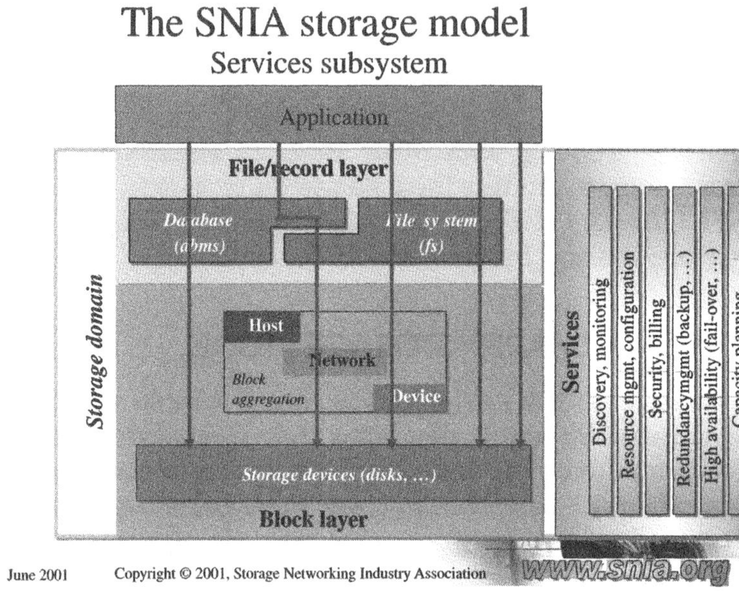

Figure 9.1   SNIA shared storage model.

9.3.2   Components of the Shared Storage Model

The file/record layer, the block layer, and the services subsystem may be implemented by a combination of physical and logical components. These normally include the following:

- *Interconnection network* – the network infrastructure that connects the elements of the shared storage environment. This network may be dedicated for storage purposes, or shared with other applications. Fibre Channel and Gigabit Ethernet networks are common examples. Various types of redundancy may be used to protect against data loss or network failure.

- *Host computer* – the host computer provides the environment in which application clients execute. Its storage requirements are met by the shared storage environment. A host computer connects to storage domain components by means of an HBA or NIC card.

- *Physical storage resources* – physical storage resources are shared storage environment components that are attached by the interconnection network. Physical storage resources include disk drives, disk arrays, storage controllers, tape drives, tape libraries, and storage appliances.

- *Storage device* – a storage device is a specific type of physical storage resource that persistently stores data, such as tape or disk storage.
- *Logical storage resources* – abstractions or services used to perform storage functions within the storage environment. Volumes, files, and data movers are examples of logical storage resources.

Storage Management components are also part of the shared storage environment. This includes components that observe, control, report on, or implement logical storage resources.

9.3.3 Layer Definitions

Each of the layers of the SNIA Shared Storage Model is defined in the following sections.

9.3.3.1 File/Record Layer

The file/record layer performs a translation function between the file or record representation of data seen by the application, and the volume or logical unit representation of data utilized by the storage domain. Database management systems typically map records or tuples into tables, and tables into volumes, while file-based applications map bytes of data into files, and files into volumes.

File/record layer functions may be performed completely in the host, or shared between a client and server. Traditional file management systems and database management systems perform file/record layer functions in the host; network file sharing applications like NFS and CIFS share file/record functions between a host client and a server. Different implementations may use a *file server*, a *NAS head*, or the storage device itself as the server. A file server is a host computer with block storage devices dedicated to the shared file serving application. A NAS head is a special-function computer acting as a file server that is connected to external block storage through a storage network.

9.3.3.2 Block Layer

The block level provides multiple levels of block aggregation between the data organization presented to the application and the device-level blocking employed by the storage device. Different aggregation techniques can be used to improve the performance and reliability of shared storage environments. Common aggregation functions include:

- *Space management* – constructing a large block vector by assembling several smaller ones. A common example of this is the creation of a virtual volume by aggregating multiple sectors of data from several disk storage devices.
- *Striping* – apportioning the load across several lower-level block vectors to increase throughput and reduce latency. Striping is sometimes referred to as a *scatter-write, gather-read* function, in which the gather-read portion is an aggregation function.
- *Redundancy* – increasing the availability of stored data. Redundancy involves creating multiple copies of data to ensure availability. Recovery procedures may involve aggregating data from both primary storage and secondary storage sites.

Block aggregation functions are not confined to specific components, and may be implemented in a variety of ways. In the host computer, aggregation functions may be performed by virtual volume managers, device drivers, or HBAs. Block aggregation may be performed in the storage network itself by storage appliances. Storage devices such as RAID controllers may also perform aggregation functions.

9.3.3.3 Services Subsystem

The services subsystem consists of management functions, including:

- *Discovery* – the ability to use a nameserver or similar function to discover storage network entities.
- *Monitoring* – the ability to monitor significant system events, such as failures and configuration changes.
- *Resource management* – the ability to manage resource utilization and prioritize resource assignment.
- *Configuration management* – the ability to add, modify, or delete network components.
- *Security* – the ability to administer security functions such as password protection and access control.

- *Billing* – the ability to bill customers for specific services.
- *Redundancy management* – the ability to manage redundancy functions such as backup and mirroring.
- *High availability* – the ability to specify criteria for performing availability functions such as failover.
- *Capacity planning* – the ability to automate capacity planning functions, such as resource utilization monitoring.

9.3.4   Integrating the Block and File/Record Layers

Figure 9.2 integrates the file/record architecture and the block-based architecture to create a generic architecture that is vendor- and protocol-neutral. Moving from left to right, this figure illustrates the following integrated storage architectures:

- *Direct attachment,* in which local private storage is directly attached to a single host. This is shown at (1) on the left side of Figure 9.2 by a host computer running a Logical Volume Manager (LVM), which provides software RAID functionality at the host block aggregation level on non-shared directly attached storage.

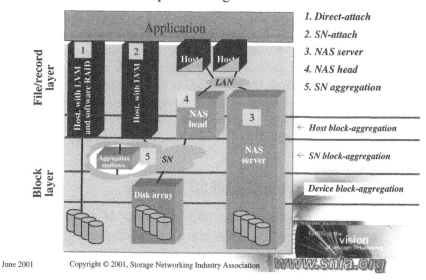

Figure 9.2   Integrated file/record and block architectures.

- *Storage network attachment*, in which a host is connected to a storage array through a storage network. A host computer is shown at (2) in Figure 9.2 attached to a storage network providing shared access to a disk array. Multiple levels of block aggregation may be taking place in this configuration, as it is possible to have aggregation taking place both in the host LVM and in the disk array controller itself. (For example, the disk array might be providing RAID 1 redundancy to improve the availability of the LVM's virtual volume.) Additionally, aggregation (e.g. striping) may be performed at the storage network level by an aggregation appliance, as at (5) in Figure 9.2.
- *NAS head attachment*, in which a NAS head at (4) in Figure 9.2 is used to provide storage access for LAN-connected hosts.
- *NAS server attachment*, in which storage access is provided by a NAS head/file server at (3) in Figure 9.2 and its own private storage.

9.3.5 The Multi-Site Model for Distributed Storage Networking

One of the strengths of the SNIA model is that it can be extended to represent multi-site distributed storage. As shown in Figure 9.3, peer-to-peer remote replication functions can be performed at the host, network, or device blocking levels. Replication at the host blocking level includes the processor-centric model discussed in Section 1.5.2, in which the host processor is aware of the remote image and issues commands to write to it. Replication at the device blocking level includes the storage-centric model discussed in Section 1.5.2, in which the replication is performed at the device controller level. (Replication at the network level using aggregation appliances represents a 'middle-path' approach which could be termed 'network-centric.')

9.4 THE SNIA MANAGEMENT MODEL

To demonstrate interoperability and the value of vendor-neutral management solutions, the SNIA has developed prototype storage management systems and test suites using existing management tools and technologies. Some of the key elements of these management solutions include:

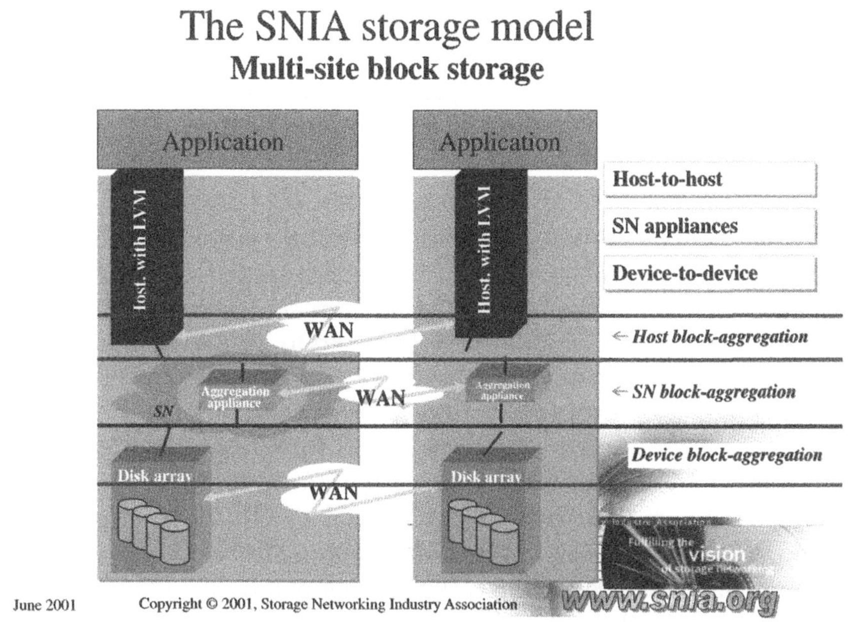

Figure 9.3   SNIA model for multi-site storage networking.

- The Common Information Model (CIM) schema to organize data and provide semantics.
- Web Based Element Model (WBEM) to exchange data and management requests.
- XML DTD for CIM and XML Stylesheet Language (XSL) for display.

9.4.1   Common Information Model (CIM)

The Common Information Model (CIM) was developed by the Distributed Management Task Force (DMTF) to provide an object-oriented paradigm for the management of systems and networks. The use of object-oriented constructs and a uniform modeling formalism makes the CIM well-suited for modeling vendor- and protocol-neutral storage networks.

CIM defines a management schema that consists of three parts:

- A *Core Model* that is applicable to all management domains.
- *Common Models* that are applicable to a specific management domain (such as systems, applications, devices, networks) but

technology-independent. Common models are subclassed from the core model.

- An *Extension Schema* that provides technology-specific (and vendor-specific) extensions to the common models.

The CIM enables all of the components of a managed storage network, such as systems, networks, physical equipment, and software, to be managed as entities in an object model, and it permits enterprise-level management to be performed across management domains. Use of a CIM eliminates the need to 're-invent the wheel' each time a new component is introduced into a storage network, or a new management application is developed.

Figure 9.4 shows the CIM core model for storage management in Unified Modeling Language (UML) format. CIM may also be expressed in Managed Object Format (MOF) or in Extensible Markup Language (XML). The XML mapping for CIM is defined in a Document Type Definition (DTD) developed by the DMTF.

The classes in the CIM model use conventional UML notation. The lines with an arrow pointing toward the superclass represent inheritance. The lines with the name of the association in the middle of the line represent associations. The lines with the diamond symbol pointing toward the aggregate entity represent aggregation. In the CIM core model, system elements may be *physical* or *logical*. Physical elements are objects in the real world that occupy space and obey the laws of physics. Logical elements are abstractions that are used to manage the physical environment and/or represent system state or capabilities. Some logical elements in the model include:

- *Systems*. A grouping of other logical elements. Since systems themselves are logical elements, a system can comprise other systems.
- *Network Components*. Network components are used to provide a topological view of a network.
- *Services and Access Points*. Services and access points provide a mechanism for accessing the capabilities of a system.
- *Devices*. Devices are abstractions of hardware entities that may or may not be realized by physical hardware.

A *Managed System Element* class provides a base class for the system element hierarchy. Any system component may be included in

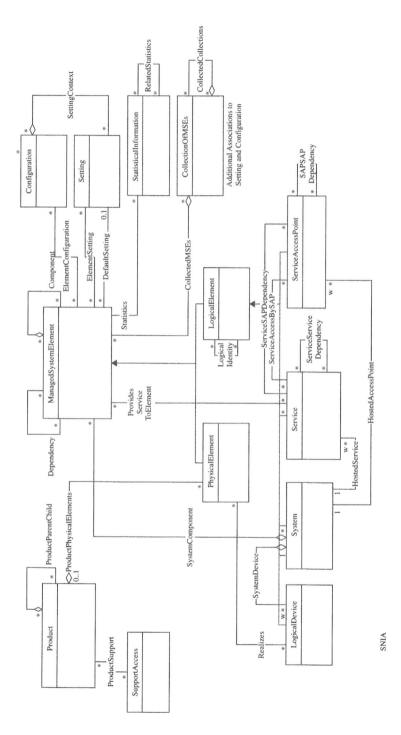

Figure 9.4   CIM core model.

this class, including software components, files, disk drives, and integrated circuits. A *Statistical Information* class provides a base class under which all statistical properties are placed.

A *Logical Element* is the base class for all abstract system components, such as profiles, processes, or capabilities. A *System* is a logical element that aggregates an enumerable set of managed system elements. A *Service* is a logical element that contains the information necessary to represent and manage the functionality provided by a device and/or software feature.

The CIM Core Model was used to create an object model for a disk resource manager (DRM) prototype, to be used for demonstration purposes. A portion of the object model developed by SNIA is shown in Figure 9.5.

9.4.2 Web Based Enterprise Management (WBEM)

Web Based Enterprise Management (WBEM) is a set of technologies that enable web-based management of enterprise networks. WBEM is actually a unifying architecture which was specified by the DMTF to enable data to be accessed from a variety of underlying platforms and technologies, and presented in a consistent manner. The set of technologies comprising WBEM includes:

- The CIM schema.
- An XML DTD to encode the schema.
- Support for CIM operations over HTTP.

Figure 9.6 shows the generic WBEM architecture. *Object Providers* are software functions written by storage device vendors to provide instrumentation, or management functions, for their products. A number of different protocols are in common use for instrumentation, including SNMP/MIB for network devices, DMI/MIF for desktop devices, and CMIP/GDMO for telecommunications devices. Support of multiple instrumentation protocols enables WBEM to support heterogeneous systems in a transparent fashion. The *CIM Object Manager* (CIMOM) provides access to CIM managed objects for update or retrieval purposes. Object providers communicate with CIMOM using either Remote Method Invocation (RMI) for Java-based implementations, or Distributed Component Object Model (DCOM) for the Windows Management Instrumentation (WMI) implementation. The CIMOM interface to management applications or clients uses XML over HTTP.

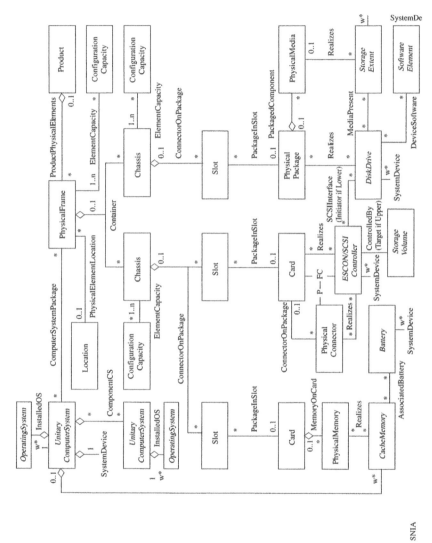

Figure 9.5 CIM object model for disk resource manager prototype.

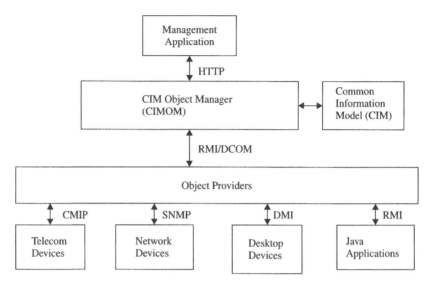

Figure 9.6 Web Based Enterprise Management (WBEM) architecture.

9.4.3 XML

Extensible Markup Language (XML) is a subset of Standard Generalized Markup Language which has found wide usage for data interchange among applications. The syntax and rules for XML have been standardized in recommendations developed by the World Wide Web Consortium (W3C). The application-specific vocabularies for XML are defined in Document Type Definitions (DTDs). The XML mapping for CIM and the CIM XML DTD were developed by the DMTF. An example of XML representation for CIM objects is shown in Figure 9.7.

Unlike HTML, XML elements do not contain information on how to display the data. In order to display XML data items, as, for example, in a web browser, an XML Stylesheet Language (XSL) must be used to specify formatting of the displayed data. The prototype management functions developed by the SNIA make use of XSL to display CIM data in a browser.

9.5 THE SNIA PROTOTYPE

To demonstrate that storage management of a heterogenous multi-vendor storage network using existing tools and technologies is possible, the SNIA has developed a prototype application for retrieving the physical inventory of a network, and doing capacity

```
<?XML Version="1.0"?>
<!DOCTYPE CIM SYSTEM
    "http://www.dmtf.org/cim-v2.dtd/">
<CIM VERSION="2.0">
  <CLASS NAME="ManagedSystemElement">
    <QUALIFIER NAME="abstract"
     TYPE="boolean">
      <VALUE>TRUE</VALUE></QUALIFIER>
    <PROPERTY NAME="Caption" TYPE="string">
      <QUALIFIER NAME="MaxLen" TYPE="sint32">
      <VALUE>64</VALUE></QUALIFIER>
    <\PROPERTY>
    <PROPERTY NAME="Description" TYPE="string">
    <\PROPERTY>
  </CLASS>
</CIM >
```

Figure 9.7   Example XML representation of CIM object.

analysis. In this prototype application, inventory information about each vendor's equipment is stored in a separate WBEM server. A resource manager maintains a directory of WBEM servers. Directory entries may be added or deleted using a web browser-based add/delete function.

A web-based physical inventory function first discovers the existence of a WBEM server for a specific vendor by using a discovery function to do a directory lookup in the resource manager. The physical inventory function then may access the WBEM server directly, and obtain the inventory data for that vendor's equipment. The data is displayed to the user in a format determined by the web pages and style sheets served by the resource manager. Figure 9.8 shows a diagram of the SNIA prototype application.

The prototype demonstrates some of the strengths of the SNIA/WBEM management model:

- It is web-based, and thus management may be performed wherever it is required.
- The architecture may be geographically distributed in terms of both servers and browsers.
- It is scaleable, in terms of the number of vendors supported and the number of elements in each vendor.
- The CIM object model is capable of supporting multiple management applications using the same set of objects and attributes.
- It is management-protocol neutral, since separate providers can be developed for each required management protocol, and the

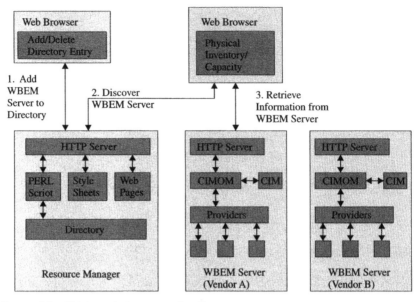

Figure 9.8   SNIA prototype application.

CIMOM is capable of mapping each management protocol to the CIM.

The SNIA prototype was developed for demonstration purposes only, and provides just one management capability – the ability to display an inventory of equipment and the characteristics of each unit. However, the prototype also enables some capacity planning to be done, based on this information. Creating a complete set of management functions would require additional development. For example, adding an event management function would require adding state information for each managed element, and providing notifications of state change. A security management function would require the ability to set and change user passwords, add users to access control lists, and administer functions such as public key encryption. Servers would need the ability to authenticate clients before permitting access. All of these functions could be built around the same management model.

9.6   DISTANCE CONSIDERATIONS FOR STORAGE MANAGEMENT

The SNIA/WBEM management model makes it possible to manage a distributed storage network from any physical location by using a web browser. Some specific design considerations arise when developing a storage management application for a distributed network:

- *Clearly identifying physical location.* The application should identify not only the frame and slot location of components, but also the geographic location, in terms of city, address, building, and room number. Installation and maintenance of physical components often requires a site visit by support personnel, and ensuring that this level of information is clearly presented by the user interface is an important design consideration.

- *Accurately timestamping system events.* It is important to remember that system events may take place in different parts of the world, and in different local time zones. Accurate event correlation is of critical importance in determining the root cause of system failures. Additional functionality may need to be developed to ensure that timestamping is correctly synchronized.

- *Coordination and synchronization of scheduled activities.* Backup windows may be scheduled at different times in different parts of the network, and master scheduling algorithms must take local considerations into account.

- *Security.* Use of a web-based interface creates a requirement for controlling access to the management functions. Password protection, access control lists, and encryption are all elements to be considered.

9.7 SUMMARY

The SNIA shared storage model provides a generic layered architectural model which enables management to be performed transparently in a vendor- and protocol-neutral manner. Use of the CIM and WBEM management models developed by the DMTF provides the necessary tools to design and implement an integrated management system that is secure and scaleable, and provides management of geographically distributed components in a transparent manner.

Design of an integrated management system for distributed storage systems should focus on operational workflow. Items to consider include:

- Automatic provisioning and configuration.
- Discovery of system elements.

- Realtime statistics reporting.
- Alarms and alarm reporting.
- Chargebacks for storage requests.
- Secure access from multiple locations.

10

Security Considerations

Storage protocols were originally intended to be used inside a frame or cabinet, or at most to remain within the bounds of a secure computing facility. Thus, security features for protocols such as bus/tag or SCSI were largely nonexistent. With the advent of storage protocols that operated over greater distances, and might be transported over public networks, the need arose for additional security features to ensure the integrity and privacy of critical customer data.

10.1 OVERVIEW

Ensuring that a storage network is secure, however, requires more than just implementing the built-in features of the protocols. It involves developing a security policy, and incorporating it into the architecture of the storage system.

In general, the architecture of the distributed storage network will determine the level of security planning that is required. The first level of security planning is represented by the enterprise network, in which all of the network components are owned and operated by the enterprise itself, including the site-to-site WAN. This can be considered to be the most 'friendly' environment from a security risk analysis standpoint.

The next level is represented by the distributed network which makes use of a public carrier for WAN connectivity. In this case,

Distributed Storage Networks   Thomas C. Jepsen
© 2003 John Wiley & Sons, Ltd   ISBN: 0-470-85020-5

the public carrier is expected to provide guarantees of data privacy, security, and non-intrusion, and the enterprise may want to consider additional routing measures to protect data integrity.

The third level is represented by networks which make use of the Internet for transport of storage data, such as IP storage. In this environment, no security guarantees can be expected, and a high level of security consciousness should be maintained. In this environment, measures such as firewalls, encryption, and public key authentication should be considered.

As noted previously, use of a distributed storage network, together with proper encryption techniques, provides good data security by randomizing the physical location of critical data. Rather than placing all of a customer's critical financial data, for example, on one storage device, where it might be accessible to hackers, the data can be broken into fragments, encrypted, and distributed across a global network to provide additional security and integrity.

10.2 PHYSICAL SECURITY

A good place to start is with physical security. Storage facilities should have controlled-access policies, so that only personnel with a need to physically access the equipment are allowed to enter. Badges, card readers, and biometric detectors should all be considered as a means to control access to the equipment and fiber interconnect facilities.

Another area of physical security is tape media management. Tape vaults are often maintained in a separate physical location from the storage facility; access to the tape storage area should be controlled, and tape checkin/checkout should be managed and logged.

A less obvious aspect of physical security involves network sharing. If the same network is used for both routine business operations and storage networking within the enterprise, it creates opportunities for unauthorized access and intrusion. If possible, dedicated networks should be used for storage networking. If not appropriate safeguards should be put in place to prevent security breaches.

Network capacity across the MAN or WAN may be provided by carriers or storage service providers. In both cases, it is a good idea to review security policies with the carrier or service provider as part of the contract negotiation. It is also a good idea to ask for details of the actual physical route of the site-to-site links, and information on any sharing of physical facilities that may occur in the network.

10.3 USER LOGIN AND ADMINISTRATION

Providing secure access to the management system is of critical importance, since the management system exposes important infrastructure data to the user, and provides the ability to modify the system configuration. This becomes especially important when web-based management allows management to be performed from multiple physical sites that may have varying levels of security. Password protection should be provided for all users, and user access should be restricted to the degree of control required for each function. Public Key Infrastructure (PKI) authentication and digital certificates may also be used to ensure that users possess the proper credentials when logging in. If users are allowed to log in remotely, protection should be provided by means of a firewall.

Validation should be provided at three levels:

- *user level:* each user login should be validated using passwords and access control lists. Each user should be assigned to an administrative group with specific access privileges.
- *application level:* each time a user attempts to invoke a management application, the attempt should be validated to ensure that the user is entitled to access this function, based on the user's role and permissions.
- *transaction level:* each management transaction should be validated to ensure that the user and application are entitled to perform the transaction.

10.4 MANAGEMENT INTERFACES

In addition to validation of user login, attention should also be paid to the interfaces between the management system and the managed elements. Referring to the SNIA/DMTF model described in Chapter 9, this would include both the HTTP-based client/server interfaces and the protocols used by the providers to communicate with the network elements. Each protocol has its own individual set of security features which must be considered. For the web interfaces, SSL/TLS or IPSec may be used to provide a secure interface. Provider protocols such as SNMP, CMIP, and DMI each have individual security features. Protocol security features are described below.

10.4.1 SSL/TLS

Secure Sockets Layer (SSL) is a protocol for managing message transmission security over the Internet, in order to prevent eavesdropping, message tampering, or message forgery. From a protocol architecture standpoint, SSL operates as a layer between TCP and the application level protocol, which is normally HTTP for Internet applications. SSL has gained wide acceptance, and is included in most common web browsers and web servers.

SSL was originally developed by Netscape, Inc. and is specified in the Netscape SSL3.0 Specification[1]. SSL3.0 has been superceded by an IETF standard, RFC2246, Transport Layer Security (TLS) 1.0. SSL3.0 and TLS1.0 are functionally similar, but do not interoperate; however, TLS1.0 includes a fallback mechanism that enables SSL3.0 authentication if one of the parties involved does not support TLS1.0. The remainder of this description focuses on TLS1.0.

The TLS1.0 protocol consists of two sublayers: the TLS Record Protocol, and the TLS Handshake Protocol. The TLS Record Protocol provides privacy and reliability, as well as encapsulating the higher-level Handshake Protocol. Symmetric cryptography, such as the Data Encryption Standard (DES) defined in ANSI X3.92, is used for data encryption. Keys are generated uniquely for each connection, and are based on a secret negotiated by the Handshake Protocol.

The TLS Handshake Protocol allows the server and client to authenticate each other, to negotiate an encryption algorithm, and to exchange cryptographic keys before data transfer begins. Peers authenticate each other using asymmetric public key cryptography, such as RSA (named after its developers, Rivest, Shamir, and Adleman)[2] or Digital Signature Standard (DSS)[3]. The Handshake Protocol also provides secure negotiation of a shared secret which is unavailable to eavesdroppers and 'man-in-the-middle' attacks.

---

[1] SSL3.0 Specification, November 1996, http://wp.netscape.com/eng/ssl3/draft302.txt.
[2] RSA FAQ, http://www.rsasecurity.com/rsalabs/faq/.
[3] 'Announcing the Standard for Digital Signature Standard (DSS),' https://www.itl.nist.gov/fipspubs/fig186.htm.

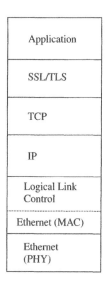

Figure 10.1   Protocol architecture of TLS1.0.

One of the advantages of TLS (and SSL) is that it is protocol-independent. It sits on top of the TCP layer, and therefore requires no operating system or kernel changes to implement. SSL/TLS may provide adequate security for web browser access to management systems, if other security precautions are implemented. For enhanced security at lower protocol levels, IPSec may be used (see below). Figure 10.1 shows the protocol architecture of TLS.

10.4.2   Simple Network Management Protocol (SNMP)

The Simple Network Management Protocol (SNMP) is a management protocol that is widely used for management of IP-based networks and LANs. Architecturally, it consists of a *manager*, usually associated with a management application server, and *agents*, which are associated with the individual managed clients. To implement management application functions, the manager issues commands, typically GET or SET commands, to the agents, and the agents perform the requested function and/or return requested data. The data managed by SNMP-based applications is referred to as the *Management Information Base*, or MIB.

The IETF has specified three versions of SNMP. Version 1 was specified in RFC1157, which was released in 1990. Version 2 was defined in a number of specifications in 1993–1996. The architecture of the current version, 3, is specified in RFC3411, which was released in 2002.

10.4.2.1 SNMP Version 1 Security Features

SNMP Version 1 employed weak authentication procedures, and therefore is not considered to have adequate security capabilities. Vulnerabilities have been discovered in both trap messages (sent from agents to managers) and in request messages (sent from manager to agents).

A specific SNMPv1 vulnerability has been identified in the use of community strings. A *community string* provides a weak authentication mechanism for the SNMP protocol. Agents are configured to provide read-only, read-write, or no access to their data, based on the community string in a request. However, community strings are transmitted in clear text, making them vulnerable to 'sniffing attacks,' in which an attacker gains entry to the system by reading the content of packets. Adding to the problem is the fact that community strings are often left with default settings, instead of implementing the recommended procedure of changing them to site-specific settings.

For new management applications, it is recommended that SNMPv3, which features improved authentication and encryption, be employed. However, a large number of existing management applications still employ SNMPv1. The CERT® Coordination Center at Carnegie Mellon University has issued an advisory on the use of SNMPv1 which contains the following recommendations:[4]

- Check with your vendor to ensure that the proper patches have been applied.
- Disable all non-essential SNMP software.
- Filter SNMP access to managed devices to ensure the traffic originates from known management systems.

---

[4] CERT Advisory CA-2002-03, "Multiple Vulnerabilities in Many Implementations of the Simple Network Management Protocol (SNMP)," February 12, 2002 (revised November 5, 2002), CERT Coordination Center, http://www.cert.org/.

- Filter SNMP services at your network perimeter (ingress/egress filtering).
- Change SNMP community strings from their defaults.
- Segregate network management traffic onto a separate network.

10.4.2.2   SNMP Version 3 Security Features

SNMP Version 3 implements a security subsystem that provides both strong authentication protocols and privacy through the use of encryption. The security subsystem is described in RFC3414. The security features of SNMPv3 are intended to provide protection against the following threats:

- *Modification of information* – altering of in-transit messages.
- *Masquerade* – assuming the identity of a valid user in order to gain access to management operations.
- *Disclosure* – eavesdropping on messages passed between manager and agent.
- *Message stream modification* – the malicious re-ordering, replaying, or delaying of messages.

For messages to be authenticated in SNMPv3, they must first pass an authentication check using HMAC-MD5-96 authentication protocol, and then pass a 'timeliness check' which guards against message replay or delay. A second authentication protocol, HMAC-SHA-96, is optionally supported.

Privacy is provided by means of the CBC-DES encryption protocol.

10.4.3   Common Management Information Protocol (CMIP)

The Common Management Information Protocol (CMIP) is an OSI-based network management protocol which is primarily used in conjunction with the Common Management Information Service Element (CMISE) application layer service for the management of telecommunications network devices. CMIP has a number of built-in security features, including access control, authorization, and security logging.

OSI security requirements related to CMIP are detailed in the following International Telecommunications Union (ITU) specifications:

- ITU-T Recommendation X.811 – Information technology – Open Systems Interconnection – Security frameworks for open systems: Authentication framework
- ITU-T Recommendation X.812 – Information technology – Open Systems Interconnection – Security frameworks for open systems: Access control framework
- ITU-T Recommendation X.813, Information technology – Open Systems Interconnection – Security frameworks for open systems: Non-repudiation framework
- ITU-T Recommendation X.814 – Information technology – Open Systems Interconnection – Security frameworks for open systems: Confidentiality framework
- ITU-T X.815 – Information technology – Open Systems Interconnection – Security frameworks for open systems: Integrity framework
- ITU-T X.816 – Information technology – Open Systems Interconnection – Security frameworks for open systems: Security audit and alarms framework

Requirements for access control are based on the framework for access control defined in ITU-T Recommendation X.812. An initiator who wishes to perform an operation on a target must supply access control information to an access control enforcement function. This function decides whether or not to grant access, based on predetermined access decision information, such as identification, and security policies relevant to the request.

Application service element level security requirements are provided by ITU-T Recommendation Q.813, *Security Transformations Application Service Element for Remote Operations Service Element (STASE-ROSE)*. STASE-ROSE enables security functions such as symmetric encryption, public encryption, hashing algorithms, and digital signatures to be negotiated.

10.4.4 Desktop Management Interface (DMI)

The Desktop Management Interface is a management interface developed by the Distributed Management Task Force (DMTF) to provide management capabilities for a variety of network components using both Windows and Unix operating systems. The DMI consists of four basic parts:

- A Management Information Format (MIF) for describing management information.
- A Service Provider entity.
- APIs to enable Service Provider-to-management application and Service-Provider-to-component communication.
- A set of services to facilitate remote communications.

The DMI is specified in the DMI Specification. The current version, DMIv2.0s, specifies access control capabilities for both local and remote access. The remote access control uses standard Remote Procedure Call (RPC) capabilities, while the local access control uses operating system functions. DMI does not specify formats for identification or encryption; these are RPC and operating system dependent.

The DMIv2.0s Specification also defines security extensions which include authentication, role-based authorization, flexible policy, security indications, and logging. The security extensions are conditionally required (i.e. if the Service Provider implements access control, the security extensions must be implemented). DMIv2.0s provides the following access control and security capabilities:

- Controlled access of remote management applications to DMI information.
- Security of component instrumentation.
- Security of MIF database.
- Security of local management applications.
- Event generation for security-related operations.
- Logging of security-related operations.
- A role-based authorization model.
- A flexible, remotely configurable authorization policy.
- Authentication interface on top of the operating system or third-party product.

DMIv2.0s does not specify a specific authentication protocol; a simple operating system login could be used, or an authentication system such as Kerberos or X.509 certificates could be used.

DMIv2.0s enables role-based access privileges to be assigned. A *role* is a set of privileges associated with a group of users. Each administrative group can be assigned a specific group of privileges based on their function. A *policy* determines which commands may be performed on which objects by each role. *Authorization* is the mechanism whereby DMI decides whether to accept or reject a command, based on the command and parameters, the user's role, and the policy.

The DMIv2.0s Service Provider can be configured to log commands and generate events when certain critical system functions are performed, such as component installation and application registration. Logging and event generation are useful in detecting security breaches, tracking actions that affect system configuration, and keeping users accountable for their actions.

10.5   FIREWALLS

A *firewall* is a set of programs, located at a network gateway server, that is used to protect the resources of a private network located inside the firewall. A firewall examines each packet and decides whether or not to deliver it to its destination, based on security policy algorithms. A standard screening function is to examine each request to ensure that it comes from a known domain name and/or IP address. A firewall may contain a proxy server to process requests on behalf of the protected network users.

A firewall may also allow remote access to the private network through the use of secure logins and authentication procedures. Firewalls are recommended if users are allowed to log in remotely to perform maintenance and administrative functions.

10.6   ENCRYPTION AND IPSEC

The use of encryption at the packet level is recommended to protect critical storage data, and is a requirement for IP storage protocols such as iSCSI. IPSec, as defined in RFC2401, protects packets by providing cryptographic integrity, authentication, and confidentiality. IPSec operates at the IP level of the protocol stack, and thus provides protection for the IP layer as well as upper layers.

10.6.1 Authentication Header (AH) and Encapsulating Security Payload (ESP)

IPSec consists of two data packet encoding protocols, the Authentication Header (AH) and the Encapsulating Security Payload (ESP), and a key distribution management function, such as Internet Key Exchange (IKE). The AH provides connectionless integrity, data origin authentication, and an optional 'anti-replay' capability. ESP provides confidentiality through encryption, and limited traffic flow confidentiality; it may optionally provide connectionless integrity, data origin authentication, and an anti-replay service. AH and ESP may be used individually or in combination with each other.

AH and ESP both support two modes of use: *transport mode* and *tunnel mode*. Transport mode provides host-to-host security for IP packets, and provides encryption for the payload only. AH and ESP primarily provide protection for upper layer protocols in transport mode. Tunnel mode encapsulates packets within IP headers for delivery to some final destination, and provides encryption of both the header and the payload. Tunnel mode must be employed if either the source or destination is a security gateway. AH and ESP provide different levels of protection for tunnel mode, as described below.

One of the primary functions of IPSec is to provide a security association between two hosts. A security association is a conceptual 'connection' that provides security services for the traffic it carries. Security associations in IPSec are simplex; one must be created in each direction. Security associations may exist for transport mode or for tunnel mode. In transport mode, a security association exists between two hosts. IPv4 IP packets passing between the hosts will have a transport mode security protocol header after the IP header and any options present, but before any upper-level (e.g. TCP) header and data. Ipv6 packets passing between the hosts will have a transport mode security protocol header that is after the base IP header and extensions, and may be before or after the destination options, but before any higher-layer protocol header and data. Exact location depends upon whether AH or ESP is supported.

For tunnel mode, there is an 'outer' IP header that specifies the IPSec processing destination (e.g. security gateway), and an 'inner' IP header that specifies the final packet destination. The tunnel mode security protocol header appears after the outer IP header, but before the inner header. If AH is used, parts of the outer header, as well as the encapsulated packet, are protected. If ESP is used, only the tunneled IP packet is protected.

10.6.2   Internet Key Exchange (IKE)

The Internet Key Exchange (IKE) is defined in RFC2409 and uses a key, such as a shared secret key, or the public keys of the two parties, to authenticate the parties and establish a session key. Once the session key is established, the rest of the session is cryptographically protected.

IKE has two phases. The first phase happens only once. In the first phase, it is assumed that each of the parties has an identity known to the other party, and that each identified party has a secret that can be verified by the other party. The first phase does mutual authentication based on the secret key, and establishes a session key for use in the rest of the session. In the second phase, multiple security associations may be set up between the parties, using the session key established in the first phase. Second phase session keys are established to protect the actual data transferred in the second phase.

10.6.3   SSL/TLS and IPSec Compared

SSL/TLS and IPSec can both be thought of as real-time security protocols that may be employed in a TCP/IP-based network. However, they operate at different levels in the protocol stack, provide different types of protection, and have different implementation requirements.

SSL/TLS operates above layer 4 (normally TCP), and therefore is operating-system independent, since the lower protocol layers are normally implemented in the operating system. This makes SSL/TLS easy to implement, and many browsers have built-in SSL/TLS support. However, this also means that packets must pass through TCP before the SSL/TLS layer can determine if they are cryptographically valid. If an attacker puts a duplicate packet with a valid sequence number into the stream, TCP will accept it and pass it along to SSL/TLS, which will reject it as invalid. When the 'real' packet with the same sequence number arrives, TCP will reject it and the connection will be broken.

IPSec, on the other hand, operates above the IP level, but below layer 4. Thus IPSec can detect and discard invalid packets before they reach the TCP layer, and all packets received by TCP are guaranteed to be cryptographically valid.[5] IPSec operating in tunnel mode can provide encryption for the source and destination addresses in the IP header as well as the data payload, and thus is well suited for use with a secure VPN. However, since IPSec is implemented at the layer 3/layer 4 intersection, it has operating system specific dependencies, and different versions must be implemented for different operating systems. Thus deciding which security protocol to use must depend on system security requirements, the need for operating system independence, and the quality of service requirements for the data being protected.

10.7   PUBLIC KEY INFRASTRUCTURE AND DIGITAL CERTIFICATES

A Public Key Infrastructure (PKI) enables users of an insecure network (such as the Internet) to securely exchange data through the use of a public and a private cryptographic key pair that are obtained from a trusted authority. The PKI allows for the use of a *digital certificate* that can uniquely identify an individual or organization, and a directory service that can store (and, when necessary, revoke) the certificates.

PKI assumes the use of public key cryptography. Message encryption may be based on a *private key* (referred to as *symmetric cryptography*), or on a *public key* (referred to as *asymmetric cryptography*). For private key cryptography, the same key is known to the sender and the receiver. The sender uses the key to encrypt the message, and the receiver uses it to decrypt the message. The disadvantage of the private key approach is that if the private key is discovered, then all encrypted messages may easily be decoded.

For public key cryptography, a user, whom we shall call User A, requests a certificate authority to create a public key and a private key. The two keys are created simultaneously, using an algorithm such as RSA. The private key is given only to User A, but the public key is made available as part of a digital certificate which can be

---

[5] This issue is discussed in R. Perlman and C. Kaufman, 'Key Exchange in IPSec: Analysis of IKE,' *IEEE Internet Computing*, November/December 2000, pp. 50–56.

obtained from a public directory. A second user, User B, may then encrypt a message using the public key obtained from the directory, and send it to User A. User A then uses his or her private key to decrypt the message that was encrypted using the public key. User A may then authenticate him/herself to User B by using the private key to encrypt a signature, and sending it to User B. User B may decrypt the signature by using the public key.

PKI is recommended for authentication of users, especially users who may be accessing the system remotely.

10.8   VIRTUAL PRIVATE NETWORKS (VPNs)

A Virtual Private Network (VPN) enables the use of a public network for secure communication between geographically separated locations. A tunnelling protocol is used to encapsulate the packets that are to be sent through the network from one location to the other. A security protocol provides encryption and authentication capabilities. Common tunneling protocols include Generic Routing Encapsulation (GRE), Layer 2 Formatting (L2F), Point to Point Tunneling Protocol (PPTP), and Layer 2 Tunneling Protocol (L2TP). VPNs use either SSL/TLS or IPSec for security; IPSec is generally preferred, since it supports tunneling and IP header encryption. In a distributed storage network context, VPNs may be used for implementing secure management networks over a wide area.

10.9   SAN SECURITY

A common technique for improving data integrity in Fibre Channel-based SANs is to use zoning. Zoning allows administrators to create closed groups of devices, ports, or WWNs which are only allowed to communicate with other devices, ports, or WWNs in the same group.

10.9.1   Zoning and Security

Zoning may be implemented in two basic ways:

- *Soft zoning* makes use of the nameserver provided by the fabric to create zones based on WWN. Soft zoning is simpler to administer, since no re-configuration is required when a device is moved from one port to another.

- *Hard zoning* uses routing tables maintained by the fabric switch or director to create zones based on ports. Hard zoning does not allow zones to overlap, and is somewhat more complex to administer, since re-configuration is required when a device is moved from one port to another.

Soft zoning is vulnerable to a type of attack referred to as *WWN spoofing*. In WWN spoofing, a rogue port uses a WWN assigned to a legitimate port to gain unauthorized access to data. Since soft zoning does not bind WWNs to physical location, the false WWN will be allowed access to stored data. Many vendors support an improvement to soft zoning which binds WWNs to specific ports and thereby prevents WWN spoofing.

10.9.2   LUN Masking

An additional level of security may be provided by Logical Unit (LUN) masking. (Note that for Fibre Channel, the acronym 'LUN' refers to a logical volume, rather than to a physical storage device, as in SCSI networks.) Users should only be aware of those files that they legitimately have a need to access. This is accomplished by filtering storage accesses and masking off the LUNs that they do not have access to. Three different implementations are possible:

- *LUN masking at the HBA level* – utilities supplied by HBA vendors can determine which LUNs an HBA allows the operating system to see. These utilities make use of the WWN supplied with each HBA. However, since this approach is hardware-device-specific, if an HBA has to be replaced due to a hardware fault or similar maintenance action, it is necessary to change the permissions for all the LUNs controlled by that HBA.
- *LUN masking using switch zoning* – use zoning to allow only certain servers to access certain storage elements. However, this will not allow multiple servers to share storage ports.
- *LUN masking using storage controller mapping* – the controller for a storage subsystem maps access privileges from the requestor to the appropriate LUNs, typically using the WWN at each HBA.

10.9.3   iSCSI Discovery Domains

IP storage protocols employ a concept referred to as a *discovery domain*. Discovery domains (see Section 8.2.10) function similarly to Fibre Channel zones, and allow storage nodes to be grouped into manageable domains, and limit logins to members of specific domains.

10.9.4   Switch Authentication

It may be desirable to perform some level of authentication on a switch that is being added to a fabric in a Fibre Channel switched configuration, to ensure that the switch ports being configured are legitimate parts of the configuration. One way to do this is to use an authentication process in which a private key and digital certificate are used to validate the switch before it is added to the configuration. Some fabric switch manufacturers incorporate switch authentication procedures into their management functions.

The ANSI/INCITS T11 Technical Committee's Fibre Channel Security Protocols (FC-SP) Working Group is currently developing a security standard for Fibre Channel. This standard will include the definition of protocols to authenticate Fibre Channel entities, set up secret keys, provide frame-by-frame integrity checking, and enable distribution of security policies across a Fibre Channel fabric.[6]

10.10   NAS SECURITY

The file sharing protocols used for NAS must support security functions, in order to limit file access to legitimate users. The following paragraphs describe security capabilities for the Network File System (NFS) and the Common Internet File System (CIFS).

10.10.1   NFS

NFS version 4 requires the implementation of RPCSEC_GSS, as described in RFC2623. Use of RPCSEC requires that mechanism, quality of protection and service be selected; service includes authentication, integrity, and privacy. The Kerberos V5 mechanism as described in RFC1964, the LIPKEY GSS-API as described in

---

[6] Fibre Channel Security Protocols, Rev. 1.1, April 2003 (work in progress). ftp://ftp.t11.org/t11/pub/fc/sp/03-149v1.pdf.

RFC2847, and the SPKM-3 GSS-API as described in RFC2847 must be implemented. Access control lists for files and directories are also supported.

10.10.2   CIFS

The CIFS protocol requires server authentication of users before users are allowed to access server resources. Authentication is provided by a user ID and password. Granularity of access is determined on a per-server basis; a server may maintain access control lists on individual files, or grant the user access to all files. Plain text password and challenge/response authentication are both supported, but the use of a plain text password is discouraged. For the challenge/response protocol, the server sends a challenge to the client, and the client must respond with a message created from the challenge and a 168-bit session key computed from the user's password.

Messages are authenticated by computing a message authentication code (MAC) for each message and attaching it to the message. The MAC is similar to that used in IPSec and described in RFC1828.

10.11   ANALYZING NETWORK ARCHITECTURE FOR SECURITY ISSUES

The key to creating a secure storage network lies in designing security into the network. A security risk analysis should be performed as part of the network architecture development process, and an action plan should be created to deal with any security exposures identified. Figure 10.2 illustrates some critical points in the network where security risks should be analyzed and appropriate measures taken.

Table 10.1 lists some security checkpoints and security features which may be implemented.

When implementing a multi-vendor network, it is important to verify that the equipment from different vendors uses compatible encryption and authentication standards. Two vendors may claim to implement the same standard, such as IPSec, for example, but may use different options for authentication and encryption. This can cause lost time and confusion during integration.

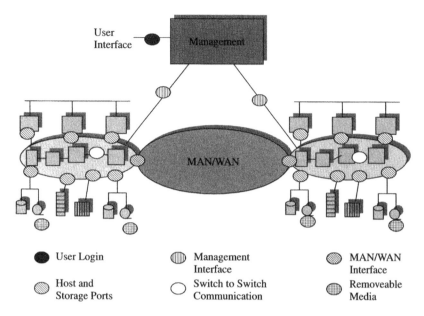

Figure 10.2   Security checkpoints for a storage network.

Table 10.1   Security checkpoints and preventative actions

Checkpoint location	Possible preventative action
User Login	Passwords, Levels of Access, PKI, Digital Certificates, Firewalls for remote access
Management Interface	SSL/TLS, encryption, VPNs
Host and Storage Ports	Zoning, Access Control Lists, LUN Masking, Discovery Domains
Switch to Switch Communication	Digital Certificates, Access Control Lists
MAN/WAN Interface	Use of separate physical media, encryption, VPNs
Removable Media	Checkin/Checkout Procedure, physical security measures

10.12   SUMMARY

Security should be designed into the network, rather than added as an afterthought. Security can be designed into the network architecture by analyzing the network for potential exposures, and applying the correct technology response to each security checkpoint.

Maintaining security, however, requires the development of security policies and procedures to be carried out after the network is installed and operational. Security planning should include not only preventative measures, but also ongoing security checks and reviews, breach response plans, and business continuity procedures in the event that security is compromised.

11

Planning Distributed Storage Networks

Planning a distributed storage network requires selecting an archi-tecture based on factors such as cost, performance, scaleability, and security. This section analyzes some of the factors to consider when planning a distributed storage network.

11.1 SELECTING AN ARCHITECTURE

One of the first considerations in planning a distributed storage net-work is selecting an architecture. Selecting the proper architecture for a storage network will depend on the architecture of the exist-ing computing infrastructure, as well as the desired scaleability, reliability, and performance.

11.1.1 Mainframe Architectures

Mainframe-based distributed storage architectures typically em-ploy either channel extension techniques or parallel processing. Channel extension is used when there is a requirement to locate storage remotely for purposes such as backup or mirroring, or

Distributed Storage Networks   Thomas C. Jepsen
© 2003 John Wiley & Sons, Ltd   ISBN: 0-470-85020-5

to operate remotely located peripheral devices such as printers. Channel extension enables data processing centers to be relocated or consolidated without requiring them to be colocated with a mainframe computer; it also allows data processing and data storage operations to be outsourced.

Parallel processing is used for high-performance computing, applications requiring distributed processing, business continuity, and disaster recovery applications requiring duplication of processing capability at a remote site.

11.1.1.1 Channel Extension

Channel extension planning begins with calculating the number and type of remotely located devices. Based on this, it should be possible to calculate the number of links and control units required at the remote site. Requirements for redundant paths should be factored in as well. Redundancy can be provided by using multiple fibers and using a storage director at the remote site to provide any-to-any connectivity between the fibers and the control units. As a rule of thumb, there should be at least four paths between the processor and each storage subsystem. Consideration should be given to scaleability; the initial architecture should be extensible so that it can support future expansion requirements.

If the current mainframe storage architecture uses bus/tag channels, then conversion to ESCON or FICON will be required for distance extension. If the distance is greater than 10 km for FICON, or 20 km for ESCON, then repeaters or link extenders will be required. If the distance is greater than 100 km, protocol conversion and transport over ATM, SONET, or IP may be required. For operations requiring real-time performance and low data loss, such as synchronous mirroring, ATM/SONET may be preferable. For operations where real-time performance and data loss are less critical, such as asynchronous mirroring and scheduled backup, IP solutions may be appropriate.

If a large number of channel links are required, WDM technology may be employed to reduce the number of fiber optic links needed. The cost-effectiveness of a WDM solution can be determined by simply comparing the cost of running multiple fibers to the remote site to the cost of WDM multiplexers and a single fiber. Be sure to include redundancy requirements in your calculations.

Channel extension planning should consider management of the remote links and equipment. The management system should clearly indicate the physical location of the remotely located equipment, and provide adequate status monitoring. Arrangements should be made for scheduled maintenance and repair.

Another aspect of planning that should be considered is physical security at the remote site. Access to the remote equipment should be controlled, as well as access to any backup media stored at the remote site.

Figure 11.1 shows a channel extension architecture and some planning considerations.

11.1.1.2 Parallel Processing

Sysplex, or Geographically Dispersed Parallel Sysplex (GDPS), configurations are used when high-capacity processing, multisite distributed processing, and rapid recovery from failure are required. In the Sysplex architecture, the processors at each site are connected using coupling links and timing links, as well as channel links, in order to provide parallel processing and remote copy capabilities.

Each site in a GDPS requires a processor, a coupling facility, a Sysplex timer, and disk storage. Each processor may be configured as multiple system images. To plan a total GDPS requires calculating the number of channel links, HiPerLinks, and CLO links required to interconnect the systems. Each system image must have a HiPerLink to each coupling facility; for a two-site configuration, this means

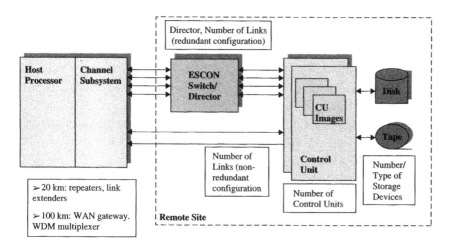

Figure 11.1   Channel extension architecture planning considerations.

that each system image must have one HiPerLink to the local coupling facility, and one to the remote facility. Each Sysplex timer must have an ETR link to each processor, and two CLO links to synchronize it with the Sysplex timer at the remote site.

It is recommended that at least four storage links exist between each processor and each storage subsystem. (This assumes that storage directors exist at each site.) Also, connections between systems are required for cross-system coupling facility (XCF) communication. This communication may be provided by using the coupling links for XCF signaling, or by using ESCON channel-to-channel (CTC) links. Each system image must support one CTC link to each other image.

As an example, a GDPS configuration consisting of two sites, each with a processor with a single image, a coupling facility, a sysplex timer, and two storage subsystems, would require the following number of site-to-site links:

2 images × 2 coupling facilities = 4 HiPerLinks
2 processors + 2 = 4 timer (CLO) links
2 storage subsystems × 4 = 8 storage links
1 image × 1 image × 2 = 2 CTC links (if coupling links are not used for XCF signaling).

Native mode timer links over multimode fiber are limited to a distance of 3 km for 62.5 mm MMF, and 2 km for 50 mm MMF. Native mode HiPerLinks are limited to 10 km for SMF, and 550 meters for 50 mm MMF. However, since all Sysplex configurations require a large number of HiPerLinks, timer links, and storage links, WDM is generally employed to reduce the total number of site-to-site optical fibers that must be deployed, and to increase the allowable distance. WDM multiplexers generally will support a distance of up to 50 km, which is sufficient for all Sysplex and GDPS configurations. GDPS configurations are normally limited to a distance of 20 km, and timer links are specified for a maximum distance of 40 km.

Figure 11.2 shows Sysplex architecture planning considerations.

11.1.1.3 Upgrading from ESCON to FICON

Upgrading from ESCON to FICON can result in improvements in both I/O performance and improved data transfer rate over longer

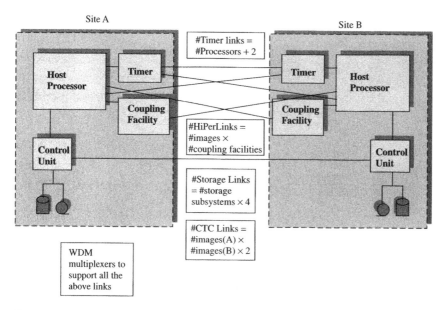

Figure 11.2 Sysplex architecture planning considerations.

distances. While ESCON can support 400–500 I/O operations per second, FICON can support ten times as many, or 4000–5000 I/Os per second, depending on blocksize employed. FICON also extends the distance at which data droop becomes significant from 10–100 km.

A single FICON link supports an instantaneous bidirectional data rate of 100 MB/s, or approximately 6 times the data rate of a single ESCON link (17 MB/s). Thus, FICON may be up to 6 times more cost-effective than ESCON for a specific network, due to the reduced amount of fiber links and interface hardware required.

There are several options for migrating existing ESCON networks to FICON. If the average traffic rate is high, or multiple remote sites must be connected, it is usually best to convert the entire network.

If the network traffic rate is not a critical factor, it is possible to use a bridge between a FICON adapter at the mainframe and an existing ESCON director to provide the benefits of FICON between mainframe and director without having to upgrade peripheral devices. Another option is to run both simultaneously by adding a FICON director to the configuration and migrating performance-critical applications to FICON. Figure 11.3 shows these migration options.

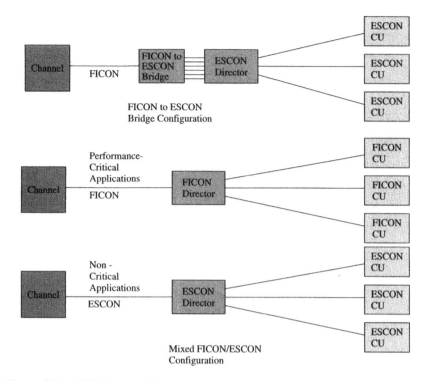

Figure 11.3 ESCON to FICON migration options.

11.1.1.4 Mainframe/Open Systems Connectivity

If the distributed storage network provides connectivity between mainframe and open systems architectures, appropriate protocol translators (e.g. ESCON to Fibre Channel) must be provided. Data conversion and/or load balancing software may also be required in some applications.

11.1.2 SAN vs. NAS – Choosing an Architecture

If no managed storage architecture exists, it may be necessary to choose between implementing a SAN and implementing a NAS. Each architecture has its pros and cons, which should be considered when making an implementation decision:

- *SAN Pros:* SAN provides better performance, since it operates at the block level. It is scaleable, can be grown to any required size, and can be extended over the MAN and WAN. Storage protocols are implemented in the HBA, and do not consume processor cycles.

- *SAN Cons:* SANs are more expensive to implement. There are still interoperability problems among vendors.
- *NAS Pros:* NAS is less expensive to implement. It uses familiar technology (Ethernet, TCP/IP) which may reduce the learning curve among administrators.
- *NAS Cons:* NAS is not as scaleable as SAN. Performance is not as good as SAN due to overhead of supporting file system, and use of TCP/IP. LAN bandwidth may be a limitation.

Neither architecture should be regarded as the ultimate answer; both are appropriate solutions to different storage problems. NAS is a front end technology that solves the problem of providing shared file access to multiple clients on a LAN, while SAN is a back end technology that provides efficient management of stored data at the device and block level.

NAS is generally appropriate when a short-term tactical solution to a storage problem is needed, and the existing Ethernet LAN infrastructure must be used to support the storage application. NAS performance is generally adequate for smaller (<1–5 terabyte of stored data) installations.

SAN is usually the architecture of choice for large installations (>1–5 terabyte of stored data) that plan for continued data growth, and where management and reliability are key factors. The use of SANs to provide multi-site data sharing and replication are also important factors. SAN can be seen as the long-term strategic solution that enables the enterprise to manage continued growth.

SAN and NAS should be regarded as complementary technologies that solve different problems for the enterprise planner. Also, the two architectures are beginning to converge as NAS file managers become more specialized and use managed SAN storage for backend storage. It is worth noting that a NAS head with a SAN back end is functionally identical to a SAN using a metadata controller to provide file-based access. In the future, the distinction may disappear completely, and NAS and SAN will simply be seen as two different 'views' of the same stored data.

11.1.3 SAN Architecture

Developing a SAN architecture should include planning for scaleability and growth. Enough storage capacity should be provided to handle current system needs and anticipated growth; the selected topology should allow for the graceful addition of switches and ports for future expansion. Chapter 1 provides overview descriptions of SAN topologies.

The architecture of a distributed SAN depends largely on the distance between sites. If the distance is less than 10 km, native-mode Fibre Channel links can be used. If the distance is less than 100 km, various types of link extenders and repeaters may be used. For distances greater than 100 km, ATM, SONET, or IP protocol translation is generally used. WDM may also be used economically if there are many links. Enterprise-level WDM equipment typically may be used over MAN distances of up to 50 km, while carrier-level WDM (DWDM) employs EFDA to provide virtually unlimited distance over the WAN.

11.1.3.1   Required WAN Bandwidth

If WAN transport is required, the amount of bandwidth needed must be determined. As a first step, the system designer should determine how much data will typically be transferred on a day-to-day basis. A good rule of thumb is that 10 megabits of bandwidth will be needed for every megabyte of data to be transferred per second. Thus, a T3 link can support about 5 megabytes of data per second; an OC3 link can support about 15 megabytes of data per second; and a 1 Gb/s Fibre Channel link can support about 100 megabytes of data per second.

11.1.3.2   Distance and Performance

However, bandwidth estimates can vary greatly due to blocksize, receive buffer availability, and distance. The throughput of a 1 Gb/s Fibre Channel link over a 100 km distance may be as little as 10 megabytes per second if data streaming is not employed and small sequences of frames (<8 KB) are sent. The manufacturers of gateway devices and multiplexers offer a variety of optimizations, including buffering, 'protocol spoofing,' and compression, to minimize the effects of distance and provide improved performance. Given the proper combination of optimizations, the bandwidths listed above can be sustained over distances as great as 3000 km.

Fibre Channel class of service may also affect performance in distributed SANs. Class 1 connections require that an end-to-end connection be set up across the SAN; this adds propagation delay and protocol acknowledgments to data transfer latency. Class 1 service is most efficiently employed in applications that require a high degree of reliability, constant transfer latency, low data loss, and high sustained transfer rate. If the total transfer size is large enough, the connection setup time becomes insignificant.

Consideration should also be given to the fact that Class 1 connections dedicate system resources for the duration of the connection. If a site-to-site link is used for a Class 1 connection, its bandwidth will not be available for other applications, even if the bandwidth dedicated to the Class 1 connection is not fully utilized. For this reason, Class 2, Class 3, and Intermixed classes of service are preferable from a resource utilization standpoint.

For IP Storage (iSCSI, FCIP, and iFCP) bandwidth and delay are difficult to predict, especially if the public Internet is used for transport. Available bandwidth and delay can only be deterministically calculated if the entire network is dedicated, and the bandwidth of the individual links is known. Data loss is also difficult to predict, since TCP discards packets under congested conditions. However, for applications where latency and throughput are not critical (such as scheduled backup over a time interval, or some types of asynchronous mirroring), IP storage protocols can provide almost unlimited distance.

For WAN distances, special attention must be paid to Fibre Channel E_D_TOV and R_A_TOV timeout values. See Sections 7.2.5.1, 7.3.7.1, and 8.3.3.7 for details.

11.1.3.3 Replication Strategies

Distance is a factor in selecting replication strategies, since performance and throughput decrease as distance increases. Synchronous mirroring is generally employed over distances of 100 km or less; at greater distances, asynchronous mirroring is generally used.

Another issue to consider in planning replication is the number and types of licenses required. Commercially available replication software may require separate licenses for each server at each site. If multiple operating systems are supported, separate licenses may be needed for each operating system.

11.1.3.4 Planning for Business Continuity/Disaster Recovery sites

Planning for a business continuity or disaster recovery site requires creating a configuration that is capable of performing all the processing that is normally done at the primary site. Some of the issues that need to be addressed include:

- *floor space* – there must be enough floor space for servers, storage devices, and media storage;
- *servers* – enough servers must be provided to handle application processing;
- *staff* – the business continuity/disaster recovery site must be adequately staffed;
- *storage hardware* – enough storage must be provided to handle existing and future application processing;
- *power supplies* – uninterruptible power, generators;
- *licenses* – licenses must be obtained for all required software;
- *network links* – links to the primary site must either be installed by the enterprise or leased from a carrier;
- *network extension, multiplexer, or gateway equipment* – the necessary distance extension equipment must be provided;
- *management* – the management system must be able to monitor the health of both primary and recovery sites, and provide transparent failover of applications;
- *security* – access to the remote site must employ the same security functions and procedures as the primary site.

11.1.3.5 Backup Planning

Planning a remote backup site requires calculating the required number of servers, storage devices, and gateways to be located at the remote backup location. If tape vaulting is to be supported, space must be allocated for this as well. Adequate floor space must be available for all the hardware and all operations to be performed at the remote site.

The use of magnetic tape devices for backup creates special requirements for the storage protocol. Tape drives must come up to the proper speed before performing write operations, and it is critical that the data be available when the correct speed is attained. This requires that the protocol used should support real-time data transfer, or that special buffering arrangements be used to guarantee availability of write data.

Backup schedules should be developed as part of backup site planning. If backup is fully automated (server-free), it will have little effect on normal system operations. If backup requires LAN bandwidth (LAN-based or LAN-free) it is a good idea to schedule backups for times when the production workload is low. Backup scheduling may also consider MAN/WAN network utilization, if bandwidth is shared with other applications, and the work schedules in effect at the remote site.

The SAN management function should provide remote management and fault detection for the remotely located equipment, and provide operators and maintenance personnel with a clear indication of remote site equipment location. Automated recovery functions should also be planned and implemented. And, as with all remote sites, access security must be considered.

11.1.3.6 Migration Planning

Migration of data from one site to another is typically a short-duration operation, and therefore it is desirable to perform it using non-permanent resources. If another application has unused network bandwidth capability, this can be used; or the network connectivity can be leased from a carrier or service provider on a short-term basis. Another possibility is to include a remote backup facility in the initial plan, and use the resources allocated for the backup facility to implement the migration as well. Figure 11.4 summarizes planning considerations for SANs.

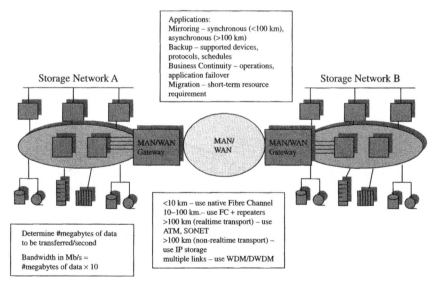

Figure 11.4 SAN planning considerations.

11.1.4   NAS Architecture

One of the primary concerns in implementing NAS is the capacity of the LAN to be used for file requests. If traffic is already near capacity, it may be a good idea to upgrade the LAN to a higher bandwidth – for example, from 10 Mb/s Ethernet to 100 Mb/s Fast Ethernet, or from Fast Ethernet to Gigabit Ethernet.

Two basic NAS architectures are possible. If storage is to be managed by a new or existing SAN, a NAS head appliance may be used. If the NAS will manage its own private storage, a NAS server with direct attached storage may be used. The NAS head approach is preferable, since it provides the benefits of managed storage and scaleability.

The NAS head or server may be attached directly to the LAN, or it may be remotely located and connected to the LAN using an Ethernet switch. Use of Gigabit Ethernet enables the NAS head or server to be located as much as 5 km from the switch or LAN; this may be useful in cases where storage is most economically consolidated in a single location in a business park or campus. Figure 11.5 illustrates planning considerations for NAS.

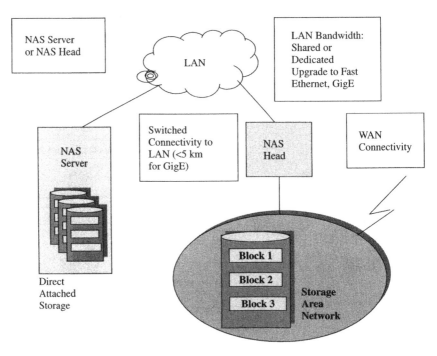

Figure 11.5   Planning considerations for NAS.

11.2   OPTICAL FIBER PLANNING

Site-to-site fiber connectivity must be planned for all types of storage architectures. If there is already existing fiber, a determination must be made if it is adequate to support the application. If not, installation of new fiber must be planned.

For distances greater than a few kilometers, SMF must be used. MMF may be adequate if used within a building, campus, or business park. Refer to the specifications in Chapters 3 and 5 for distance and attenuation specifications for the various types of fiber and protocols.

For new fiber installations, it may be a good idea to install extra fiber capacity to allow for future growth and new applications. If a large number of links are required, however, it may be more economical to use WDM multiplexers to concentrate traffic on a smaller number of fibers. Also, if there are not enough installed fibers to handle the required number of links, and it is not economical to add more fiber, WDM may be a cost-effective option.

Outside plant cabling should be designed with survivability and reliability in mind. Planning should include measures to avoid failures due to accidental backhoe cuts and shelter damage.

11.2.1   Redundancy Planning

The choice of WAN technologies should include redundancy considerations. SONET networks and carrier-level DWDM networks normally have redundancy built in; if one path fails, another path is automatically placed into service. Enterprise-level WDM generally requires provisioning of multiple paths to provide redundancy.

Redundancy and security should also be considered when planning the fiber infrastructure. If a carrier or service provider is used to supply the fiber connectivity, ensure that the carrier's network provides actual physical redundancy for the individual links. While fibers may enter the carrier's network as separate physical links, the carrier may multiplex both primary and redundant paths onto the same physical path at some point in the network, thus reducing the reliability of the network. It is a good idea to require the carrier to provide a diagram showing the entire site-to-site path through the network for each fiber link.

A similar issue exists for security. A carrier or service provider should be able to identify the security measures implemented in the network, and to demonstrate that the fiber path through the network is secure from intrusion, eavesdropping, or malicious reconfiguration.

11.3 SECURITY PLANNING

Planning for all storage architectures should include security planning. Specific areas to cover include:

- *Physical security* – controlled access to critical resources; use of passcards, ID badges, and biometric security.
- *Network security* – use of secure networks and private networks; encryption; use of security partitions.
- *User access security* – use of logins, passwords, and controlled access.
- *Protocol level security* – use of protocol-specific authentication and privacy features.

11.4 OUTSOURCING STORAGE

One possible solution to the problem of providing remote data storage is by using a Storage Service Provider (SSP). SSPs can provide additional capacity without requiring a major investment in equipment, and can satisfy requirements for remotely located business continuity centers without the need to purchase or lease additional building space. SSPs typically can provide outsourced storage and network connectivity, and can supply either fixed capacity or 'storage on demand' for short-term requirements. SSPs may be able to provide specialized services, such as scheduled backup, replication, or business continuity.

Enterprise customers must determine outsourcing requirements on an individual basis. Important factors to consider include the type of services provided, security and quality of service guarantees, and network connectivity.

11.5   RETURN ON INVESTMENT (ROI)

An important consideration in planning a distributed storage network is determining the Return On Investment (ROI) to be realized
from implementing and operating it. Studies have shown that the
cost of managing storage over time far exceeds the initial cost of the
storage system; distributed storage systems reduce management
costs by automating or eliminating many management functions,
and improving the reliability of the network. Some factors to be
considered in ROI calculation include:

- *Reduced total cost of ownership due to improved storage utilization.*
- *Reduced downtime for installation of storage upgrades.* Utilizing a
  switched network architecture enables additional storage to be
  installed with no server downtime.
- *Reduced cost of manual backup.* Automating backup functions eliminates the need for backup windows and labor costs associated
  with manual backup functions.
- *Reduced downtime due to fault and/or data recovery.* Downtime due
  to system failures or loss of data is prohibitively expensive for
  many business functions; a remote backup or business continuity
  center can largely eliminate this exposure.[1]
- *Reduced maintenance time due to integrated management.* Implementing an integrated management system reduces the time spent on
  configuring and maintaining the storage resources.
- *Ability to build a cost-efficient multi-vendor solution.* Industry-
  standard storage network architectures enable cost-effective
  multi-vendor solutions to be developed, reducing initial cost
  of implementation.

11.6   SUMMARY

As data storage requirements continue to grow at annual rates
in excess of 30%, storage management becomes a necessity, not

---

[1] An up-to-date listing of the cost of downtime for various business applications can
be found in 'Disk Mirroring – Local or Remote,' http://www.cnt.com/literature/
documents/pl512.pdf.

an option. SAN, NAS, and mainframe-based architectures are mature, practical technologies which offer managed multi-site storage solutions now. Effective planning requires coordination among enterprise IT planners, network engineers, and telecommunications engineers, who must work together to build storage networks that are scaleable, reliable, and secure.

12

Glossary of Terms

8B/10B – line coding standard, in which each 8 bits of data to be transmitted is encoded into a 10-bit transmission character and sent serially over the fiber link.

add/drop multiplexer (ADM) – SONET element which adds or drops lower-level tributary signals.

ADM – see *add/drop multiplexer.*

American National Standards Institute (ANSI) – a standards institute responsible for generating technical standards in the U.S. Affiliated with the International Committee on Information Technology Standards (INCITS).

ANSI – see *American National Standards Institute.*

arbitrated loop topology – Fibre Channel topology (FC-AL) in which up to 127 nodes operate on a shared-bandwidth loop.

assured forwarding (AF) – DiffServ class of service which is divided into four relative classes of service, each subdivided into three levels of packet drop precedence.

Asynchronous replication – 'semi-realtime' mirroring of data in which groups of changes are cached and committed to storage at preset intervals.

Asynchronous Transfer Mode (ATM) – a circuit-based, connection-oriented technology developed to provide a single packet-based format for transport of digital voice and data across telecommunications networks.

Distributed Storage Networks   Thomas C. Jepsen
© 2003 John Wiley & Sons, Ltd   ISBN: 0-470-85020-5

ATM – see *Asynchronous Transfer Mode.*

backbone architecture – a SAN architecture which uses core fabric switches to provide connectivity among groups of edge switches.

Backup – the practice of periodically making copies of application data and transferring them to a storage device that is kept physically separate from the original copy, such as a tape cartridge or a RAID.

backup server – a separate server node attached to the same LAN as the application servers, which manages backup for all application nodes in a centralized fashion.

backup window – a segment of time specifically allocated for performing backup operations, during which time application processing is suspended.

BER – see *Bit Error Rate.*

best effort – IP class of service in which the network will attempt to deliver each packet to its destination, but no guarantees about performance are made.

Bidirectional Link Switched Ring (BLSR) – SONET ring architecture which performs link switching if a fault occurs.

Bit Error Rate (BER) – the statistical probability of a transmitted bit being erroneously received in a communications system.

BLSR – see *Bidirectional Link Switched Ring.*

Bridge – a hardware device used to interwork two protocols or networks.

Business Continuity – same as disaster recovery.

cable skew – same as clock skew.

Carrier Sense Multiple Access/Collision Detect (CSMA/CD) – IEEE802.3 access method which enables multiple stations to share a common transport medium without requiring a central arbitration function to determine which station is allowed to send at any time.

CBR – see *Constant Bit Rate.*

CCW – see *Channel Command Word.*

CD-ROM – see *Compact Disk-Read-Only Memory.*

Channel Command Word (CCW) – an individual command in a channel program used by a mainframe computer.

channel extension – mainframe term for extending storage device connectivity over geographically dispersed areas.

Chromatic Dispersion – an optical fiber impairment in which different wavelengths travel through the optical media at different velocities and therefore spread out.

CIFS – see *Common Internet File System.*

CIM – see *Common Information Model*.

clock skew – differences in bus propagation time due to differences in the length of the individual wires in a cable which may cause timing errors.

CMIP – see *Common Management Information Protocol*.

Common Information Model (CIM) – information model developed by the Distributed Management Task Force (DMTF) for representing storage network components and functions in an object-oriented fashion.

Common Internet File System (CIFS) – a network file sharing application used by NT/Windows systems; CIFS is TCP/IP based and uses an open-systems version of server message block (SMB) protocol.

Common Management Information Protocol (CMIP) – an OSI-based network management protocol which is primarily used in conjunction with the Common Management Information Service Element (CMISE) application layer service for the management of telecommunications network devices

Compact Disk-Read-Only Memory (CD-ROM) – compact and economical plastic storage medium used to store computer data as well as audio.

Constant Bit Rate (CBR) – ATM service category intended for real-time applications requiring tightly controlled delay variation, such as voice, video, or circuit emulation.

controlled load – IntServ class of service which provides an approximation of best-effort service over an uncongested network.

Control unit – in mainframe architecture, a unit which interprets and executes channel commands, provides a data path between the CPU and the individual storage device, and furnishes status information on the data transfer.

CRC – see *Cyclical Redundancy Check*.

CSMA/CD – see *Carrier Sense Multiple Access/Collision Detect*.

Cyclical Redundancy Check (CRC) – a field computed using a generating polynomial and written into the transmitted data. It is used by the receiving facility to detect errors that may have occurred during transmission.

DASD – see *Direct Access Storage Device*.

Data Encryption Standard (DES) – standard for symmetric cryptography, defined in ANSI X3.92 and used for data encryption.

Data migration – moving large volumes of data from one physical location to another.

data mover – software function used to extract data from one storage partition in flat file format, process it into the proper format, and load it into the storage partition of another operating system.

data droop – a performance impairment in distributed storage systems resulting from the propagation delay associated with individual packet acknowledgements.

data streaming – a Fibre Channel technique for reducing data droop in which multiple frames are sent in one I/O exchange requiring only one acknowledgment.

DCD – see *Duty Cycle Distortion*.

DCS – see *Digital Cross-connect*.

Dense Wavelength Division Multiplexing (DWDM) – wavelength division multiplexing with improved channel density.

DES – see *Data Encryption Standard*.

Desktop Management Interface (DMI) – a management interface developed by the Distributed Management Taskforce (DMTF) to provide management capabilities for a variety of network components using both Windows and Unix operating systems.

Deterministic jitter – timing distortions caused by normal circuit effects in the transmission system.

Differential Mode Delay (DMD) – pulse-spreading phenomenon which limits both bandwidth and distance for multimode fiber.

Differentiated Services (DiffServ) – Internet architecture developed by IETF which classifies service requests at the edge of the network and aggregates individual flows into a few service classes for transport through the network.

digital certificate – an electronic document that can uniquely identify an individual or organization; used for security purposes.

Digital cross-connect (DCS) – a SONET element used to cross-connect SONET tributaries and change payload data from one SONET payload envelope to another.

Digital Signature Standard (DSS) – asymmetric public key cryptography standard.

Direct Access Storage Device (DASD) – mainframe terminology for a disk storage unit.

direct attachment – see *point to point topology*.

Disaster Recovery – a strategy for recovering from data loss due to disaster and continuing business operations.

Distributed Management Task Force (DMTF) – an industry organization which promotes development of management standards for distributed desktop, network, enterprise, and Internet environments.

DMI – see *Desktop Management Interface.*

DMTF – see *Distributed Management Task Force.*

Document Type Definition (DTD) – application-specific vocabulary for XML.

DSS – see *Digital Signature Standard.*

DTD – see *Document Type Definition.*

Duty Cycle Distortion (DCD) – component of deterministic jitter; caused by propagation differences between two transitions of a signal.

DVD – Digital Video Disk.

DWDM – see *DenseWavelength Division Multiplexing.*

EDFA – see *Erbium Doped Fiber Amplifier.*

electronic tape vaulting – same as *remote backup/restoral.*

End Of Frame (EOF) – an ordered set used to indicate the end of a frame of user data.

Enterprise Systems Connection (ESCON) – a serial optical fiber based protocol for connecting mainframe computers to storage sub-systems.

Erbium Doped Fiber Amplifier (EDFA) – an optical amplifier used in WDM/DWDM networks that enables amplification to be performed optically, without the need to regenerate the electrical signals.

Error Checking and Correction (ECC) – a technique for improving the reliability of stored data by including encoded information which may be used to detect and correct data errors.

ESCON – see *Enterprise Systems Connection.*

Ethernet – IEEE802.3 LAN protocol supporting a data rate of 10 Mb/s.

exchange – multiple Fibre Channel sequences which may flow in one direction, or both directions, between the originator and the responder.

Expedited Forwarding (EF) – DiffServ class of service which supports low packet loss, low delay, and low jitter.

Extensible Markup Language (XML) – a subset of Standard Generalized Markup Language which has found wide usage for data interchange among applications.

Extinction ratio – the ratio, measured in dB, of the average optical energy in a logic level one to a logic level zero.

Eye opening – time interval across the eye, measured at the 50% normalized eye amplitude.

fabric switch – a switching device enabling any fabric storage device to be connected to any fabric computing device for the duration of a data transfer operation.

Fall time – time interval required for the falling edge of an optical pulse to transition between specified percentages of the signal amplitude. For lasers, transitions are measured between the 80% and 20% points; for LEDs, transitions are measured between the 90% and 10% points.

Fast Ethernet – IEEE802.3 LAN protocol supporting a data rate of 100 Mb/s.

FC-AL – see *Fibre Channel Arbitrated Loop*.

FCP – see *Fibre Channel Protocol*.

Fiber Connection (FICON) – high-performance 1 Gb/s storage protocol used in mainframe systems.

Fibre Channel – a serial optical fiber and copper based protocol used to increase the bandwidth and extend the reach of storage connectivity.

Fibre Channel Arbitrated Loop (FC-AL) – a protocol enabling up to 127 nodes to be connected in a loop topology network.

Fibre Channel Protocol (FCP) – a layer 4 Fibre Channel protocol used to provide SCSI command set emulation.

FICON – see *Fiber Connection*.

firewall – a set of programs, located at a network gateway server, that is used to protect the resources of a private network located inside the firewall.

F_Port – Fibre Channel fabric port.

gateway – a device which provides SAN/WAN interworking and protocol translation in distributed SAN applications.

GDPS – see *Geographically Dispersed Parallel Sysplex*.

Geographically Dispersed Parallel Sysplex (GDPS) – a multisite Sysplex configuration, developed by IBM, in which all data is remote-copied from one location to another.

Gigabit Ethernet – IEEE802.3 LAN protocol supporting a data rate of 1000 Mb/s.

guaranteed service – IntServ class of service which supports real-time traffic with bounds on delay.

Hard zoning – Fibre Channel device-level zoning in which certain servers are allowed to access specific storage devices

HBA – see *Host Bus Adapter*.

Host Bus Adapter (HBA) – interface card used to terminate Fibre Channel on a storage or computing node.

Hub – hardware device used to improve reliability and cabling requirements for Fibre Channel Arbitrated Loops.

IBA – see *Infiniband Architecture*.

IDE/ATA – see *Integrated Drive Electronics/AT Attachment*.

idle character – 8B10B special character used to perform the idle function.

IETF – see *Internet Engineering Task Force*.

iFCP – see *Internet Fibre Channel Protocol*.

Infiniband Architecture (IBA) – a network architecture for connecting multiple host processor nodes, I/O platforms, and I/O devices together to form a system area network.

immediate commands – ESCON/SBCON commands which are typically completed as a single operation.

initiator – SCSI node, normally the host processor, which initiates a bus operation.

Integrated Drive Electronics/AT Attachment (IDE/ATA) – shared bus used in home PCs for connection of storage devices.

Integrated Services Architecture (IntServ) – architecture developed by IETF to provide additional classes of service for IP with guaranteed QoS.

International Telecommunications Union (ITU) – international standards organization for telecommunications.

Internet Engineering Task Force (IETF) – group formed to develop standards for the Internet.

Internet Fibre Channel Protocol (iFCP) – standard being developed by the IETF IP Storage Working Group which specifies an implementation of Fibre Channel fabric functionality for an IP network.

Internet Protocol (IP) – the networking layer of the TCP/IP protocol suite; the most commonly used internetworking protocol in the world today.

Internet Protocol Version 6 (ipv6) – next-generation IP addressing scheme which provides a 128-bit address, and incorporates some additional functionality, such as integrated multicasting and IPSec security.

Internet SCSI (iSCSI) – an IP storage protocol, developed by the IETF, that maps the SCSI protocol over TCP/IP.

Internet Storage Name Service (iSNS) – IP storage discovery mechanism, developed by the IETF.

Intersymbol Interference (ISI) – the effect on a sequence of symbols in which the symbols are distorted by transmission through a limited bandwidth medium to the extent that adjacent symbols begin to interfere with each other.

IntServ – see *Integrated Services Architecture*.

IP – see *Internet Protocol*.

IPSec – security mechanism defined in RFC2401, which protects packets by providing cryptographic integrity, authentication, and confidentiality.

IPv6 – see *Internet Protocol Version 6*.

iSCSI – see *Internet SCSI*.

iSNS – see *Internet Storage Name Service*.

ISI – see *Intersymbol Interference*.

ITU – see *International Telecommunications Union*.

JBOD – see Just a Bunch of Disks.

Jitter – deviations from the ideal timing of an event which occur at a high frequency.

Just a Bunch Of Disks (JBOD) – a management technique in which a group of hard disk units are managed as a single logical drive.

LAN – see *Local Area Network*.

LAN-based backup – a backup operation performed by transferring the data through the application server, across the LAN, and through the backup server to the dedicated backup storage.

LAN-free backup – a backup operation in which the LAN is used only for the purpose of sending backup commands to the individual servers.

Launched power – the power level at which laser or LED light is injected into an optical fiber; measured in dBm.

link extender – same as repeater.

Local Area Network (LAN) – a network, usually Ethernet-based, used for computer-to-computer communication to support functions such as file transfer, remote procedure calls, and client/server applications.

Logical Unit (LUN) masking – Fibre Channel access and security mechanism that limits users' access to storage that they legitimately have a need to access.

Logical Unit Number (LUN) – a SCSI storage unit associated with a Device ID; or a Fibre Channel logical volume.

Logical Volume Manager (LVM) – a software function providing virtualization of disk storage.

loss budget – a value which specifies the maximum allowable loss in an optical fiber link, given a minimum input power and a specified receiver sensitivity for a given signal to noise level.

L_Port – Fibre Channel port used to provide interconnection between arbitrated loop and switched configurations.

LUN – see *Logical Unit Number*.

LVM – see *Logical Volume Manager*.

Metropolitan Area Network (MAN) – a term generally used to describe network connectivity over an urban area in which distances between end points are assumed to be 100 km or less.

Mirroring – a technique to improve reliability by writing each block redundantly to two different locations in physical disk storage.

MMF – see *MultiMode Fiber*.

Modal Bandwidth – a bandwidth/length product, specified in MHz-km, which can be used to determine how far a system can operate at what bandwidth.

MultiMode Fiber (MMF) – optical fiber which allows multiple modes of transmission to exist in the fiber.

nameserver – Fibre Channel server function which enables lookup of any node on a Fibre Channel network using a World Wide Name.

Network Attached Storage (NAS) – a storage architecture which uses a file manager to transfer file-structured data between an application processor and LAN-attached storage.

Network File System (NFS) – Network file sharing system used by UNIX systems; NFS is TCP/IP-based and uses remote procedure call (RPC) protocol.

NFS – see *Network File System*.

non-immediate commands – ESCON/SBCON commands which require multiple operations, such as transfer of multiple data frames.

N_Port – Fibre Channel node port.

OC-1 – see *Optical Carrier 1*.

OC3 – see *Optical Carrier 3*.

OMA – see *Optical Modulation Amplitude*.

Optical Modulation Amplitude (OMA) – the absolute difference between the optical power of a logic one and a logic zero.

Optical Carrier 1 (OC-1) – SONET optical equivalent of STS-1 51.84 Mb/s frame.

Optical Carrier 3 (OC3) – SONET optical equivalent of STS-3 155.52 Mb/s frame.

Optical path power penalty – a link penalty to account for effects other than attenuation.

ordered set – a group of transmission characters that cannot occur in an error-free frame of user data; used for control functions and frame delimiters.

Overfilled Launch – an optical fiber transmission condition in which many paths, or "modes", exist in the fiber; occurs when LED sources are used.

Path Terminating Element (PTE) – SONET element which provides service mapping and concentration of lower-level (e.g. DS-1, DS-3) signals.

Permanent Virtual Circuit (PVC) – ATM virtual circuit established by provisioning.

PKI – see *Public Key Infrastructure*.

point to point topology – a storage network topology in which links are used to connect servers directly to storage devices; same as *direct attachment*.

private loop profile – membership in a Fibre Channel private loop profile enables loop devices to communicate only with other loop nodes.

processor centric mirroring – a mirroring technique in which the server or computer node is aware of the existence of a primary disk and a mirror disk, and simply issues duplicate write commands to each to create mirror copies.

PTE – see *Path Terminating Element*.

Public Key Infrastructure (PKI) – a security mechanism which enables users of an insecure network (such as the Internet) to securely exchange data through the use of a public and a private cryptographic key pair that are obtained from a trusted authority.

public loop profile – membership in a Fibre Channel public loop profile enables switched or loop nodes to communicate with other loop or fabric ports.

PVC – see *Permanent Virtual Circuit*.

QoS – see *Quality of Service*.

Quality of Service (QoS) – a measure of network performance in terms of bandwidth, throughput, delay, packet loss, and error rate; the ability to provide service guarantees based on these measures.

RAID – see *Redundant Array of Independent Disks*.

Random jitter – jitter due to thermal noise.

real time variable bit rate (rt-VBR) – ATM service category intended for realtime applications with controlled delay.

Receiver Sensitivity – the minimum acceptable value of average received signal to achieve a Bit Error Ratio (BER), typically 10^{-12}.

Redundant Array of Independent Disks (RAID) – a term used to describe a technology for managing a group of disk units to provide increased performance, reliability, or both.

Relative Intensity Noise (RIN) – noise caused by Rayleigh backscattering and optical reflections.

Remote backup/restoral – the use of distributed storage networks to provide non-realtime backup and restoral of user data from a remote location

Repeater – a device which regenerates a storage protocol signal at the physical layer.

Resource Reservation Protocol (RSVP) – reservation protocol used by IntServ to create a path and reserve resources for a flow.

Restoral – using a backup copy to replace data which has been lost.

Return loss – the ratio, expressed in dB, of optical power incident upon a component port or assembly to the optical power reflected by that component.

RIN – see *Relative Intensity Noise.*

Rise time – time interval required for the rising edge of an optical pulse to transition between specified percentages of the signal amplitude. For lasers, transitions are measured between the 80% and 20% points; for LEDs, transitions are measured between the 90% and 10% points.

RSA – asymmetric public key cryptography standard named after its developers, Rivest, Shamir, and Adleman.

Running Disparity – for 8B/10B encoding, the relative number of ones and zeroes in the transmission character.

SAN – see *Storage Area Network.*

SBCON – see *Single-Byte Command Codes Sets Connection.*

SCSI – see *Small Computer Systems Interface.*

SDH – see *Synchronous Digital Hierarchy.*

Secure Sockets Layer (SSL) – a protocol for managing message transmission security over the Internet, in order to prevent eavesdropping, message tampering, or message forgery.

sequence – one or more related Fibre Channel data frames, transmitted unidirectionally, and their link control frame responses.

server-free backup – backup operation in which backups are performed by moving data directly from the application backend storage to the backup storage without the involvement of the application server.

Shadowing – same as synchronous replication.

Simple Network Management Protocol (SNMP) – a management protocol that is widely used for management of IP-based networks and LANs.

Single-Byte Command Codes Sets Connection (SBCON) Architecture – open systems version of ESCON.

Single Mode Fiber (SMF) – optical fiber which allows light to travel along only one path, or mode, through the center of the fiber.

Small Computer Systems Interface (SCSI) – open systems bus and protocol developed to enable external storage devices to be connected to small computers.

SMF – see *Single Mode Fiber*.

SNIA – see *Storage Networking Industry Association*.

SNMP – see *Simple Network Management Protocol*.

SOF – see *Start Of frame*.

soft zoning – Fibre Channel zoning in which only specific WWNs are allowed to access stored data.

SONET – see *Synchronous Optical Network*.

SPE – see *Synchronous Payload Envelope*.

special characters – in 8B/10B encoding, transmission characters which are used for purposes that require them to be distinct from frame contents.

Spectral Width – Full Width Half Maximum (FWHM): The absolute difference between the wavelengths at which the spectral radiant intensity is 50% of the maximum power; typically used for LED sources. Root Mean Square (RMS): The weighted room mean square width of the optical spectrum. Typically used for laser sources.

Split mirror copy – a specialized form of disk mirroring that provides increased reliability and minimal impact on application performance.

SSL – see *Secure Sockets Layer*.

Start Of Frame (SOF) – an ordered set used to indicate the start of a frame of user data.

Storage Area Network (SAN) – a storage network that provides shared access to storage by multiple computers and servers.

storage centric mirroring – a mirroring technique in which the server is aware only of the primary disk, and the disk controller is responsible for copying the data to the mirror disk.

Storage consolidation – managing storage using a network (SAN or NAS), as opposed to direct attached storage.

storage director – a specialized type of fabric switch which provides enhanced management and reliability features.

Storage Integration – the use of distributed storage networks to share disks and integrate storage across a wide geographical area

Storage network – a special-purpose network that transports data between storage devices, such as tape or disk, and computing devices, such as mainframes or servers.

Storage Networking Industry Association (SNIA) – a storage industry trade association that sponsors working groups and conferences to promote storage networking.

storage sharing – same as storage integration.

storage virtualization – a function which enables applications to access data in 'virtual volumes' or 'virtual disks,' rather than accessing the physical devices containing the data directly.

Striping – a technique for enhancing I/O performance by dividing up the blocks of data that constitute an I/O write request and writing a portion of the total number of blocks (i.e. a stripe) to each physical disk.

STS-1 – see *Synchronous Transport Signal, Level 1.*

SVC – see *Switched Virtual Circuit.*

Switched Virtual Circuit (SVC) – ATM virtual circuit established by signaling.

Synchronous Digital Hierarchy (SDH) – an optical transmission interface developed for synchronous digital transport of voice telephony; used in Europe.

Synchronous Optical Network (SONET) – an optical transmission interface developed for synchronous digital transport of voice telephony; used in United States.

Synchronous Payload Envelope (SPE) – SONET STS-1 payload.

Synchronous replication – near-realtime mirroring of data.

Synchronous Transport Signal, Level 1 (STS-1) – 51.84 Mb/s SONET frame.

Sysplex – mainframe architecture, developed by IBM in 1994, using high-speed fiber optic links to couple processors together for parallel processing.

Target – SCSI node, generally a storage device, which performs a storage operation.

TCP – see *Transmission Control Protocol*.

TCP/IP Offload Engine (TOE) – a hardware implementation of the TCP/IP protocol, used to improve performance.

TDM – see *Time Division Multiplexing*.

third party copy – same as server-free backup.

Time Division Multiplexing (TDM) – multiplexing scheme in which each data stream is assigned a time slot on the transport medium.

TLS – see *Transport Layer Security*.

TOE – see *TCP/IP Offload Engine*.

Transmission Control Protocol (TCP) – a connection-oriented transport protocol designed to provide reliable communications between processors across a variety of reliable and unreliable networks. Part of the TCP/IP protocol stack.

Transport Layer Security (TLS) – security mechanism developed by IETF as a successor to Secure Sockets Layer (SSL).

Underfilled Launch – an optical fiber transmission condition in which few paths, or "modes", exist in the fiber; occurs when laser sources are used.

Unidirectional Path Switched Ring (UPSR) – SONET ring architecture which performs path switching in the event of a fiber fault.

UPSR – see *Unidirectional Path Switched Ring*.

VCC – *see Virtual Channel Connection*.

virtualization layer – a function used by mass storage devices to translate between operating system-specific protocols and the generic storage format employed internally.

Virtual Channel Connection (VCC) – a concatenation of VCIs across an ATM network.

Virtual Path Connection (VPC) – a concatenation of VPIs across an ATM network.

Virtual Private Network (VPN) – a virtual network that enables the use of a public network for secure communication between geographically separated locations.

Volume Manager – a software component which performs storage virtualization.

VPC – see *Virtual Path Connection*.

VPN – see *Virtual Private Network*.

WAN – see *Wide Area Network*.

Wavelength Division Multiplexing (WDM) – a technology for mid- and long-range transport of optical signals in which a group of wavelengths around the 1550 nm region are combined onto a single mode fiber and transmitted to the far end as a group.

WBEM – see *Web Based Enterprise Management*.

WDM – see *Wavelength Division Multiplexing*.

Web Based Enterprise Management (WBEM) – a set of technologies that enable web-based management of enterprise networks; developed by the DMTF.

Wide Area Network (WAN) – network used to transport data across a large area, typically >100 km.

World Wide Name (WWN) – a unique 64-bit Fibre Channel unsigned name identifier.

XML – see *Extensible Markup Language*.

XML Stylesheet Language (XSL) – stylesheet language used to specify formatting of XML displayed data.

XSL – see *XML Stylesheet Language*.

zoning – a Fibre Channel capability, which partitions switch ports into port groups for resource allocation and security purposes.

Bibliography

This section lists all references and recommendations for further reading.

ARTICLES AND WHITE PAPERS

Building Enterprise SANs Through Intelligent Networking. Brocade Communications Systems, Inc., 2001.

Class of Service: Optimizing Data Transport in Fibre Channel Systems. McData Corporation, 2001.

Connecting SANs Over Metropolitan and Wide Area Networks. Brocade Communications Systems, Inc., 2001.

Daoust M, Lavallee B. Designing and Planning Metropolitan DWDM Solutions. *NFOEC 2000 Technical Proceedings*, v. 1, 733–741.

DeCusatis CM, Stigliani DJ, Mostowy WL, Lewis ME, Petersen DB, Dhondy NR. Fiber Optic Interconnects for the IBM S/390 Parallel Enterprise Server G5. *IBM Journal of Research and Development*, September/November 1999, 807–828.

Dhillon A, Diminico C, Woodfin A. Optical Fiber and 10 Gigabit Ethernet, Version 2. 10 Gigabit Ethernet Alliance, May 2002. http://www.10gea.org/SP0502OpticalFiberand10GbE_Final.pdf.

Enrique Hernandez-Valencia, Michael Scholten, Zhenyu Zhu, 'The Generic Framing Procedure (GFP): An Overview,' *IEEE Communications Magazine*, May 2002, 63–71.

Ethernet Technologies. Cisco Systems, Inc. http://www.cisco.com/univercd/cc/td/doc/cisintwk/itd_doc/ethernet.pdf.

Fibre Channel and Ethernet: Different Approaches Meet Different Computing Needs. Brocade Communications Systems, Inc., 2001.

Distributed Storage Networks   Thomas C. Jepsen
© 2003 John Wiley & Sons, Ltd   ISBN: 0-470-85020-5

Gray, RC, McArthur, J, Turner, V. *Storage Consolidation: A Business Value Analysis*. IDC Whitepaper, 02-072STORAG3437, August 2002.

Gibson GA, Van Meter R. Network Attached Storage Architecture. *Communications of the ACM*, November 2000, 37–45.

Gigabit Data Transport – Technologies for Today's Applications. McData Corporation, 2001.

Gigabit Ethernet: Accelerating the Standard for Speed. Gigabit Ethernet Alliance, 1998.

Humblet PA, Miller B, Nair S, Babu S. Protecting DWDM Metropolitan Mesh Networks. *NFOEC 2000 Technical Proceedings*, v. 1, 100–109.

Landis H. *I/O Channels*, Storage Technology Corporation, 1979.

Malavalli K. *Fibre Channel Classes of Service for Data Transport*. Brocade Communications Systems, Inc., 1997.

Metz C. IP QOS: Traveling First Class on the Internet. *IEEE Internet Computing*, March/April 1999, 84–88.

Nag D, Yuhn M. Reliability, Protection, Survivability in the Optical Core. *NFOEC 2000 Technical Proceedings*, v. 1, 94–99.

Perlman R, Kaufman C. Key Exchange in IPSec: Analysis of IKE. *IEEE Internet Computing*, November/December 2000, 50–56.

The Business Case for a Storage Virtualization Engine. Aberdeen Group, September 2000.

The Essential Elements of a Storage Networking Architecture. Brocade Communications Systems, Inc., 2001.

Westerinen A. *CIM and the DRM Prototype*. Storage Networking Industry Association, 1999.

BOOKS

Barker R, Massiglia P. *Storage Area Network Essentials*. New York: John Wiley & Sons, 2002.

Raman LG. *Fundamentals of Telecommunications Network Management*. Piscataway, NJ: IEEE Press, 1999.

Stallings W. *Data and Computer Communications*. Upper Saddle River, New Jersey: Prentice-Hall, 1997.

STANDARDS

ANSI INCITS

ANSI INCITS 131-1994 (R1999), *Small Computer System Interface – 2*, American National Standards Institute, 1994.

ANSI INCITS 230–1994 (R1999), *Fibre Channel – Physical and Signaling Interface (FC-PH)*, American National Standards Institute, 1994.

ANSI INCITS 272–1996 (R2001), *Fibre Channel – Arbitrated Loop (FC-AL)*, American National Standards Institute, 1996.

ANSI T1. 105–1995, *Telecommunications – Synchronous Optical Network (SONET)* – Basic Description Including Multiplex Structures, Rates and Formats, American National Standards Institute, 1995.

ANSI INCITS 296–1997, *Single Byte Command Code Sets CONnection (SBCON) Architecture*, American National Standards Institute, 1997.

ANSI INCITS Fibre Channel Security Protocols, Rev 1.1, April 2003 (work in progress). ftp://ftp.t11.org/t11/pub/fc/sp/03-149v1.pdf.

ANSI INCITS Project 1331D, *Fibre Channel Framing and Signaling (FC-FS)*, Rev 1.90, April 2003, (work in progress) ftp://ftp.t11.org/t11/pub/fc/fs/03-173v1.pdf.

ATM Forum

af-bici-0013.003, *B-ICI 2.0 Specification*, ATM Forum, 1995.
af-sig-0061.002, *UNI SIG 4.1 Specification*, ATM Forum, 2002.
af-tm-0121.000, *TM 4.1 Specification*, ATM Forum, 1999.
af-uni-0010.002, *ATM UNI 3.1 Specification*, ATM Forum, 1994.

Bellcore/Telcordia

GR-253-CORE. *Synchronous Optical Network (SONET) Transport Systems: Common Generic Criteria, Issue 3*. Telcordia Technologies, September 2000.

Distributed Management Task Force (DMTF)

DSP0004. *Common Information Model Specification, Version 2.2*. Distributed Management Task Force, Inc., June 14, 1999.

DSP0005. *Desktop Management Interface Specification, Version 2.0.1s*. Distributed Management Task Force, Inc., January 10, 2003.

InfiniBand

InfiniBand Architecture Specification, Volumes 1 and 2, General Specifications, Release 1.1. InfiniBand Trade Association, November 6,
2002.

Institute of Electrical and Electronics
Engineers (IEEE)

IEEE 802.1D Part 3: Media Access Control (MAC) Bridges, Institute
of Electrical and Electronics Engineers, 1998.
IEEE 802.1Q, Virtual Bridged Local Area Networks, Institute of
Electrical and Electronics Engineers, 1998.
IEEE 802.3-2002, Carrier sense multiple access with collision detection (CSMA/CD) access method and physical layer specifications, Institute of Electrical and Electronics Engineers, 2002.
IEEE 802.3ae-2002, Part 3, Amendment: media access control (MAC)
parameters, physical layers, and management parameters for
10Gb/s operation, Institute of Electrical and Electronics Engineers, 2002.

International Telecommunications Union (ITU)

ITU-T G.707, *Network Node Interface for the Synchronous Digital Hier-
archy (SDH)*, International Telecommunications Union, October
2000.
ITU-T G.708, *Sub STM-0 Network Node Interface for the Synchronous
Digital Hierarchy (SDH)*, International Telecommunications
Union, July 1999.
ITU-T G.709, *Interfaces for the Optical Transport Network*, International
Telecommunications Union, February 2001.
ITU-T G.711, *Pulse Code Modulation of Voice Frequencies*, International
Telecommunications Union, November 1988.
ITU-T G.7041/Y.1303, *Generic Framing Procedure (GFP)*, 2001.
ITU-T I.361, *B-ISDN ATM Layer Specification*, International Telecom-
munications Union, February 1999.
ITU-T I.363.5, *B-ISDN ATM Adaptation Layer Specification, Type 5
AAL*, International Telecommunications Union, August 1996.
ITU-T I.371, *Traffic Control and Congestion Control in B-ISDN*, Inter-
national Telecommunications Union, March 2000.

ITU-T Q.813, *Security Transformations Application Service Element for Remote Operations Service Element (STASE-ROSE)*. International Telecommunications Union, June 1998.

ITU-T Q.2110, *B-ISDN ATM Adaptation Layer, Service Specific Connection Oriented Protocol*, International Telecommunications Union, July 1994.

ITU-T Q.2130, *B-ISDN ATM Adaptation Layer, Service Specific Coordination Function*, International Telecommunications Union, July 1994.

ITU-T Q.2931, *Digital Subscriber Signalling System No. 2, UNI Layer 3 Specification for Basic Call/Connection Control*, International Telecommunications Union, July 1994.

ITU-T X.811, *Information technology – Open Systems Interconnection – Security frameworks for open systems: Authentication framework*. International Telecommunications Union, April 1995.

ITU-T X.812, *Information technology – Open Systems Interconnection – Security frameworks for open systems: Access control framework*. International Telecommunications Union, November 1995.

ITU-T X.813, *Information technology – Open Systems Interconnection – Security frameworks for open systems: Non-repudiation framework*. International Telecommunications Union, October, 1996.

ITU-T X.814, *Information technology – Open Systems Interconnection – Security frameworks for open systems: Confidentiality framework*. International Telecommunications Union, November, 1995.

ITU-T X.815, *Information technology – Open Systems Interconnection – Security frameworks for open systems: Integrity framework*. International Telecommunications Union, November, 1995.

ITU-T X.816, *Information technology – Open Systems Interconnection – Security frameworks for open systems: Security audit and alarms framework*. International Telecommunications Union, November, 1995.

Internet Engineering Task Force (IETF)

Blake S, Black D, Carlson M, Davies E, Wang Z, Weiss W. *An Architecture for Differentiated Services*, IETF RFC 2475, December 1998.

Braden B, Shenker S, Clark D. *Integrated Services in the Internet Architecture: An Overview*, IETF RFC 1633, June 1994.

Braden R, Zhang L, Berson S, Herzog S, Jamin S. *Resource Reservation Protocol (RSVP)*, IETF RFC2205, September 1997.

Csse J, Fedor M, Schoffstall M, Davin J, *A Simple Network Management Protocol (SNMP)*, IETF RFC 1157, May 1990.

Deering S, Hinden R. *Internet Protocol, Version 6 Specification*, IETF RFC2460, December 1998.

Diercks T, Allen C. *The TLS Protocol, Version 1.0*, IETF RFC2246, January 1999.

Eisler M, *NFS Version 2 and Version 3 Security Issues and the NFS Protocol's Use of RPCSEC_GSS and Kerberos V5*, IETF RFC 2623, June 1999.

Eisler M, *LIPKEY - A Low Infrastructure Public Key Mechanism Using SPKM*, IETF RFC 2847, June 2000.

Harkins D, Carrel D, *The Internet Key Exchange (IKE)* IETF RFC 2409, November 1998.

Harrington D, Presuhn R, Wijnen B, *An Architecture for Describing Simple Network Management Protocol (SNMP) Management Frameworks*, IETF RFC 3411, December 2002.

Heinanen J, Baker F, Weiss W, Wroclawski J. *Assured Forwarding PHB Group*, IETF RFC2597, June 1999.

Jacobsen V, Nichols K, Poduri K. *An Expedited Forwarding PHB*, IETF RFC2598, June 1999.

Kent S, Atkinson R, *IP Authentication Header*, IETF RFC 2402, November 1998.

Kent S, Atkinson R, *IP Encapsulation Security Payload (ESP)*, IETF RFC 2406, November 1998.

Kent S, Atkinson R. *Security Architecture for the Internet Protocol*, IETF RFC2401, November 1998.

Krueger M, Haagens R, Sapuntzakis C, Bakke M. *Small Computer Systems Interface Protocol over the Internet (iSCSI) Requirements and Design Considerations*, IETF RFC3347, July 2002.

Linn J, *The Kerberos Version 5 GSS-API Mechanism*, IETF RFC 1964, June 1996.

Mankin A, Ed. *Resource Reservation Protocol (RSVP) Version 1 Applicability Statement: Some Guidelines on Deployment*, IETF RFC 2208, September 1997.

Monia, C, Mullendore, R, Travostino, F, Jeong, W, Edwards, M. draft-ietf-ips-ifcp-14, *iFCP – A protocol for Internet Fibre Channel Storage Networking*, December 2002 (work in progress).

Nichols K, Blake S, Baker F, Black D. *Definition of the Differentiated Services Field (DS Field) in the IPv4 and IPv6 Headers*, IETF RFC2474, December 1998.

Postel J. Ed. *Transmission Control Protocol*, IETF RFC 793, September 1981.

Rajagopal, M, Rodriguez E, Weber R. draft-ietf-ips-fcovertcpip-12, *Fibre Channel Over TCP/IP (FCIP)*, August 2002 (work in progress).

Satran, J, Meth, K, Sapuntzakis, C, Chadalapaka, M, Zeidner, E. draft-ietf-ips-iscsi-20, *iSCSI*, 19 January 2003 (work in progress).

Shenker S, Partridge C, Guerin R. *Specification of Guaranteed Quality of Service*, IETF RFC2212, September 1997.

Tseng, J, Gibbons, K, Travostino, R, Du Laney, C, Souza, J. draft-ietf-ips-isns-16, *Internet Storage Name Service*, January 2003.

Wroclawski J. *Specification of the Controlled-Load Network Element Service*, IETF RFC2211, September 1997.

Java Community Process

Federated Management Architecture (FMA) Specification, Version 1.0, Revision 0.4. Java Community Process, Sun Microsystems, January 21, 2000.

Secure Sockets Layer (SSL)

SSL3.0 Specification, November 1996. http://wp.netscape.com/eng/ssl3/draft302.txt.

Storage Networking Industry Association (SNIA)

Common Internet File System (CIFS) Technical Reference, Revision 1.0. Storage Networking Industry Association, March 1, 2002.

Shared Storage Model: A Framework for Describing Storage Architectures. SNIA Technical Council, June 5, 2001. (Draft SNIA TC proposal document).

Storage Management Initiative Specification (SMI-S), public review draft, Storage Networking Industry Association, April 15, 2003 (work in progress).

WEB SITES

CIM, http://www.dmtf.org/spec/cims.html

Fibre Channel – Overview of the Technology, http://www.fibre-channel.org/technology/

Gary Field's SCSI Info Central, http://scsifaq.org:9080/scsi_faq/

History and Technology of Wavelength Division Multiplexing, http://www.spie.org/web/oer/october/oct97/multiplex.html.

IEC: Synchronous Optical Network (SONET), http://www.iec.org/online/tutorials/sonet/

SCSI,   http://www.ba-stuttgart.de/~schulte/htme/ebuss12.htm #REF1.1

The SONET Homepage, http://www.sonet.com

WBEM, http://www.dmtf.org/spec/wbem.html

XML, http://www.w3.org/XML/

Index

Distributed Storage Networks   Thomas C. Jepsen
© 2003 John Wiley & Sons, Ltd   ISBN: 0-470-85020-5

Printed and bound in the UK by
CPI Antony Rowe, Eastbourne

Printed and bound by CPI Group (UK) Ltd, Croydon, CR0 4YY

27/10/2024

14580218-0003